Environmental Performance Reviews

UNITED KINGDOM

OECD

ORGANISATION FOR ECONOMIC CO-OPERATION AND DEVELOPMENT

ORGANISATION FOR ECONOMIC CO-OPERATION AND DEVELOPMENT

Pursuant to Article 1 of the Convention signed in Paris on 14th December 1960, and which came into force on 30th September 1961, the Organisation for Economic Co-operation and Development (OECD) shall promote policies designed:

– to achieve the highest sustainable economic growth and employment and a rising standard of living in Member countries, while maintaining financial stability, and thus to contribute to the development of the world economy;

– to contribute to sound economic expansion in Member as well as non-member countries in the process of economic development; and

– to contribute to the expansion of world trade on a multilateral, non-discriminatory basis in accordance with international obligations.

The original Member countries of the OECD are Austria, Belgium, Canada, Denmark, France, Germany, Greece, Iceland, Ireland, Italy, Luxembourg, the Netherlands, Norway, Portugal, Spain, Sweden, Switzerland, Turkey, the United Kingdom and the United States. The following countries became Members subsequently through accession at the dates indicated hereafter: Japan (28th April 1964), Finland (28th January 1969), Australia (7th June 1971), New Zealand (29th May 1973), Mexico (18th May 1994), the Czech Republic (21st December 1995), Hungary (7th May 1996), Poland (22nd November 1996), Korea (12th December 1996) and the Slovak Republic (14th December 2000). The Commission of the European Communities takes part in the work of the OECD (Article 13 of the OECD Convention).

Publié en français sous le titre :
Examens des performances environnementales
ROYAUME-UNI

FOREWORD

The principal aim of the OECD's Environmental Performance Reviews is to help *member countries improve their individual and collective performances in environmental management*. The primary goals for this programme are:

- to help *individual governments* assess progress;

- to promote a continuous policy *dialogue among member countries*, through a peer review process; and

- to stimulate *greater accountability* from member countries' governments towards their public opinion, within developed countries and beyond.

Environmental performance is assessed with regard to the degree of achievement of *domestic objectives and international commitments*. Such objectives and commitments may be broad aims, specific qualitative goals, precise quantitative targets or a commitment to a set of measures to be taken. Assessment of environmental performance is also placed within the context of historical environmental records, the present state of the environment, the physical endowment of the country in natural resources, its economic conditions and demographic trends.

These systematic and independent reviews have been conducted for all member countries as part of the first cycle of reviews. The OECD is now engaged in the second cycle of reviews directed at *promoting sustainable development*, with emphasis on implementation of domestic and international environmental policy, as well as on the integration of economic, social and environmental decision-making.

The report was peer-reviewed by the Working Party on Environmental Performance (Paris, June 2002). The conclusions and recommendations of the report are approved by the Working Party.

GENERAL INTRODUCTION

This review of the United Kingdom's environmental performance *examines results* in the light of domestic objectives and international commitments. Three countries assisted particularly with this review: Australia, Japan and Poland.

The report is organised in three parts:

– Part I is entitled: "Environmental Management" and focuses on air, water, and waste management, as well as nature conservation and biodiversity;

– Part II is entitled: "Sustainable Development" and focuses on environment and the economy, environmental-social interface and sectoral integration: construction;

– Part III is entitled: "International Commitments" and focuses on international commitments and co-operation.

The OECD extends its most sincere thanks to all those who helped in the course of this review, to the representatives of member countries to the Working Party on Environmental Performance, and especially to the examining countries (Australia, Japan and Poland) and their experts. The OECD is particularly indebted to the Government of the United Kingdom for its co-operation in expediting the provision of information and the organisation of the experts' missions to Reading and Edinburgh, and in facilitating contacts with many individuals both inside and outside administrative and governmental structures of the country.

The OECD Working Party on Environmental Performance conducted the review at its meeting on 17-19 June 2002 and approved its conclusions and recommendations. This report is published under the authority of the Secretary-General of the OECD.

TABLE OF CONTENTS

Part II
SUSTAINABLE DEVELOPMENT

Part III
INTERNATIONAL COMMITMENTS

ANNEXES

LIST OF FIGURES AND TABLES

Figures

Tables

ABBREVIATIONS AND SIGNS

Abbreviations

ASSI	Area of special scientific interest
BATNEEC	Best available technology not entailing excessive cost
BREEAM	Building Research Establishment Environmental Assessment Method
CAP	Common Agricultural Policy of the European Union
CFP	Common Fisheries Policy of the European Union
CHP	Combined heat and power
DEFRA	Department for Environment, Food and Rural Affairs
DETR	Department for Environment, Transport and the Regions
DFID	Department for International Development
EAC	Environmental Audit Committee of the House of Commons
EEA	European Economic Area
ELV	End-of-life vehicle
EMEP	Co-operative Programme for Monitoring and Evaluation of the Long-range Transmission of Air Pollutants in Europe
EQS	Environmental Quality Standards
FAO	Food and Agriculture Organization
GDP	Gross domestic product
GEF	Global Environment Facility
GHG	Greenhouse gas
GIS	Geographic information system(s)
GMO	Genetically modified organism
GNI	Gross national income
HCB	Hexachlorobenzene
HEES	Home Energy Efficiency Scheme
HFC	Hydrofluorocarbon
HMIP	Her Majesty's Inspectorate of Pollution
ICES	International Council for the Exploration of the Sea
IEA	International Energy Agency
IMO	International Maritime Organization
IPC	Integrated pollution control
IPPC	Integrated pollution prevention and control
IPRI	Industrial Pollution and Radiochemical Inspectorate

IUCN	International Union for the Conservation of Nature (The World Conservation Union)
LEV	Low-emission vehicle
LPG	Liquefied petroleum gas
MARPOL	International Convention for Prevention of Pollution from Ships
MCA	Marine and Coastguard Agency (formerly MSA)
MOX	Mixed oxide fuel
MtC	Million tonnes of CO
MWh	Megawatt hours
NFFO	Non-fossil fuel obligation
NGO	Non-governmental organisation
NMVOCs	Non-methane volatile organic compounds
NVZ	Nitrate vulnerable zone
ODA	Official development assistance
ODS	Ozone-depleting substance
OFGEM	Office of Gas and Electricity Markets
OFWAT	Office of Water Services
OSPAR	North East Atlantic Treaty
PAC	Pollution abatement and control
PAH	Polycyclic aromatic hydrocarbon
PCBs	Polychlorinated biphenyls
p.e.	Population equivalent
PFC	Private final consumption
PFCs	Perfluorocarbons
PIC	Prior informed consent
POPs	Persistent organic pollutant
PRN	Packaging-waste recovery note
RDA	Regional development agency
RIA	Regulatory impact assessment
RSPB	Royal Society for the Protection of Birds
RWA	Regional water authority
SAP	Standard Assessment Procedure
SEPA	Scottish Environment Protection Agency
SSSI	Site of special scientific interest
TFC	Total final energy consumption
TPES	Total primary energy supply
TWh	Terawatt hour
UNCTAD	United Nations Conference on Trade and Development
UNECE	United Nations Economic Commission for Europe

UNEP	United Nations Environment Programme
UNFCCC	United Nations Framework Convention on Climate Change
VAT	Value-added tax
WRAP	Waste Resources Action Programme
WWF	World Wide Fund for Nature

Signs

The following signs are used in Figures and Tables:
. .: not available
– : nil or negligible
. : decimal point

Country Aggregates

OECD Europe: All European member countries of the OECD, i.e. countries of the European Union plus the Czech Republic, Hungary, Iceland, Norway, Poland, the Slovak Republic, Switzerland and Turkey.

OECD: The countries of OECD Europe plus Australia, Canada, Japan, the Republic of Korea, Mexico, New Zealand and the United States.

Country aggregates may include Secretariat estimates.
The sign * indicates that not all countries are included.

Currency

Monetary unit: pound (GBP).
In 2000, GBP 0.661 = USD 1.
In 2001, GBP 0.692 = USD 1.

Cut-off Date

This report is based on information and data available up to June 2002.

LIST OF TEAM MEMBERS

Mr. Andrew Ross	Expert from reviewing country: Australia
Ms. Jadwiga Sienkiewicz	Expert from reviewing country: Poland
Mr. Motoharu Yamazaki	Expert from reviewing country: Japan
Mr. Christian Avérous	OECD Secretariat
Ms. Martha Heitzmann	OECD Secretariat
Mr. Heino von Meyer	OECD Secretariat
Mr. Gérard Bonnis	OECD Secretariat
Mr. Takahiko Hasegawa	OECD Secretariat

CONCLUSIONS AND RECOMMENDATIONS*

The United Kingdom has experienced almost a decade of *steady GDP growth*, exceeding both the OECD and EU averages. Since the early 1990s, per capita GDP has grown 20% in real terms. This expansion was primarily driven by rapid growth in services (e.g. transport, communication, finance and business services). Services now exceed 70% of total output, while industry's contribution has dropped to 25% of GDP, despite growth in the high technology and light manufacturing sectors. This dematerialisation of the economy, along with changes in energy supply and an increasingly mobile lifestyle, has helped reshape UK production and consumption patterns in ways that eased some traditional pollution pressures and raised some new environmental challenges.

Since the early 1990s, the UK has made noteworthy progress in *decoupling* a number of environmental pressures from economic growth. It achieved strong decoupling for major air pollutants and CO_2, for water withdrawals and for agro-chemical consumption. This progress reflects both the reshaping of the economy and the strengthening of UK environmental policies in the EU context. The UK is committed at the highest level of government to environmental protection and sustainable development. Yet, it could still improve its ranking among OECD and EU countries with respect to a number of indicators of environmental pressure intensity. Today, *priority environmental issues* include diffuse pollution, waste management, soil and water management, landscape and biodiversity conservation, and climate protection.

To meet these challenges, the UK will need to: i) expand its environmental infrastructure (e.g. for waste and waste water treatment) and continue implementing its environmental policies; ii) further integrate environmental concerns into economic and social decisions; and iii) reinforce its international environmental

---

* Conclusions and Recommendations reviewed and approved by the Working Party on Environmental Performance at its meeting in June 2002.

co-operation. This report examines progress made by the UK *since the previous OECD Environmental Performance Review* in 1994, and the extent to which the country's *domestic objectives and international commitments* are being met. It also reviews progress in the context of the *OECD Environmental Strategy.** Some 51 recommendations are made that could help strengthen the UK's environmental performance in the context of sustainable development.

1.   Environmental Management

Implementing environmental policies

Since the 1994 review, the UK has made noteworthy progress in achieving a number of its *environmental objectives* and in expanding its *environmental infrastructure*, although at the pace allowed by relatively limited pollution abatement and control expenditure. Targets related to emissions of conventional air pollutants, persistent organic pollutants and heavy metals, and to quality of drinking and surface water, were reached. Large-scale investment in waste water treatment infrastructure has accompanied privatisation of water services in England and Wales. The UK has extended the range of its environmental objectives, partly in response to EU and other international commitments, and partly as a consequence of its own sustainable development commitments. The mix of policy measures used has become more balanced, with more use of economic instruments in recent years, and continued effective use of regulation and land use planning. Regulation of significant point sources of industrial pollution has been carried out in an *integrated pollution control* (IPC) framework since 1990, with cost-effectiveness as a guiding principle (BATNEEC). Lesser industrial point sources and urban waste water treatment are subject to media-specific regulatory regimes. Modifications to the pollution control system, initiated to conform with provisions of the EU directive on integrated pollution prevention and control (IPPC), are encompassing previously excluded installations and introducing additional objectives of pollution prevention and resource efficiency. For water supply and waste water treatment, the *polluter pays and user pays principles* are applied fairly consistently in England and Wales, although less so in Scotland. The UK has developed and begun to apply new economic instruments such as a landfill tax, an aggregates levy, a climate change levy and emission trading systems. A reform is under way to enhance integration of environmental objectives with land use planning.

---

*   The objectives of the 2001 OECD Environmental Strategy covered in these Conclusions and Recommendations are maintaining the integrity of ecosystems (Section 1), decoupling environmental pressures from economic growth (Section 2), the social and environmental interface (Section 2) and global environmental interdependence (Section 3).

Notwithstanding the revival of environmental management in the late 1980s and the real progress just described, there is considerable *margin for further environmental progress*, as the UK is in the middle range of EU or OECD countries for many environmental indicators, has not yet achieved a number of its environmental objectives and still presents a deficit of environmental infrastructure (e.g. waste and waste water treatment infrastructure). Municipal waste generation has continued to parallel GDP growth, with recycling and recovery rates trailing those of comparable EU countries and landfilling rates remaining high. Developing the infrastructure necessary to implement best practices concerning *hazardous waste disposal* will require considerable investment. There is a need to further develop policy instruments to address *diffuse pollution concerns*, particularly as regards agriculture and urban runoff; the nitrogen surplus of the UK, although reduced, still exceeds the EU average by nearly 50% and the number of declared nitrate vulnerable zones is still insufficient to comply with the nitrate directive. Measures to conserve marine habitats and biodiversity should be reinforced. Significant expansion in *inspection and enforcement* will be required to accommodate the extended scope of IPPC regulation. Pollution abatement and control expenditure continues to represent 0.8% of GDP, and will probably need to be increased to meet future infrastructure investment requirements. The use of cost-benefit analysis to support decision making is part of the administrative culture in the UK, but limited information on costs and benefits makes it difficult to assess the cost-effectiveness of the IPC system. Also, the extended efficiency criteria have to be made compatible with the international and sustainable development

It is *recommended* to:

- strengthen *inspection and enforcement* and related monitoring efforts, as necessary to implement revised environmental regulations;
- review present *systems of charging users* for waste and waste water services, identifying opportunities to strengthen economic incentives for resource conservation and efficiency;
- review *environmental expenditure* and increase investment in environmental infrastructure (e.g. waste and waste water treatment facilities);
- develop and apply *economic and regulatory instruments* so as to meet reduction targets for diffuse pollution, particularly from agriculture and transport;
- continue to integrate environmental concerns into *land use planning*.

objectives that are increasingly shaping the UK's environmental policies. In summary, considerable effort and investment will be necessary for the UK to consolidate and extend implementation of environmental policies.

Air

In the 1990s, urban air quality continued to improve in the UK. Very strong *decoupling of emissions of conventional air pollutants from GDP* was achieved: while GDP rose by 26%, emissions decreased by 68% for SO_x, 42% for NO_x, 34% for NMVOCs and 33% for CO. This achievement mainly resulted from energy intensity gains, large-scale fuel switching (e.g. from coal and heavy oil to gas) and improved pollution control devices such as catalytic converters on gasoline cars and flue gas desulphurisation systems at coal-fired power stations. SO_x and NO_x emissions from large combustion plants were reduced below the EU's 1998 limits several years early. This brought the UK energy and emission intensity figures closer to EU averages, but room for further progress exists. *Large reductions in emissions of toxic chemicals* were also achieved (e.g. by 77% for polycyclic aromatic hydrocarbons [PAH], 70% for dioxins and furans, 73% for heavy metals). The sale of leaded gasoline was banned at the beginning of 2000. A statutory *national air quality strategy* with quantitative, dated targets for eight air pollutants has been implemented and regularly reviewed. An area-wide air quality management system introduced in 1997 launched a more holistic approach to addressing local air quality problems. Parking regulation and pricing continue to be effective traffic management tools in UK cities. Integration of air quality concerns into *energy and transport policies* has further progressed with measures such as promotion of combined heat and power generation, the automotive fuel duty escalator, reform of company car taxation, and the differentiation of vehicle excise duty based on CO_2 emission factors and of motor fuel excise duties based on sulphur content. Coal subsidies ceased in 1995. Cost-benefit analyses and estimates of health effects of air pollution are systematically considered in policy decisions. Overall, the UK has proceeded very well with its air agenda, in the context of its EU and other international commitments.

Despite these very positive intentions, actions and results, the UK faces a number of air management challenges. Metropolitan areas still contain "hot spots" where NO_x and PM_{10} concentrations frequently exceed national standards and cause *air quality concerns*, particularly affecting the poor. In some urban areas heavily exposed to road traffic, the UK's proposed national long-term standards for benzene would be exceeded at many roadside locations; exceedances of the proposed national standard for PAH would also occur in a few industrial and domestic coal burning areas. This suggests that additional local measures would be needed to achieve the proposed national standards (which would be more stringent than the EU limit values) by 2010. At the local level, implementation of the national air quality strategy has been rather slow, in part due to insufficient commitment and capacity on the part of local authorities. *Decoupling road transport use from GDP growth*, for both passengers and freight, remains the biggest challenge. Despite increased use of rail for passenger and freight transport in recent years, its modal share is still lower than that in many other OECD countries. The latest national transport programme is predicated upon major investment in the current decade, after years of underinvestment. A significant proportion of the public appears to perceive *taxes on fuels and vehicles* as fulfilling a revenue raising function, rather than as tools to help achieve environmental goals. Local authorities have not yet used their recently extended road pricing powers. Natural gas and oil prices for industry and households, compared to EU and OECD averages, leave room for increased internalisation of environmental externalities. Investment in new and cleaner transport, including low-emission vehicles, is relatively limited and has not been integrated into efforts to "green" government operations in practical terms.

It is *recommended* to:

- continue efforts to reduce *NO_x, particulate and NMVOC emissions*, in light of persistent problems with high concentrations of NO_2, PM_{10} and ozone in some areas;
- implement *area-wide emission control* more consistently, providing more precise guidance to local authorities and taking measures to reinforce their management capacity where necessary;
- work to increase public perception of *fuel- and vehicle-related taxes* as tools for achieving environmental goals, improving public transport and promoting low-emission vehicles and their refuelling infrastructure;
- strengthen *transport demand management* measures, including through the use of local authorities' new powers to set road use charges and workplace parking levies;
- improve integration of air management concerns into *transport policies and plans*, particularly at the local level through better land use planning;
- continue to integrate local, regional and global atmospheric management concerns into *energy policies*.

Water

The UK made *significant progress* during the 1990s on improving the quality of surface, bathing, drinking and estuary waters and controlling discharges from point sources. River quality objectives have been adopted for all rivers, as recommended during the 1994 Environmental Performance Review, though they are not statutory. This progress was made possible by a significant increase in *water infrastructure investment* (e.g. GBP 3 to 4 billion per year from 1990 to 2000 in England and Wales) to reduce urban point source pollution. Sewage treatment infrastructure has been upgraded and storm overflows constructed. Disposal of sewage sludge at sea has been discontinued. These achievements came about through a *major shift in water policy*, responding to a decade of underinvestment and stimulated in large part by EU water directives. *Water pricing policies*, supervised by an independent regulator, have led to full cost recovery of public water supply and sewage treatment services by privatised water companies in England and Wales. Continued increased investment is planned until 2005 to complete sewage treatment infrastructure. In response to a recent increase in the frequency and severity of floods, flood prevention and defence are evolving towards more integrated *flood management*, making greater use of specific planning tools (catchment flood plans, shoreline plans, water level plans), general land use planning and flood damage liability. Serious droughts have led to proposals to increase withdrawal charges.

Despite this overall progress and a well-established policy framework, much remains to be done. Addressing *drinking water quality* breaches (e.g. for iron and manganese) and meeting the EU requirements on lead content will require considerable investment. Even after significant improvements, 16% of *river length* in north-western England is of poor quality. Eight cities of more than 150 000 people still lack treatment plants. The number of water pollution incidents remains high. Controls on sewage sludge used for land application need to be strengthened. The quality of coastal waters remains a concern, largely because of *diffuse pollution* leading to nitrate, phosphate and pesticide contamination. Little has been done to address this issue; in particular, no strategy exists to deal with nutrient management in agriculture, despite EU directives and a recommendation in the 1994 OECD review. However, a review of diffuse pollution of waters by agriculture in England is under way to identify pollution control measures, including regulations, economic instruments and voluntary actions. The *interface between water and nature*, including wetland management and river revitalisation, has received relatively little attention, although there is a growing number of programmes to rehabilitate or restore river habitats. Building on a long tradition of monitoring/enforcement and service provision at the river basin level, and of planning at the catchment level (local environment agency plans), priority should be given to addressing water quantity and quality issues in an integrated manner, in line with requirements of the new EU water framework directive. Control of industrial effluent discharges has remained mainly regulatory, with little use of economic incentives such as *pollution charges*. Metering should be extended to further support modernisation of *water pricing*. A large amount of water-related investment is to be made in the next ten years (e.g. for drinking water supply, urban waste water treatment, nitrate and pesticide control and more ecological management of water bodies). Financing this investment will require a water pricing policy with a longer-term perspective, along with better integration of environmental concerns into sectoral policies, notably those for agriculture.

It is *recommended* to:

- increase the number of designated sensitive areas and complete *urban waste water treatment infrastructure*, especially that needed to reduce pollutant discharges to coastal waters;
- complete delineation of *nitrate vulnerable zones*, in which codes of good agricultural practice and nutrient management plans should be binding;
- further develop the *river basin approach to water management* (e.g. by setting statutory water quality and quantity objectives), extending responsibilities of subnational environment agencies accordingly;
- continue to develop a policy framework for *sewage sludge management* based on economic and environmental analysis;
- further explore the possibility of introducing *taxes on nutrients and pesticides* as a means of internalising external costs of diffuse pollution;
- explore the possibility of introducing industrial *water pollution charges*, with efficiency and financing objectives in mind.

Waste

In 1999 and 2000, the UK established *national waste management strategies* that, for the first time, included quantitative targets. It initiated data collection on municipal waste generation and management in the mid-1990s. Mechanisms to improve local authorities' performance on municipal waste management (e.g. "Best Value" duty) were introduced. The UK developed several *economic instruments* for waste management in the 1990s, including the landfill tax and the aggregates levy. A system of tradable permits for the land-filling of biodegradable municipal waste has been proposed. For some waste streams, recycling rates gradually increased over the decade. The UK transposed the EU packaging directive into national legislation, and progressed with prepa-rations to implement EU directives on waste electrical and electronic equipment and on end-of-life vehicles. *Regulations* on hazardous waste were strengthened with, for instance, a broader definition of "special waste" and the obligatory attachment of consignment notes. A new regime for the identification and remediation of contaminated land was introduced.

The *rate of municipal waste generation* showed no sign of decoupling from GDP growth in the 1990s. Furthermore, given the relatively low cost of landfilling, there is little incentive to reduce waste generation or increase recycling. Measures to encourage waste minimisation remain very weak, and charges on household waste management have not been introduced despite a recommendation in the 1994 OECD review. An official *data collection system for non-municipal waste* is still lacking, rendering analysis of waste generation, management and

It is *recommended* to:
- establish a systematic *data collection and information system* concerning the generation, recovery and disposal of non-municipal waste;
- introduce effective measures to encourage *waste minimisation* (e.g. waste charges for household waste, material resource efficiency standards) and accelerate efforts to increase *material recovery* rates;
- strengthen measures to prevent and discourage *illegal disposal of waste*, with emphasis on inspection and enforcement;
- review and revise *landfill-related measures* (e.g. landfill tax rates, exemptions; inspection and enforcement) so as to more effectively support objectives related to reduction of landfilling and diversion of waste to unlicensed sites;
- accelerate measures to ensure that treatment and disposal of *hazardous waste* are organised in an environmentally sound and economically efficient manner (e.g. eliminating "co-disposal"), and clearly identify infrastructure needs;
- assure implementation of new legislation on remediation of *contaminated land*.

disposal trends impossible, except for selected waste streams. The controversial practice of "*co-disposal*" (landfilling hazardous waste with other waste) continues, though it is supposed to be phased out by 2004 to comply with the EU landfill directive. Full compliance with EU legislation will require considerable investment to expand waste treatment capacity. Recycling rates continue to be among the lowest in OECD countries due to low public awareness and a lack of recycling infrastructure. *Regulatory inspection* of waste management sites should be made more systematic and consistent, and efforts to control illegal disposal should be further strengthened.

Nature and biodiversity

Since the 1994 OECD review, the UK has steadily strengthened *protection of special sites* by increasing their area (e.g. a 22% increase in areas and sites of special scientific interest between 1993 and 2001), enacting new legislation (e.g. the 2000 Countryside and Rights of Way Act) and promoting positive, rather than compensatory, management agreements with landowners/occupiers. Some trends of *habitat loss* seen before 1990 have been slowed, halted or reversed, including those affecting plant diversity in arable fields, area of fen/marsh/swamp and biological condition of small rivers. Forest cover increased by 16% between 1990 and 2000. A framework for implementing "*Biodiversity: The UK Action Plan*" was established with the preparation of individual action plans for 45 priority habitats and 391 species, as well as for 160 local areas, under highly successful voluntary public-private partnerships. The first five-year progress report was published in 2001. Incorporation of biodiversity concerns into other policy fields was further advanced through national initiatives such as sustainable development indicators and the UK forestry standard, although there is still need for improvement. Land area subject to agri-environmental programmes continued to increase, as did related public expenditure (from GBP 9 million in 1990 to GBP 150 million in 2000). Environmental NGOs play a major and influential role in managing nature and biodiversity in the UK.

Nevertheless, the UK still faces significant challenges concerning bio-diversity and nature conservation. It is uncertain whether nature and biodiversity protection efforts are sufficient to balance the multiple pressures from densely clustered economic activities. There is still considerable room for improvement in the *condition of protected areas*, as only 60% are in either "favourable" or "unfavourable but recovering" condition (the national target is 95% by 2010). The deterioration of some habitats and species has continued (e.g. plant diversity in grasslands, population of farmland birds, number of shrubs and bogs), largely because of intensive agriculture. Runoff from agricultural sources still causes *eutrophication* of sensitive habitats (e.g. over 80% of riverine habitats). *Fertiliser and pesticide application intensities* for the UK are higher than OECD Europe averages by 100% and 70%, respectively. Intensive grazing causes major habitat deterioration, especially in uplands. Statutory mechanisms for *marine nature conservation* are patchy, and an overall policy framework is lacking. Information is still insufficient to allow the recent biodiversity status of some animal species to be known.

It is *recommended* to:
- extend and strengthen the use of *management agreements* for protected areas;
- fully implement the *biodiversity action plan* through local action plans, and improve monitoring of the condition of individual species and habitats;
- continue to encourage the expansion of *woodland and forest cover* and to promote sustainable forestry in line with the UK forestry standard;
- further promote *agri-environmental programmes*, as allowed for under the EU Common Agricultural Policy (CAP);
- develop and implement comprehensive legislative and institutional mechanisms for *marine nature conservation*, fully implementing the EU habitat directive in the 200-mile exclusive economic zone;
- continue to promote measures to conserve *wildlife species* that are in decline, and regularly monitor their status as a basis for establishing related conservation measures.

2.   Towards Sustainable Development

Integration of environmental concerns in economic decisions

The UK economy has grown by almost 2.5% per year since the early 1990s. *Strong decoupling* from GDP growth has been achieved for emissions of major air pollutants and CO_2, as well as for water withdrawals and application of agrochemicals. A sustainable development strategy is in place. Progress towards sustainable development has been aided by institutional and market-based integration in several sectors. *Institutional integration* of sustainable development has been fostered by a range of high-level co-ordination committees (e.g. Green

Ministers Committee, Environmental Audit Committee) and advisory bodies (e.g. Sustainable Development Commission). Strengthened procedures for taking environmental issues into account have been built into policy-making processes. The traditional filtering of policy measures through cost-benefit analysis has been extended, with a stronger focus on objective setting and monitoring of progress through indicators. Substantial progress in policy integration has been achieved with respect to energy, transport, construction and agriculture. The UK has begun to use the modulation mechanism of the CAP, strengthening integrated rural development approaches, including through targeted support for environmental management and biodiversity. A number of *market-based instruments* have been introduced, such as the climate change levy, that apply the principle of taxing "bads" and using the revenue to support "goods". In transport, the fuel duty escalator influenced the modal split, shifting the trend back towards rail and water, and thus helped the UK reduce air pollutant emissions. At project level, environmental impact assessments are carried out for large projects, and recent legislative changes are expanding their scope, in compliance with EU legislation.

On the other hand, many UK indicators of environmental pressure intensity are still in the OECD middle range. Changes in consumption patterns are generating and/or accentuating environmental concerns. For instance, traffic volumes continue to grow, and municipal waste generation closely tracks GDP growth. Decoupling of diffuse pollution from economic growth will require continued efforts. Much remains to be done to translate sustainable development

It is *recommended* to:
- reflect sustainable development objectives more systematically in *public service agreements* and through integrated analysis (e.g. extended cost-benefit analysis) of policy measures;
- ensure that central government initiatives for improved environmental integration and sustainable development are effectively translated into *regional development priorities and local action*;
- strengthen the incentive role of economic instruments in inducing targeted *modal shifts in transport*, with appropriate phasing and consultation;
- further extend the shift of CAP resources towards integrated rural development programmes, including through *agri-environmental measures*;
- study and develop the extension of the *climate change levy* into a broader based tax on greenhouse gas (GHG) emissions.

orientations into practice and to achieve full integration of economic, social and environmental considerations in important *sectoral policies*. Although such efforts have been fairly comprehensive on the part of the central government, translation of general intentions into *regional development priorities* and local action is patchy. The integration of environmental objectives into the policies of *economic regulators* such as OFGEM should be improved. The guidance function of important environment-related *energy and transport taxes* should be reviewed. Progress toward national goals concerning renewable forms of energy, waste management and agri-environmental concerns remains slower than what is needed to reach them.

Integration of environmental and social concerns

The environmental-social interface has taken on new importance in the UK's sustainable development strategy. Improving environmental quality and resource efficiency is among the objectives of local initiatives to combat *social exclusion and deprivation*. Disparities in exposure to pollution and the distributive effects of environment-related measures are increasingly considered in policy design and assessment. Legislation concerning countryside access and rights of way has been reinforced. *Access to environmental information* has improved, and broad-based consultation is current practice. Extensive databases on the state of the environment have been established, and particular emphasis has been put on developing and using "headline" indicators of sustainable development. Consumer campaigns have helped raise *environmental awareness* and influence behaviour. Partnership approaches are promoted, and have helped improve environmental management and integration. *Environmental NGOs* are major actors in the environmental and sustainable development debate and activities, not only at the local, regional and national levels but also in international contexts such as the EU and the IUCN. Environmental and sustainable development *education* and learning have been reinforced by a wide range of measures, including an update of the national curriculum.

However, substantial *disparities in environmental quality* persist and generally are associated with socio-economic imbalances, resulting in significant inequality in health status and death rates. Distributive effects of environmental or environment-related policies are not systematically taken into account in planning. Countryside access and rights of way still require significant improvement to meet objectives. Regional development agencies have missed opportunities to promote truly integrated approaches to sustainable development with a strong environmental-social dimension. Local partnership approaches (e.g. Local Agenda 21 and community strategies) should be further strengthened, and performance assessment of local authorities in programmes such as Best Value should include systematic reviews of progress in environmental management and sustainable development. *Public support* for use of economic instruments is fading, partly because of inadequate communication strategies (e.g. concerning the roles of energy and transport taxation in achieving environmental objectives). Recent legislation concerning access to environmental information needs to be fully implemented. *Access to courts* is limited, de facto, for NGOs, which have no explicit right to stand on behalf of nature and the environment. Stakeholder participation in the *planning* of large-scale investment projects should not be restricted, but rather made more effective.

It is *recommended* to:

- take concerted action to reduce *disparities in risk exposure* and access to environmental services;

- monitor implementation and assure proper enforcement of *countryside access and rights of way*;

- further strengthen the *integration of environmental targets and actions* in initiatives to combat social exclusion and deprivation, and seek to ensure that social *compensation measures* do not undermine the effectiveness of environmental policies;

- assure effective integration of environmental objectives in *local partnership approaches* to sustainable development;

- provide for improved *legal standing of NGOs* in courts and pursue implementation of recent legislation concerning access to environmental information.

Sectoral integration: construction

The UK recently adopted a *strategy for more sustainable construction* and has established institutions and procedures for improving the integration of environmental concerns into construction activities and policies. In close co-operation with the industry, several initiatives for technology diffusion have been set up. With respect to material use, a quantified target of increasing the use of construction waste and *recycled aggregates* was set: an increase of more than 80% by 2006, from the 1989 level. Landfilling of construction and demolition waste has fallen since the introduction of the *landfill tax*. The 2002 *aggregates levy*, which increased prices of sand, gravel and crushed rock by some 30%, is expected to provide additional incentive for recycling. The 2001 climate change levy should help improve energy efficiency in commercial buildings. Standards for *energy efficiency* in new buildings have gradually been raised through the application of revised building regulations, and there is now more technical flexibility in meeting them. To improve energy efficiency in the existing housing stock, an investment programme targeted at *"fuel poor" households* was launched. In the private sector, builders now have to display energy ratings for new homes. The environmental performance of buildings is rated through the Building Research Establishment Environmental Assessment Method (BREEAM). Already applied to about 25% of new office buildings, this *labelling system* has helped raise awareness of energy efficiency issues.

However, there is still considerable scope for progress. Despite repeated upgrades, energy efficiency standards for new dwellings remain below those of comparable EU countries, while the large potential for improved energy efficiency in the *existing building stock* is only now beginning to be addressed. Translation of positive experiences from pilot projects into standard practice should be accelerated. Awareness of energy saving potential is still low. Rating and labelling systems for buildings, such as BREEAM, should be promoted more actively. The public sector has not yet fully integrated sustainable

---

It is *recommended* to:

- further promote the *integration of environment-related measures* into strategies and programmes devoted to improving performance in the construction sector;

- amend the Building Act to address the operational *energy efficiency of existing buildings*, and launch a comprehensive policy, with clearly defined targets, to substantially upgrade energy efficiency in existing buildings;

- continue efforts to improve *resource efficiency and conservation* through increased recycling and reuse of construction materials and sites, and strengthen control of illegal disposal of construction and demolition waste;

- ensure that the public sector, through its *procurement policy*, sets a good example for sustainable construction and operation of buildings and infrastructure;

- add environmental indicators to the set of *construction performance indicators* and promote public awareness of *rating and labelling systems* such as SAP and BREEAM.

construction objectives into its procurement policies as regards construction. Concerning waste streams, information is insufficient to review the impact of recent measures, though there is growing concern about *illegal disposal* of construction and demolition waste at unlicensed sites. The sustainable construction strategy does not contain *specific quantified targets*, but calls on the industry to measure baselines, set targets and publish results. The industry is developing sector- and product-specific performance indicators, yet the development and use of environmental indicators needs to be further encouraged. Environmental and sustainable development concerns and criteria are often not sufficiently integrated into decisions on the design, construction, operation and assessment of buildings. Overall, the restructuring and reorientation of the sector has been primarily driven by economic priorities and perspectives.

3. International Co-operation

Concerning *climate change*, the UK reduced its GHG emissions by 13.5% from 1990 to 2000. The country thus has already made very good progress towards meeting its ambitious national target of cutting CO_2 emissions by 20% between 1990 and 2010, as well as its international target under the Kyoto Protocol (a 12.5% reduction in GHG emissions between 1990 and 2008-12). A comprehensive climate change programme was launched in 2000, with the aim of sustaining these emission reductions and meeting the national CO_2 target. Concerning *transboundary air pollution*, the UK has met all of its international reduction targets for NO_x, SO_x and NMVOC emissions. Concerning *marine issues*, the UK extended prohibitions regarding ocean dumping to industrial waste and sewage sludge in the 1990s, and has consistently ensured that at least 25% of the foreign ships calling at its ports are inspected for compliance with the Paris Memorandum of Understanding on Port State Control. It has also upgraded waste management facilities in its ports, anticipating international requirements. Performance on transposing and applying EU directives on environment has improved overall, although several issues of non-compliance have been taken to court (e.g. on nitrates and marine habitats). A major review in 2000 of *export credit programmes* led to the adoption of a Statement of Business Principles that determines how applications for support are assessed, taking into account sustainable development concerns.

However, to ensure that the *GHG reductions* are sustained, the country needs to vigorously pursue implementation of additional policies and measures outlined in the climate change programme. Attaining its targets concerning wider use of renewables and combined heat and power production would also help assure the country's longer-term performance (post-2010) with respect to climate protection, and to transboundary air pollution control (in line with the EU acidification strategy and national emission ceiling directive). Additional measures will also be necessary to moderate demand for road transport and electricity. Further technological control of air emissions at *refineries and offshore installations* will be necessary to meet future international emission reduction targets for SO_x, NO_x and NMVOCs. The UK's performance in reducing *nitrate discharges to regional seas* has fallen short of international commitments. Offshore installations have been slow in complying with OSPAR limits on oil content in discharges of produced water. As in other North Sea countries, about half the *fish stocks* exploited by the UK fishing fleet are classified as outside of biologically sustainable limits. Programmes aimed at reducing fishing capacity have had moderate impact. The UK's *official development assistance* (ODA) totals 0.32% of GNI, well under the Rio target of 0.7%. Attempts to "mainstream" environmental concerns into ODA projects have helped raise general awareness of the issues, but have so far not led to clear and practical guidelines, or use of best practices.

It is *recommended* to:

- review and adjust, if appropriate, *economic incentives in the energy and transport sectors* to facilitate full implementation of the climate change programme;

- strengthen and further expand measures to limit *nitrate inputs* into regional seas, with particular attention to diffuse sources such as agriculture;

- strengthen enforcement and pollution control measures at *offshore installations and refineries* in line with internationally agreed control targets (e.g. under OSPAR, MARPOL, EU emission ceiling directive);

- continue to reduce *fishing fleet capacity* and related subsidies, and work to ensure that precautionary management strategies are applied to overexploited fish stocks;

- monitor the implementation of voluntary initiatives designed to assure integration of sustainable development concerns into *export credits and guarantees*;

- increase *official development assistance* towards the Rio commitment of 0.7% of GNI and establish clear procedures for mainstreaming environmental objectives into projects;

- ratify and implement recently signed *international environmental agreements* (Annex II).

Part I
ENVIRONMENTAL MANAGEMENT

2

AIR MANAGEMENT*

Recommendations

The following recommendations are part of the overall conclusions and recommendations of the Environmental Performance Review of the United Kingdom:

- continue efforts to reduce *NO$_x$, particulate and NMVOC emissions*, in light of persistent problems with high concentrations of NO$_2$, PM$_{10}$ and ozone in some areas;
- implement *area-wide emission control* more consistently, providing more precise guidance to local authorities and taking measures to reinforce their management capacity where necessary;
- work to increase public perception of *fuel- and vehicle-related taxes* as tools for achieving environmental goals, improving public transport and promoting low-emission vehicles and their refuelling infrastructure;
- strengthen *transport demand management* measures, including through the use of local authorities' new powers to set road use charges and workplace parking levies;
- improve integration of air management concerns into *transport policies and plans*, particularly at the local level through better land use planning;
- continue to integrate local, regional and global atmospheric management concerns into *energy policies*.

---

* The present chapter reviews progress in the last ten years, and particularly since the previous OECD Environmental Performance Review of 1994. It also reviews progress with respect to the objective "maintaining the integrity of ecosystems" of the 2001 OECD Environmental Strategy. It takes into account the latest IEA Energy Policy Review of the United Kingdom.

Conclusions

In the 1990s, urban air quality continued to improve in the UK. Very strong *decoupling of emissions of conventional air pollutants from GDP* was achieved: while GDP rose by 26%, emissions decreased by 68% for SO_x, 42% for NO_x, 34% for NMVOCs and 33% for CO. This achievement mainly resulted from energy intensity gains, large-scale fuel switching (e.g. from coal and heavy oil to gas) and improved pollution control devices such as catalytic converters on gasoline cars and flue gas desulphurisation systems at coal-fired power stations. SO_x and NO_x emissions from large combustion plants were reduced below the EU's 1998 limits several years early. This brought the UK energy and emission intensity figures closer to EU averages, but room for further progress exists. *Large reductions in emissions of toxic chemicals* were also achieved (e.g. by 77% for polycyclic aromatic hydrocarbons [PAH], 70% for dioxins and furans, 73% for heavy metals). The sale of leaded gasoline was banned at the beginning of 2000. A statutory *national air quality strategy* with quantitative, dated targets for eight air pollutants has been implemented and regularly reviewed. An area-wide air quality management system introduced in 1997 launched a more holistic approach to addressing local air quality problems. Parking regulation and pricing continue to be effective traffic management tools in UK cities. Integration of air quality concerns into *energy and transport policies* has further progressed with measures such as promotion of combined heat and power generation, the automotive fuel duty escalator, reform of company car taxation, and the differentiation of vehicle excise duty based on CO_2 emission factors and of motor fuel excise duties based on sulphur content. Coal subsidies ceased in 1995. Cost-benefit analyses and estimates of health effects of air pollution are systematically considered in policy decisions. Overall, the UK has proceeded very well with its air agenda, in the context of its EU and other international commitments.

Despite these very positive intentions, actions and results, the UK faces a number of air management challenges. Metropolitan areas still contain "hot spots" where NO_x and PM_{10} concentrations frequently exceed national standards and cause *air quality concerns*, particularly affecting the poor. In some urban areas heavily exposed to road traffic, the UK's proposed national long-term standards for benzene would be exceeded at many roadside locations; exceedances of the proposed national standard for PAH would also occur in a few industrial and domestic coal burning areas. This suggests that additional local measures would be needed to achieve the proposed national standards (which would be more stringent than the EU limit values) by 2010. At the local level, implementation of the national air quality strategy has been rather slow, in part due to insufficient commitment and capacity on the part of local authorities. *Decoupling road transport use from GDP growth*, for both passengers and freight, remains the biggest challenge. Despite increased use of rail for passenger and freight transport in recent years, its modal share is still lower than that in many other OECD countries. The latest national transport programme is predicated upon major investment in the current decade, after years of under-investment. A significant proportion of the public appears to perceive *taxes on fuels and vehicles* as fulfilling a revenue raising function, rather than as tools to help achieve environmental goals. Local authorities have not yet used their recently extended road pricing powers. Natural gas and oil prices for industry and households, compared to EU and OECD averages, leave room for increased internalisation of environmental externalities. Investment in new and cleaner transport, including low-emission vehicles, is relatively limited and has not been integrated into efforts to "green" government operations in practical terms.

1.   Evaluation of Performance

1.1   Institutional framework and objectives

The 1990 Environmental Protection Act established a *two-tier regime* for control of air pollution from industrial sources, composed of integrated pollution control (IPC) and local air pollution control (LAPC). Most large polluting installations or technologically complex processes are regulated under the IPC system by national authorities (Chapter 6, Section 2.1). The IPC approach regulates emissions not only to air but also to other environmental media. In England and Wales, the Environment Agency implements the IPC system, while air emissions from smaller-scale processes are regulated under the LAPC system by local authorities (counties/county boroughs in Wales, districts/boroughs elsewhere). The Scottish Environment Protection Agency regulates both IPC and LAPC processes in Scotland. In Northern Ireland, the Indus-trial Pollution and Radiochemical Inspectorate regulates large processes, including IPC processes, and local authorities regulate smaller processes.

The IPC and LAPC approaches both seek to minimise pollutant releases to the environment by requiring the use of "*best available techniques not entailing excessive cost (BATNEEC)*" (Chapter 6, Section 2.1). Emission limits are usually site-specific, rather than process-specific, and thus can be adapted to reflect local conditions. A new *integrated pollution prevention and control (IPPC)* system, established under the 1999 Pollution Prevention and Control Act (which transposed the 1996 EU IPPC directive), is being phased in between 2000 and 2007, and will supersede the IPC sys-tem. The new system maintains the basic principles of the previous one, but substan-tially extends the type of processes and the range of issues subject to integrated permitting.

The UK sets out its *medium-term air quality management objectives and measures* in a national *air quality strategy*, as required by the 1995 Environment Act. Devolved administrations in Scotland, Wales and Northern Ireland help develop the national strategy. The revised strategy published in January 2000 strengthened health-related ambient air quality standards and introduced target dates for achieving them for eight pollutants. It also introduced air quality standards for the protection of vegetation and ecosystems, covering NO_2 and SO_2. The revised strategy strengthened most of the air quality standards along with objectives (e.g. target dates) for their achievement, in line with or tighter than EU limit values for the pollutants concerned (Table 2.1). The UK is considering tightening the standards and objectives for particles (PM_{10}), CO and benzene, and introducing standards for polycyclic aromatic hydrocarbons (PAHs).

The UK is committed to numerous *national emission reduction targets* through a range of international agreements, including the 1988 EU large combustion plant directive (for SO_2 and NO_x emissions from large combustion plants) and the protocols to the UNECE Convention on Long-range Transboundary Air Pollution (for SO_2 NO_x, NH_3, VOCs, persistent organic pollutants [POPs] and heavy metals). International agreements concerning the ozone layer and climate change also generate emission targets and policies with ancillary benefits for local and regional air management (Chapter 9). Fuel quality standards are largely driven by EU legislation.

The UK's performance in managing air quality can also be assessed against the recommendations of the 1994 *OECD Environmental Performance Review*, which were to:

– accelerate work to establish ambient air quality standards and to extend coverage to particulates and air toxics;

– explore the wider use of economic instruments, including road pricing;

– use more regulatory measures such as product standards, energy efficiency standards and life-cycle analysis of products;

– efficiently implement strategies to achieve emission reductions of SO_x and VOCs and to limit acid deposition;

– further integrate transport and environmental policies.

1.2   Air management

Trends in air emissions

In the 1990s, the UK achieved *large emission reductions* for a range of pollutants, including criteria air pollutants, POPs and heavy metals (Chapter 2, Section 2.1). The

Table 2.1   **Selected national ambient air quality standards and corresponding EU standards**

Pollutant	Parameter	UK national objectives		EU legislation[a]	
		Limit value	Date to be achieved[b]	Limit value	Date to be achieved[b]
For the protection of human health					
SO_2	1-hr mean	350 µg/m³, not to be exceeded more than 24 times per year	2005	350 µg/m³, not to be exceeded more than 24 times per year	2005
	24-hr mean	125 µg/m³, not to be exceeded more than 3 times per year	2005	125 µg/m³, not to be exceeded more than 3 times per year	2005
	15-min mean	266 µg/m³, not to be exceeded more than 35 times per year	2006		
PM_{10}	24-hr mean	50 µg/m³, not to be exceeded more than 35 times per year	2005	50 µg/m³, not to be exceeded more than 35 times per year	2005
	Annual mean	40 µg/m³	2005	40 µg/m³	2005
NO_2	1-hr mean	200 µg/m³, not to be exceeded more than 18 times per year	2006	200 µg/m³, not to be exceeded more than 18 times per year	2010
	Annual mean	40 µg/m³	2006	40 µg/m³	2010
CO	8-hr mean[c]	11.6 mg/m³	2004	10 mg/m³	2005
Lead	Annual mean	0.5 µg/m³	2005	0.5 µg/m³	2005
	Annual mean	0.25 µg/m³	2009		
Benzene	Annual mean[d]	16.25 µg/m³	2004	5 µg/m³	2010
1,3-butadiene	Annual mean[d]	2.25 µg/m³	2004		
Ozone	Daily maximum of running 8-hr mean	100 µg/m³, not to be exceeded more than 10 times per year	2006		
For the protection of vegetation and ecosystems					
SO_2	Annual mean	20 µg/m³	2001	20 µg/m³	2001[e]
	Winter average[e]	20 µg/m³	2001	20 µg/m³	2001[e]
NO_x	Annual mean	30 µg/m³	2001	30 µg/m³	2001[e]

a) Directive 99/30/EC for SO_2, NO_2, PM_{10} and lead; Directive 00/69/EC for CO and benzene.
b) Unless otherwise stated, date refers to beginning of year indicated.
c) Running 8-hr mean (i.e. mean of past 8 hours) for UK limit value, and maximum daily 8-hr mean for EU limit value.
d) Running annual mean (i.e. mean of past 8 760 hours) for UK limit value.
e) From 1 October to 31 March.
Source: DEFRA.

UK attained its 1998 SO_x and NO_x targets under the EU large combustion plant directive several years early. Between 1990 and 1999, national emissions of SO_2 fell by 68%, NO_x by 42%, NMVOCs by 34% and CO by 33%. The UK reversed the upward trend in its emissions of NO_x and NMVOCs, and overcame the stagnation in SO_2 and CO emission levels that occurred in the latter half of the 1980s. *Strong decoupling* of these air emissions from economic growth was achieved in the 1990s (Figure 2.1). This can be attributed to the combined effects of fuel switching, improved fuel efficiency and wider application of modern pollution abatement technologies. However, UK *air pollutant emission intensities* (kg/unit GDP) are still about average for OECD Europe countries, and are slightly higher than the EU average, leaving considerable room for further progress.

The UK met its *internationally agreed air emission reduction targets* in the 1990s, and is well on its way to meeting future targets (Chapter 9, Section 2.2). Air emissions of *organic and toxic pollutants* decreased substantially between 1990 and 1999; national emissions of benzene, 1,3-butadiene and 12 selected PAHs declined by 45%, 53% and 77%, respectively. National emissions of *dioxins and furans* decreased by 70% in the same period. In 1999, per capita dioxin emissions were around the OECD average. Over the same period, emissions of *heavy metals* declined by 73%. Despite decreased use of fertiliser in agriculture, ammonia emissions were little changed in the 1990s because management of livestock manure, the main source of ammonia, was not much improved. Once ratified or transposed, the 1999 Gothenburg Protocol and the 2000 EU national emission ceiling directive will be challenging for the UK as far as SO_x, NO_x, NMVOC and ammonia emissions are concerned.

Trends in air quality

The UK has made *major progress in reducing ambient levels of criteria air pollutants*. There was a consistent decreasing trend in the 1990s, and levels generally satisfy the national air quality standards (Chapter 2, Section 2.2). However, "hot spots" exist in some metropolitan areas, where concentrations of NO_2 and PM_{10} exceed the standards. Concerning ground-level ozone, the annual frequency of exceedances fluctuated from less than 10% of the time to over 70% in the 1990s (Figure 2.2). Concentrations of benzene and 1,3-butadiene have declined substantially since monitoring of these compounds started in the early 1990s. Present measures are expected to eliminate existing hot spots for these two toxics by 2003. If the tighter long-term standard for benzene and the new one for PAHs are adopted, however, additional measures may be necessary to meet those standards at all locations. Constant *high NO_2 levels and the existence of hot spots for PM_{10}* in metropolitan areas suggest a continuing need to reduce urban emissions from road

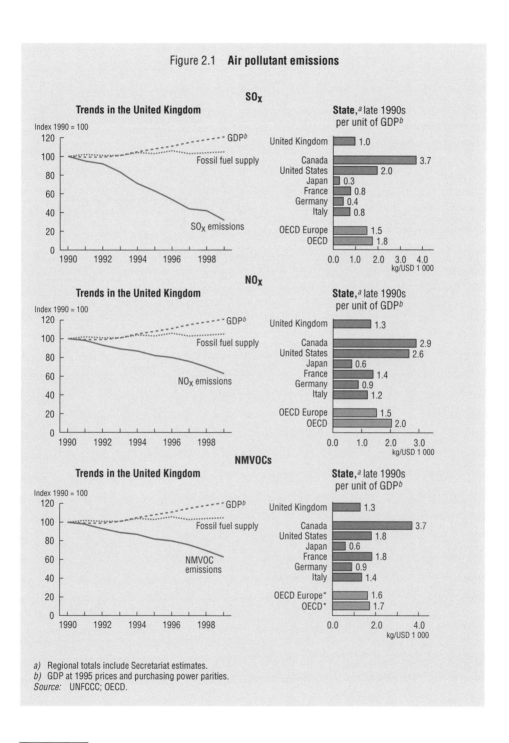

Figure 2.1 **Air pollutant emissions**

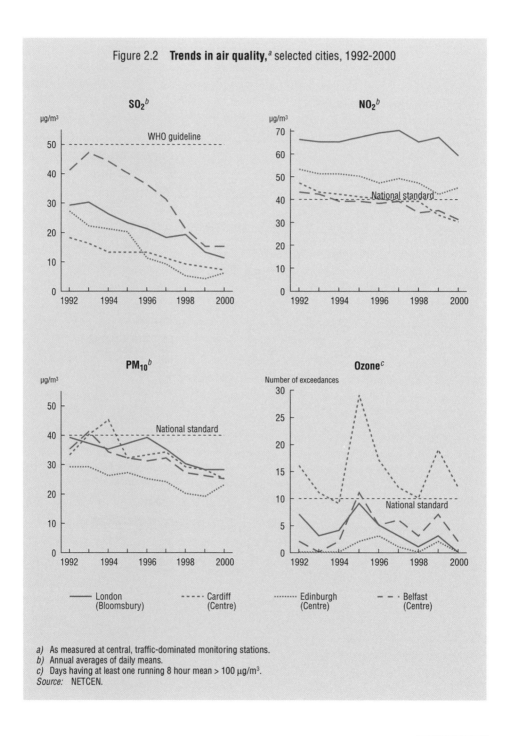

Figure 2.2   **Trends in air quality,** *a* selected cities, 1992-2000

a) As measured at central, traffic-dominated monitoring stations.
b) Annual averages of daily means.
c) Days having at least one running 8 hour mean > 100 µg/m³.
Source: NETCEN.

transport, the major source of both pollutants. High levels of ground-level ozone are consistently found in rural areas (although the severity has been declining) and sometimes in urban areas, implying a need for continued efforts to limit regional emissions of ozone precursors, especially NO_x from motor vehicles and NMVOCs from motor vehicles and industry (e.g. solvents).

The UK's *air quality monitoring* system was significantly expanded in the 1990s. The number of automatic monitoring sites for conventional air pollutants increased from about 30 in 1990 to 110 in 2000 (the number varies depending on the pollutant) as affiliation of local authority sites with the national network progressed. Automatic monitoring is complemented by several non-automatic monitoring systems run by both national and local authorities. In 2001, these included 25 sites for lead, 1 100 for NO_2, 165 for SO_2 and black smoke, 32 for acid deposition and 14 for PAHs, PCBs, dioxins and furans. Air monitoring is now carried out in some form or another at over 1 500 sites across the UK. The extension of automatic monitoring has been accompanied by expanded public access to *air quality information*. Real-time regional air quality ratings and 24-hour forecasts of air quality are provided for SO_2, NO_2, CO, PM_{10} and ozone via the Internet, toll-free telephone, TV teletext services and local news media. Hourly values for each pollutant at individual monitoring stations are also provided.

UK authorities actively pursue evaluation of *health damage caused by air pollution*. In the late 1990s, the Committee on the Medical Effects of Air Pollutants estimated that 8 100 premature deaths were caused annually by PM_{10} and 3 500 by SO_2 in urban areas (Chapter 7, Section 1.1). An interministerial review of implementation of the 1997 air quality strategy found that existing and proposed measures would likely reduce the number of respiratory deaths and hospital admissions by approximately 18 500 and 22 000, respectively, over 1996-2005. In addition, non-health benefits (e.g. avoidance of damage to historic buildings, crops and forests) were estimated to equal GBP 500 million over the same period.

Policy measures

The two-tier air pollution control regime (IPC and LAPC) was effective in many respects in the 1990s. In the late 1990s in England and Wales, about 2 000 large industrial processes (accounting for 88%, 26% and 40% of the UK's SO_2, NO_x and CO_2 emissions, respectively, in 1998) were regulated by the Environment Agency for air emissions under the IPC system, while 17 000 smaller processes were regulated by local authorities under LAPC for air emissions. *Substantial emission reductions from licensed facilities were made in the 1990s.* Between 1990 and 1998, *emissions from IPC-licensed processes* (i.e. most large polluting processes) in England and

Wales declined by 57% for SO_2, 48% for NO_x, 30% for CO_2, 59% for lead, 61% for benzene and 92% for dioxins. These processes are still the dominant emitters of SO_2 (88% of the UK total in 1998), but their shares are relatively small for other pollutants (e.g. 26% for NO_x and less than 10% for benzene and NMVOCs).

Under the IPC system, *technical guidance notes* were issued and regularly updated, describing available abatement technology, achievable emission levels and BATNEEC. Interpretation of these notes was a source of confusion in implementing the IPC system in the early years. A number of technical guidance notes were also issued and updated for smaller air pollution processes to help local authorities implement the LAPC system.

Inspection and enforcement of licensed air polluting facilities were not consistently carried out in the 1990s. The annual number of inspections of IPC-licensed processes fluctuated greatly. Inspection programmes by local authorities on LAPC processes were also criticised as unplanned, unstructured and complaint-driven. As such inconsistencies undermine the credibility of the IPC/IPCC and LAPC systems, the situation needs to be improved (Chapter 6, Section 2.1).

By 2007, when the *IPPC system* is to be completely phased in, the number of installations under integrated licensing will reach 7 000 (including 1 000 that will continue to be regulated by local authorities), compared to 2 100 now, in England and Wales. In Scotland, about 2 000 installations will be subject to the new system. The IPPC system requires "best available techniques" (BAT) rather than BATNEEC. IPC is being substantially strengthened, which should accelerate further emission reductions, but the effects of the new system remain to be seen.

An *area-wide air quality management system* was introduced in 1997 in England, Scotland and Wales. It requires local authorities to review and assess current and future air quality in their areas, to designate areas where air quality standards are likely not to be met and to develop action plans for those areas, considering all sources of air pollution, including IPC and LAPC processes, as well as road transport. The system may lead to a better mix of measures and enhanced policy integration of air quality management and land use planning (e.g. for transport development at local level). By 2001, 50 local authorities had designated air quality management areas, and a further 50 were doing so. In addition, local authorities are encouraged to utilise *land use planning* to complement local pollution control efforts, in particular through regulation of factory and road siting. The Environment Agency has also begun applying an area-wide emission control approach to assess the contribution of IPC processes to local air quality, as well as the technological feasibility and cost-effectiveness of possible improvements. For this purpose, it has identified 11 "Zones of Industrial Pollution Sources" in England and Wales where large IPC processes are grouped. However, given the delays observed in preparation of evaluation and assessment by local authorities, and the large variations in the process of area designation and in the contents of action plans, there would seem to be a need for clearer, more precise guidance from the central government. The system could also be improved by adding ground-level ozone, for which the air quality standard was established in the 2000 air quality strategy, while taking into account the transboundary nature (i.e. from and to continental Europe) of the pollutant and its precursors.

Pollution abatement and control (PAC) expenditure concerning air quality and climate protection totalled GBP 1.1 billion in 1999 (Table 6.8). Around 25% of PAC expenditure by the private sector went for air management in the 1990s. In 1999, 70% of the amount was for investment and the rest for operations. Chemicals/rubber/plastic, basic metals, non-metallic mineral products and pulp/paper accounted for two-thirds of the UK's total PAC expenditure by business in 1997. The energy sector contributed 13%. Despite the UK's strong orientation towards cost-effectiveness in pollution control, little information is available to evaluate how the IPC system and BATNEEC approach have actually affected industry's overall PAC expenditure for air pollution control.

1.3   Integration of air pollution objectives into energy policies

Trends in energy production and consumption

Since 1950, the *energy intensity* of the UK economy (total primary energy supply [TPES] per unit of GDP) has been steadily declining. This trend continued in the 1990s, with a 10% decline, roughly equalling the OECD Europe average in 1999 (Figure 9.2). Improved energy efficiency and a decline in energy intensive industry (e.g. steel) are the main causes of the downward trend and constitute the main reason for emission reduction in 1990s. Over the decade, total final energy consumption (TFC) grew strongest in the transport sector, followed by the residential sector, whereas a decreasing trend was seen in the industry sector. Consequently, the largest energy-consuming sector is now the residential/commercial sector, with 37% of TFC, followed by transport (32%), industry (26%) and agriculture (1%) (Figure 9.2).

The UK's *energy supply is dominated by fossil fuels* (88% of TPES), with coal, oil and natural gas representing 15%, 36% and 37%, respectively (Figure 9.2). Nuclear power makes up most of the rest (11%); renewable energy sources and hydropower account for less than 1%. The share of coal nearly halved in the 1990s, while that of gas increased by more than 60%; this is one major reason for the substantial emission reduction in the decade (Chapter 2, Section 1.2). In the electricity generation sector, significant *fuel switching* occurred, predominantly from coal to gas. Also, electricity generation capacity of combined heat and power (CHP) doubled, and capacity of non-hydro renewables (e.g. wind) increased eight-fold, which are encouraging trends for emission reduction. National targets are to further raise CHP capacity from 4 700 MW to 10 000 MW and the share of renewables in electricity generation from 2.8% to 10% by 2010. The share of nuclear plants in electricity generation gradually increased in the 1990s, but may decline as existing nuclear power stations reach the end of their licensed lifetimes in 2010 and beyond.

Energy prices and taxation

In the 1990s, the UK's *energy prices for industry* generally evidenced a declining trend, except for heavy fuel oil, which fluctuated significantly. The prices paid by industry for electricity, gas and coal in 2000 were over 30% lower than in 1990, in real terms. *Energy prices for households* also showed a downward trend, to a smaller degree, except for heating oil prices, which increased sharply in the late 1990s. For both industry and households, the price of electricity closely tracked the OECD Europe average, while that of gas stayed cheaper than the OECD Europe average, with a widening gap during the 1990s as domestic gas production increased. Throughout the 1990s, the price of oil was lower than the OECD Europe average. The difference became increasingly smaller for industry but remained large (more than 30%) for households (Table 2.2).

Taxes on non-automotive fuels are rather limited in the UK. Only gas oil, liquefied petroleum gas (LPG) and kerosene are subject to excise duty, with a reduced rate for the latter two when used for domestic heating. VAT on domestic fuel and power was introduced at 8% in 1994 to encourage efficient use of fuels, but the rate was reduced to 5% in 1997. A reduced VAT of 5% on energy saving materials (e.g. insulation, central heating) was introduced in 2000, and a climate change levy on non-domestic energy use was introduced in April 2001. These measures will likely stimulate emission reductions from stationary sources, not only for CO_2 but also for conventional pollutants, though their effectiveness in this respect remains to be seen. Subsidies to coal ceased in 1995.

Taxes on automotive fuels increasingly took emissions into account in the 1990s. The *automotive fuel duty escalator* introduced in 1993 was maintained until 1999, resulting in a stepwise increase in the annual rate. Consequently, the tax component of prices (sum of excise tax and VAT) reached 70% for gasoline and 75% for diesel in 2000, placing the UK's road fuel prices among the highest in OECD countries when adjusted for purchasing power parity (Figure 2.3). Road traffic growth was slower than GDP growth during the period when the fuel duty escalator was applied, though it is unclear whether, or to what degree, a causal relationship exists. Since 1998, automotive fuel duties have been loosely based on energy and carbon contents; thus, the rate for diesel fuel is slightly higher than that for gasoline. Yet, the government's position is not to favour either gasoline or diesel, but rather to encourage drivers to choose the fuel most suited to their circumstances. As a result, the final consumer price of diesel is about the same as that of gasoline, unlike in other OECD countries, where diesel is often much cheaper (Figure 2.3).

Tax differentials on automotive fuels in favour of unleaded gasoline, and ultra-low-sulphur diesel and gasoline, were introduced in 1987, 1997 and 2000, respectively, and were progressively increased. Duties on compressed natural gas (CNG) and LPG were reduced in 1999 to a level about a fifth of that on diesel, and have been frozen in real terms until at least 2004. Despite these developments, automotive fuel duties are still generally perceived simply as revenue raising instruments. Public understanding of the positive effects of recent fuel taxation policy in reducing emissions needs to be improved.

Table 2.2 **Energy prices in selected OECD countries,** 2000

	Electricity		Oil		Natural gas	
	Industry (USD[c]/KWh)	Households (USD[d]/kWh)	Industry[a] (USD[c]/toe)	Households[b] (USD[d]/1 000 l)	Industry (USD[c]/toe)	Households (USD[d]/ 10[7] kcal)
United Kingdom	0.055	0.108	194.1	328.9	104.6	295.9
Canada	. .	. .	190.0	453.9	89.8	250.1
United States	0.045	0.082	174.7	357.0	169.7	317.7
Japan	. .	0.151	233.6	308.4	452.7	911.5
France	0.036	0.113	183.6	460.2	167.8	385.2
Germany	. .	0.132	. .	411.8	187.9	408.2
Italy	0.089	0.178	230.1	1 037.5	. .	. .
OECD Europe	0.058	0.128	203.6	499.4	156.7	393.8
OECD	0.050	0.106	212.8	448.3	167.0	366.3
UK price/OECD Europe (%)	*95*	*84*	*95*	*66*	*67*	*75*
UK price/OECD (%)	*110*	*102*	*91*	*73*	*63*	*81*

a) High-sulphur oil.
b) Light fuel oil.
c) At current exchange rates.
d) At current purchasing power parities.
Source: IEA-OECD.

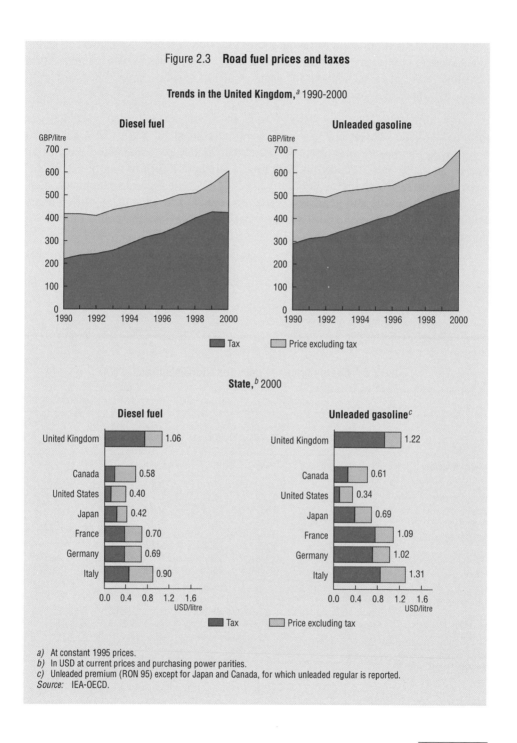

Figure 2.3   **Road fuel prices and taxes**

Trends in the United Kingdom,[a] 1990-2000

Diesel fuel

GBP/litre

Unleaded gasoline

GBP/litre

Tax   Price excluding tax

State,[b] 2000

Diesel fuel

United Kingdom	1.06
Canada	0.58
United States	0.40
Japan	0.42
France	0.70
Germany	0.69
Italy	0.90

USD/litre

Unleaded gasoline[c]

United Kingdom	1.22
Canada	0.61
United States	0.34
Japan	0.69
France	1.09
Germany	1.02
Italy	1.31

USD/litre

Tax   Price excluding tax

a) At constant 1995 prices.
b) In USD at current prices and purchasing power parities.
c) Unleaded premium (RON 95) except for Japan and Canada, for which unleaded regular is reported.
Source: IEA-OECD.

© OECD 2002

1.4   Integration of air pollution objectives into transport policies

Trends in transport modes and emissions

Road transport is the dominant *mode of transport* in the UK, for both passengers and freight (Figure 6.2). Large increases in road transport occurred in the 1990s, although its market share appears to be stabilising. Over the decade, the number of passenger cars registered rose by more than 20%, while the growth of passenger transport by car in terms of passenger-kilometres was relatively limited at 6%. The growth of road freight transport closely tracked GDP growth in the 1990s, with road freight taking market share from inland waterway shipping. Concerning public transport, a positive sign from the air emission perspective is that the use of rail has been strongly recovering since the mid-1990s, although that of buses and coaches has remained stable. After years of underinvestment in rail passenger and freight transport infrastructure, major structural reforms of the transport sector took place: privatisation of rail transport companies, revival of investment and the new national transport programme, Transport 2010: The 10 Year Plan.

Emissions from transport decreased significantly in the 1990s (Chapter 2, Section 2.1). Between 1990 and 1999, emissions of SO_2 from transport fell by 57%, NO_x by 41%, NMVOCs by 46% and CO by 35%. Nevertheless, the transport sector remained the largest source of national emissions of NO_x (56% in 1999), NMVOCs (31%) and CO (78%). The declining trend in emissions of these pollutants from road transport is projected to continue for two decades or so, then to gradually slow as continuing road traffic growth offsets engine and fuel improvements. On the other hand, CO_2 emissions from road transport rose steadily in the 1990s and accounted for 22% of total CO_2 emissions in 1999, despite increased fuel efficiency (Chapter 2, Section 2.3).

Regulations

Vehicle emission and fuel quality standards are driven at EU level by the auto-oil programmes and related EU legislation. Between 1992 and 2001, emission standards for new vehicles were tightened in three steps: Euro I (1992-4), II (1996-7) and III (2001). As a result, emission standards for new vehicles are now 45-98% tighter than before Euro I, depending on type of vehicle and pollutant. Further tightening (Euro IV) is planned for 2006. The proportion of gasoline-fuelled cars with catalytic converters, which became a de facto standard via Euro I, increased from 3% of the UK fleet in 1990 to 46% in 1998. In 2001, it was estimated that more than 70% of gasoline cars and 90% of diesel cars in the fleet complied with Euro I, II or III standards.

EU *fuel quality standards* on maximum allowable sulphur content in gasoline and diesel were tightened to 150 ppm and 350 ppm, respectively, in 2000, and a further reduction to 50 ppm for both fuels is scheduled for 2005. In the UK, by 2000, all gasoline and diesel fuels were already "ultra-low-sulphur fuels" meeting the EU 2005 standards (< 50 ppm sulphur), and the sale of *leaded gasoline* had been phased out, in compliance with EU legislation.

Annual vehicle emission tests are used to check compliance with emission standards of in-use vehicles. Introduced in 1991 for gasoline vehicles, and extended to all vehicles in the mid-1990s, the annual tests are supplemented by roadside spot tests. However, the National Audit Office estimated in 1999 that 10-20% of vehicles on UK roads did not comply with emission standards, despite the annual test. Vehicle owners pay a total of GBP 100 million a year for the testing. In its report, the Audit Office suggested that the credibility of the system could be improved if the Vehicle Inspectorate were to make ad hoc inspections to raise the standard of testing by garages.

Economic instruments

The UK took steps to ensure that the *vehicle excise duty* reflected the external costs of air emissions by the late 1990s (Table 6.2). Since 1999, buses and trucks meeting stringent particle emission standards have been eligible for excise duty concessions of up to GBP 1 000. The vehicle excise duty regime for cars and light goods vehicles was overhauled in 2001. Previously differentiated for two classes by engine size, it is now differentiated for four classes by CO_2 emission level. The new regime also introduced higher duty rates for diesel cars and lower rates for low-emission vehicles (LEVs), both differentiated by up to 10% from rates applied to gasoline cars. The strength of these economic incentives towards purchases of less polluting cars may be rather limited, given the relatively small differences. The differentiation of excise duty by air emission level could be extended to larger vehicles such as buses and haulage vehicles, considering their higher emission rates and sizable contribution to total motor vehicle emissions (e.g. about a quarter for CO_2, a third for NO_x and a half for PM_{10}).

Since *company cars* in the UK account for almost 20% of car mileage, policies concerning company cars have significant implications for air emissions from road transport. In the late 1990s, taxation related to company cars underwent a major reform to produce incentives to reduce emissions from company cars. The previous company car taxation system was widely criticised as giving a perverse incentive to drive more in order to reach the tax discount thresholds (taxable benefits declined as miles travelled increased). From April 2002, the tax rates are based on a percentage of a car's list price, graduated according to its CO_2 emissions. The tax will build up from 15% of the car's price to a maximum of 35%, in 1% steps for every 5 g/km CO_2

above a specified level. The tax on employers for providing free fuel to employees for their private use was raised in 1998 by 20% above the usual movement of pump prices. Since 1998, the cost of converting company cars to gas fuels has been tax deductible. While such policies to discourage unnecessary private use of company cars should continue to be developed, the common practice of providing company cars in the first place should be reviewed.

A range of government-backed initiatives and programmes launched in the 1990s has helped increase the use of alternative fuel vehicles and vehicle emission reduction technologies in the UK. PowerShift, a *financial support programme* for the purchase of alternative fuel vehicles, has supported the purchase of more than 10 000 gas and electric vehicles since its launch in 1996, and helped establish the growing market for LPG vehicles. In the late 1990s, about 13 000 LPG vehicles, 750 natural gas (CNG or LNG) vehicles and nearly 100 modern electric vehicles (excluding 16 000 milk delivery vehicles driven on rudimentary systems) were on UK roads. A grant programme called CleanUp, launched in 2000, will support the retrofitting of emission control equipment (e.g. particulate traps) on about 19 000 large diesel vehicles (e.g. trucks and buses) and taxis in urban areas by 2004 (Chapter 2, Section 2.4).

Road transport demand management

Emissions from road vehicles are the principal causes of chronic hot spots for PM_{10} and NO_2 in major urban areas. The 1997 *Road Traffic Reduction Act* allows local authorities to take special transport demand management measures to address this problem. *Parking restriction* policies have been used effectively and efficiently in many cities. Park-and-ride programmes also became common in the 1990s: around 70 were in operation in mid-2000. An increasing number of towns and cities are introducing *restrictions on access of motor vehicles to town/city centres* (e.g. low-emission zones, 20 mph zones) to improve air quality as well as to regenerate urban centres. Examples include Nottingham, Winchester, Reading and Camden. On the other hand, except in limited locations (e.g. bridges), *road user charging* has so far been little applied. Local authorities in England and Wales were recently given the legislative power to introduce road user charges, as well as workplace parking levies. Although several local authorities have considered such charges for city centres, most have so far been reluctant to use the instrument. London authorities recently announced their intention to establish road pricing in a significant part of the city centre. The use of such economic instruments should be more fully explored, as they can have multiple benefits, including the improvement of persistent urban air quality problems.

Efforts were made in the 1990s to better integrate environmental concerns (air quality in particular) into *freight transport*. A national strategy ("Sustainable

Distribution") issued in 1999 proposes a range of measures in this respect, including public-private partnerships to reduce urban air and noise pollution from freight transport. Such partnerships have already been established in some regions (e.g. Hampshire). Diversion of freight from roads to rail gained momentum in the late 1990s, with an increase of 38% (in tonne-kilometres) between 1995 and 1999 (Figure 6.2). This trend was backed by investment in intermodal rail-freight terminals and new locomotives, as well as by national financial support: the Freight Facilities Grants and Track Access Grants weigh environmental benefits (avoided road journeys for freight transport) when considering grant applications.

Various public and private initiatives for *raising public awareness* of the need to reduce emissions from road transport were developed in the 1990s. Encouraging the use of less polluting modes of transport and fuel-efficient driving is a core message of the government-led *"Are you doing your bit?"* campaign in England and Wales (Chapter 7, Section 1.4) and the *"do a little – change a lot"* campaign in Scotland. A government-backed award programme called Motorvate was launched in 2000 to encourage companies to pursue fuel-efficient fleet management (with a target of reducing CO_2 emissions by 12% in three years) through annual assessment and certification. A database on the fuel efficiency and CO_2 emissions of all new cars, established by the Vehicle Certification Agency, was made easily accessible on the Internet in 2000.

Improving public transport

Until a rapid increase in national rail infrastructure investment was made in the late 1990s, *investment in improving public transport* was more or less stable over the decade. Investment in road infrastructure fell by 30% between 1990 and 1999. The government's Transport 2010 plan includes a substantial boost for investment in the sector, with a strong emphasis on public transport: about 60% of the total investment of GBP 180 billion would go to improve public transport. This would represent more than twice the annual investment in public transport in the 1990s.

Public-private partnerships between local authorities and bus operators to improve the quality of bus service had been developed in over 120 towns and cities by mid-2000. This helped increase bus use by 10-20% from the 1997 level. The initiative was strengthened in late 2001 by giving statutory powers to local authorities to make such agreements and to award exclusive contracts, through bidding, with operators meeting specified conditions as regards routes, frequencies, fares, etc. The establishment of a new national railway regulator, the Strategic Railway Authority, in 2001 is expected to improve the quality of rail service and restore public confidence in rail transport.

2. Focus on Selected Topics

2.1 Steady declines in national air emissions

Criteria air pollutants

National SO_2 *emissions* declined by 68% between 1990 and 1999 (Table 2.3). The bulk of the reduction (79%) was achieved in the energy production and transformation sector (e.g. power stations and refineries) through increased use of nuclear plants and natural gas (in combined cycle gas turbines) for electricity generation. *Flue gas desulphurisation systems*, operational since 1994 at two coal-fired power stations in England, have also helped reduce SO_2 emissions in this sector. In manufacturing, major reductions had already been made by the mid-1980s with the decline in energy-intensive heavy industries such as iron and steel production. A further 71% reduction in emissions from industrial combustion in the 1990s largely reflects fuel switching from coal and oil to natural gas.

National NO_x *emissions* decreased by 42% between 1990 and 1999 (Table 2.3). The reduction mainly came from mobile sources (54% of the reduction) and from energy production and transformation (40%). Despite the increase in road traffic, penetration of cars fitted with catalytic converters, combined with tighter emission standards for trucks, brought about an emission reduction from mobile sources. Wider application of low-NO_x burners to coal-fired power plants and the increase in the proportion of nuclear and combined cycle gas turbine plants contributed to the emission reduction from power generation.

National *NMVOC emissions* fell by 34% between 1990 and 1999 (Table 2.3). About half of this reduction was achieved in transport and a quarter in solvent use. Reduced emissions from transport stem from increased penetration of catalytic converters and a rise in the use of diesel cars (from 3% of all registered cars in 1990 to 12% in 1999). The reduction in emissions associated with solvent use reflects stricter standards and technological change.

National *CO emissions* declined by 33% from 1990 to 1999 (Table 2.3). The reduction came primarily in road transport, with increased penetration of cars with catalytic converters and, to a lesser extent, switching from gasoline to diesel cars. Annual national *ammonia emissions* were stable during the 1990s at around 350 kt per year. About 70% of these emissions came from the decomposition of urea in manure.

National CO_2 *emissions* declined by about 8% between 1990 and 2000 (Chapter 9, Section 1.2). Per unit of GDP, CO_2 emissions have declined by 23% since 1990 (Figure 9.1). The bulk of the nominal reduction (84%) was made by power stations, mainly through fuel switching from coal to gas and nuclear plants, despite a rise in electricity consumption. Emissions from transport have gradually increased, since rapid growth in road transport offset improved motor fuel efficiency.

Table 2.3   **National atmospheric emissions,** by source,[a] 1990-99

Source[b]		SO$_2$ (kt)	SO$_2$ (%)	NO$_X$ (kt)	NO$_X$ (%)	NMVOCs (kt)	NMVOCs (%)	CO (kt)	CO (%)
Combustion in energy	1990	2 918	77.6	884	32.0	11	0.4	143	2.0
production/transformation	1999	884	74.5	423	26.3	10	0.6	94	2.0
Industrial combustion	1990	458	12.2	219	7.9	6	0.2	187	2.6
	1999	156	13.1	169	10.6	7	0.4	173	3.6
Non-industrial combustion[c]	1990	198	5.3	101	3.7	68	2.5	381	5.3
	1999	74	6.3	103	6.4	46	2.6	269	5.7
Production processes	1990	48	1.3	13	0.5	329	12.4	442	6.2
	1999	17	1.5	6	0.4	212	12.2	476	10.0
Extraction and distribution	1990	16	0.4	1	0.0	315	11.9	7	0.1
of fossil fuels	1999	1	0.1	1	0.1	259	14.8	1	0.0
Solvent use	1990	2	0.1	..	..	684	25.8	..	..
	1999	4	0.3	..	..	472	27.0	..	..
Road transport	1990	63	1.7	1 306	47.3	922	34.7	5 235	73.2
	1999	12	1.0	714	44.5	473	27.1	3 293	69.2
Other transport	1990	47	1.3	219	7.9	66	2.5	464	6.5
	1999	35	2.8	185	11.5	63	3.6	437	9.2
Miscellaneous[d]	1990	5	0.1	18	0.7	256	9.6	297	4.1
	1999	4	0.4	3	0.2	202	11.7	17	0.3
Total	1990	3 754	100.0	2 761	100.0	2 657	100.0	7 155	100.0
	1999	1 187	100.0	1 605	100.0	1 744	100.0	4 760	100.0
Change 1990-99 (%)		−68		−42		−34		−33	

a) For the UK as a whole.
b) Source categories defined by UNECE with some aggregations.
c) Includes residential, commercial, institutional and agricultural combustion.
d) Includes waste treatment and disposal, agriculture and forestry.
Source: Netcen; Environment Agency.

Organic and toxic pollutants

National *benzene and 1,3-butadiene emissions* decreased by 45% and 53%, respectively, between 1990 and 1999 (Table 2.4), mainly through the penetration of cars fitted with catalytic converters. Road transport is the predominant source of air emissions of both of these compounds, accounting for 62% and 88%, respectively, in 1998.

Among a vast number of *PAHs*, the UK's official emission inventory focuses on 12 priority PAHs. Their largest source is aluminium production (56% in 1990), followed by natural fires and open agricultural burning (16%), domestic and industrial coal combustion (16%) and road transport (4%). Anthropogenic emissions of each of the 12 PAHs declined in the 1990s. The simple sum of emissions of the 12 PAHs (unweighted by toxicity) decreased by 77% between 1990 and 1999 (Table 2.4), mainly through significant investment in abatement equipment in aluminium processing plants, as required by the IPC system.

National *emissions of dioxins and furans* (in toxic equivalents) decreased by 70% between 1990 and 1999 (Table 2.4). Emissions from municipal waste incinerators, which accounted for 56% of the national emissions in 1990, were significantly reduced through the replacement of old incinerators not meeting stricter standards. As a result, by 1999, emissions from municipal waste incinerators had been reduced to only 4% of the total. National *emissions of PCBs* are estimated to have declined by 70% between 1990 and 1999 with the gradual replacement of electrical equipment containing PCBs (e.g. capacitors) (Table 2.4).

Table 2.4   **Emissions of persistent organic and toxic pollutants,** 1990-99

	Benzene (kt)	1,3-butadiene (kt)	PAHs[a] (kt)	Dioxins and furans (g-Teq)	PCBs (kg)	Heavy metals[b] (tonnes)
1990	54.4	13.3	6.2	1 142	6 976	5 929
1999	29.7	6.2	1.4	346	2 071	1 599
Change 1990-99 (%)	–45	–53	–77	–70	–70	–73

a) Simple sum (unweighted by toxicity) of 16 types: acenapthene, acenapthylene, anthracene, benz(a)anthracene, benzo(a)pyrene, benzo(b)fluoranthene, benzo(ghi)perylene, benzo(k)fluoranthene, chrysene, dibenz(ah)anthracene, fluoranthene, fluorene, indeno(1,2,3-cd)pyrene, napthalene, phenanthrene and pyrene.
b) Simple sum (unweighted by toxicity) of ten elements: arsenic, cadmium, chromium, copper, mercury, nickel, lead, selenium, vanadium and zinc.
Source: Netcen.

National *emissions of heavy metals* decreased significantly, by 73%, between 1990 and 1999 (Table 2.4). The reason varies depending on the metal, but fuel switching from coal and heavy fuel oil to natural gas and tightened controls on municipal waste incinerators were the main factors. The largest reduction among the ten heavy metals in the official inventory was for lead (−80%), as the use of leaded gasoline was phased out.

2.2   *Improvements in urban air quality*

Criteria air pollutants

Monitoring in major urban areas showed a *decreasing trend in ambient air concentrations of most criteria air pollutants* in the 1990s (Figure 2.2). Between 1992 and 2000, *ambient levels of SO_2* fell by about 70% on average in urban areas (i.e. at "urban background", "urban centre" and "urban industrial" stations, by the UK's classification for automatic monitoring sites). In 2000, the average ambient SO_2 concentration in these areas was $10\,\mu g/m^3$, well below the World Health Organization's annual air quality guideline ($50\,\mu g/m^3$). The number of monitoring stations at which national limit values were exceeded was reduced to zero by the end of the 1990s.

Ambient concentrations of NO_2 in urban areas decreased by 35% between 1992 and 2000, to reach an annual average concentration of $34\,\mu g/m^3$, which is below the national limit value ($40\,\mu g/m^3$). However, concentrations in some metropolitan areas, such as London, Glasgow and Edinburgh, were still above the limit value. In London, ambient concentrations were nearly 50% above the limit value in 2000. Furthermore, kerbside monitoring showed that some areas consistently violate the air quality standard's short-term limit value (one-hour mean).

Ambient concentrations of respirable particulates (PM_{10}) decreased by a third in major urban areas between 1992 and 2000. The annual average concentration in these areas was $23\,\mu g/m^3$ in 2000. Concentrations in metropolitan areas such as London, Manchester and Glasgow were among the highest, at about $28\,\mu g/m^3$. Although the national limit value for the annual mean ($40\,\mu g/m^3$) was respected, there remained a few hot spots where the short-term limit value (24-hour mean) was violated. The number and extent of hot spots decreased substantially during the 1990s.

Ambient concentrations of CO in urban areas was halved between 1992 and 2000, reaching the annual average of $0.5\,mg/m^3$ in 2000. Not a single monitoring site has recorded exceedance of the annual limit value since 1999.

Photochemical and toxic pollution

No clear trend in *ground-level ozone concentrations* was detected in the 1990s. Weather conditions continued to show the highest correlation with ambient concentrations. Concentrations in urban areas are generally lower than in rural areas. The proportion of the monitoring sites that failed to meet the air quality standards in urban areas fluctuated from less than 10% to over 70% between 1992 and 2000, while that in rural areas consistently exceeded 70% during the same period. Concentrations in the rural parts of southern England and Wales are generally higher than elsewhere.

Data from 13 monitoring sites show that urban *concentrations of benzene and 1,3-butadiene* substantially decreased in the 1990s. The annual average concentration of benzene decreased by 70% between 1993 and 2000 to reach 1.7 μg/m^3, well below the national air quality standard (16.25 μg/m^3). That of 1,3-butadiene decreased by 40% between 1994 and 2000, to reach 0.3 μg/m^3, also well below the standard (2.25 μg/m^3). However, it is estimated that in some hot spots the standards for these pollutants are regularly exceeded. The extent of these areas can be expected to diminish by 2003 through the implementation of existing or planned policies.

2.3   Key trends in the transport sector

Motorisation, mobility and modal mix

In 2000, the UK *road vehicle fleet* comprised 24.4 million passenger cars, 2.2 million light goods vehicles, 0.8 million heavy trucks and buses, 1.0 million two-wheelers and 0.5 million other vehicles (e.g. agricultural vehicles). Between 1990 and 2000, the number of registered passenger cars increased by 21% and the rate of motorisation in the UK reached 45 cars per 100 people (Figure 6.2). Annual road traffic (in vehicle-kilometres) by all motor vehicles increased by 14% between 1990 and 1999. Road traffic in the UK, at 7 800 vehicle-kilometres per capita, is 26% higher than the OECD Europe average. The rate of increase in the number of diesel passenger cars was significantly higher than that of gasoline cars in the 1990s; in 2000, diesel cars consti-tuted 15% of all registrations.

Throughout the 1990s, the predominant *mode of passenger transport* (in passenger-kilometres) was the private passenger car (85%). Buses and coaches (6%), rail (6%) and air (1%) constituted the rest. The growth of passenger car transport was slower than GDP growth starting in 1993 (Figure 6.2). Both the annual number of trips and the average trip length by car continued to grow. Annual car travel distance per person rose by 11%, reaching more than 8 500 kilometres per person in the late 1990s. Rail use declined until 1994, but has been recovering since at 5-8% per year, possibly because rapid motor fuel price rises increased the cost of car use in the period. Use of buses and coaches was stable during the 1990s. Since there was a long period of underinvestment in public transport, the level of public transport use is still lower in the UK than in many European countries.

Road transport is the predominant *mode of freight shipment* in the UK, accounting for two-thirds of freight shipment by weight (in tonne-kilometres) in the
late 1990s. Waterways are the second most important mode of freight transport,
accounting for 22% of total tonne-kilometres. Shipment by rail and pipeline
accounted for an additional 8% and 5%, respectively. Growth in road transport of
freight has closely tracked GDP growth since the early 1990s, while shipment by
waterways has fallen (Figure 6.2).

Energy consumption

Total final energy consumption by the UK transport sector amounted to
54 million tonnes of oil equivalent in the late 1990s, with road transport accounting
for 76%, followed by air (20%), inland waterway (2%) and rail (1%). Despite rapid
growth in road traffic volume (14% in vehicle-kilometres between 1990 and 1999),
final energy consumption by road transport grew by a rather moderate 5% in
the 1990s due to increased fuel efficiency. Of the energy consumed by road vehicles,
59% was gasoline and the rest diesel. Electricity represents 59% of the energy
consumed by railways in the UK and diesel the remainder. All waterway navigation
is diesel-fuelled.

In 1998, UK automobile manufacturers, as members of the European Federation
of Automobile Manufacturers, pledged to reduce average CO_2 emissions (and related
average fuel consumption) of new passenger cars by 25% by 2008 relative to 1995
levels: to 140 g CO_2/km (5.7 litres/100 km). An indicative, intermediate target is
165-170 g CO_2/km in 2003. *Average new car fuel consumption* (registration-
weighted) in the UK was stable over the 1990s until 1997, with improving engine and
power train efficiency being offset by the effects of consumer demand for larger
engine capacity and developments in safety and utility features. Since 1997, average
new car fuel consumption has gradually improved, but it was still 9% lower than the
EU average in 2000, partly due to the smaller proportion of diesel cars (16% *versus*
37%). In 2000, new cars sold in the UK had average CO_2 emissions of 179 g CO_2/km
(7.4 litres/100 km). Also, the improvement rate from the base year was among the
lowest in EU countries (6.8% *versus* 9.1%).

2.4   *Promoting low-emission vehicles*

Since 1996, the UK has promoted the purchase of *low-emission vehicles*
(e.g. LPG, natural gas and electric vehicles) through the *PowerShift financial support
programme*, funded mainly by the national budget through the Energy Saving Trust, a
non-profit company set up by the central government. The programme provides
grants of 30-75% of the additional cost of buying an LEV or converting an existing

vehicle to cleaner fuel. For 1996-2000, the budget for the programme totalled GBP 20 million and was used mainly to support the purchase of nearly 10 000 gas and electric vehicles. A further GBP 33 million is expected for 2001-03. The programme has been particularly successful in boosting the market for LPG vehicles: in 2000, a third of new LPG vehicles entering the market were supported by the PowerShift programme. On the other hand, market penetration of natural gas and electric (including hybrid) vehicles is still low in the UK: about 200 of each were newly registered in 2000.

In 1998, the UK took the lead in launching the *Alternative Traffic in Towns Initiative*, a Europe-wide initiative in which cities define areas where only zero-emission or near-zero-emission vehicles are permitted. About 30 cities and six councils in the UK have signed the initiative. Since 1997, in the Foresight Vehicle programme, the central government has also been making substantial investments in R&D on future motor vehicles powered by cleaner fuels. Since these initiatives are relatively recent, *market penetration of natural gas, electric (except milk trucks) and hybrid vehicles has not yet gained momentum*, and the proportion of alternative fuel vehicles is still very low compared to other OECD countries.

In 2000, a new *government funding programme (CleanUp)* was launched under the auspices of the Energy Saving Trust. It aims to reduce emissions from big emitters in urban areas, complementing the PowerShift programme. Under CleanUp, up to 75% of the *capital costs of converting diesel engines* to run on LPG, CNG or LNG, or for retrofitting emission reduction equipment (e.g. oxidation catalysts and particulate traps), are funded for large diesel vehicles (e.g. buses and trucks over 3.5 tonnes) and black cabs in England. Priority is given to vehicles operated primarily in the most polluted urban areas. With a budget of GBP 66 million for 2000-04, CleanUp will support the retrofitting of about 19 000 vehicles.

3

WATER MANAGEMENT*

Recommendations

The following recommendations are part of the overall conclusions and recommendations of the Environmental Performance Review of the United Kingdom:

- increase the number of designated sensitive areas and complete *urban waste water treatment infrastructure*, especially that needed to reduce pollutant discharges to coastal waters;

- complete delineation of *nitrate vulnerable zones*, in which codes of good agricultural practice and nutrient management plans should be binding;

- further develop the *river basin approach to water management* (e.g. by setting statutory water quality and quantity objectives), extending responsibilities of subnational environment agencies accordingly;

- continue to develop a policy framework for *sewage sludge management* based on economic and environmental analysis;

- further explore the possibility of introducing *taxes on nutrients and pesticides* as a means of internalising external costs of diffuse pollution;

- explore the possibility of introducing industrial *water pollution charges*, with efficiency and financing objectives in mind.

---

* The present chapter reviews progress in the last ten years, particularly since the previous OECD Environmental Performance Review of 1994. It also reviews progress with respect to the objective "maintaining the integrity of ecosystems" of the 2001 OECD Environmental Strategy.

© OECD 2002

Conclusions

The UK made *significant progress* during the 1990s on improving the quality of surface, bathing, drinking and estuary waters and controlling discharges from point sources. River quality objectives have been adopted for all rivers, as recommended during the 1994 Environmental Performance Review, though they are not statutory. This progress was made possible by a significant increase in *water infrastructure investment* (e.g. GBP 3 to 4 billion per year from 1990 to 2000 in England and Wales) to reduce urban point source pollution. Sewage treatment infrastructure has been upgraded and storm overflows constructed. Disposal of sewage sludge at sea has been discontinued. These achievements came about through a *major shift in water policy*, responding to a decade of underinvestment and stimulated in large part by EU water directives. *Water pricing policies*, supervised by an independent regulator, have led to full cost recovery of public water supply and sewage treatment services by privatised water companies in England and Wales. Continued increased investment is planned until 2005 to complete sewage treatment infrastructure. In response to a recent increase in the frequency and severity of floods, flood prevention and defence are evolving towards more integrated *flood management*, making greater use of specific planning tools (catchment flood plans, shoreline plans, water level plans), general land use planning and flood damage liability. Serious droughts have led to proposals to increase withdrawal charges.

Despite this overall progress and a well-established policy framework, much remains to be done. Addressing *drinking water quality* breaches (e.g. for iron and manganese) and meeting the EU requirements on lead content will require considerable investment. Even after significant improvements, 16% of *river length* in north-western England is of poor quality. Eight cities of more than 150 000 people still lack treatment plants. The number of water pollution incidents remains high. Controls on sewage sludge used for land application need to be strengthened. The quality of coastal waters remains a concern, largely because of *diffuse pollution* leading to nitrate, phosphate and pesticide contamination. Little has been done to address this issue; in particular, no strategy exists to deal with nutrient management in agriculture, despite EU directives and a recommendation in the 1994 OECD review. However, a review of diffuse pollution of waters by agriculture in England is under way to identify pollution control measures, including regulations, economic instruments and voluntary actions. The *interface between water and nature*, including wetland management and river revitalisation, has received relatively little attention, although there is a growing number of programmes to rehabilitate or restore river habitats. Building on a long tradition of monitoring/enforcement and service provision at the river basin level, and of planning at the catchment level (local environment agency plans), priority should be given to addressing water quantity and quality issues in an integrated manner, in line with requirements of the new EU water framework directive. Control of industrial effluent discharges has remained mainly regulatory, with little use of economic incentives such as *pollution charges*. Metering should be extended to further support modernisation of *water pricing*. A large amount of water-related investment is to be made in the next ten years (e.g. for drinking water supply, urban waste water treatment, nitrate and pesticide control and more ecological management of water bodies). Financing this investment will require a water pricing policy with a longer-term perspective, along with better integration of environmental concerns into sectoral policies, notably those for agriculture.

1.   Evaluation of Performance

1.1   Policy objectives

The UK Government has *three broad aims* in relation to water management:

– protect and enhance the water environment, including through flood management;

– improve public health and safety as regards water;

– promote an efficient and competitive water industry.

More specifically, the government has set the following *targets*:

– in England and Wales, 91% of rivers to meet river quality targets by 2005;

– in Scotland, poor or seriously polluted rivers to be reduced to 800 km by 2006;

– at least 97% of English and Welsh bathing waters to meet mandatory coliform standards in the 2005 season;

– in England and Wales, a 15% reduction in the number of substantiated water pollution incidents by 2005, compared with 1997;

– achieving and maintaining full compliance with the EU drinking water and groundwater directives;

– all towns in England, Scotland and Wales above 15 000 population equivalent (p.e.) to have at least secondary treatment by the end of 2001;

– all cities in England, Scotland and Wales above 2 000 p.e. to have at least secondary treatment by 2005.

To strengthen water management, the *1994 OECD Environmental Performance Review* made the following recommendations:

– statutory environmental quality objectives should be adopted for individual rivers, in line with the 1991 Water Resources Act, and for groundwater. They should be based on both human health criteria and ecological considerations;

– sewage treatment should be further improved, notably to deal with discharges to coastal waters, capacity problems and storm water overflows. Water supply facilities should also be improved, aiming at removal of nitrate and pesticides, reduction of leakage and replacement of old piping (especially lead and tar-coated pipes). Charges for these services should be designed with such investment needs in mind;

– measures should be developed to deal with increasing quantities of sewage sludge, such as proper composting, incineration and landfilling. Further efforts to reduce contamination of sludge are required. Control of land application of sludge, based on adequate monitoring, is necessary to assure sustainable land use;

– economic instruments (e.g. effluent and withdrawal charges) should be used to provide increased incentives for reducing water pollution and withdrawal, and water metering should be extended to encourage customers to reduce consumption;

– control of diffuse sources of water pollution should be strengthened through integrated measures, including land use planning, protection zones, agricultural practices and better use of fertilisers and pesticides.

1.2   Protecting and enhancing the water environment

Water conservation

In England and Wales, average per capita effective rainfall (precipitation minus evaporation) is low (4 000 litres per day) by European standards due to the high population density. A high share of water withdrawal (51%) is for public water supply, leading to demand management concerns for the water industry (Figure 3.1). In 1995, following severe drought, the Environment Agency put forward a *national strategy on water conservation*, which recommended setting leakage targets, selectively metering domestic use and increasing withdrawal charges. The water industry commited itself to reducing leakage from its distribution system from 30% (national average in 1995) to 15% by 2005. The leakage rate was 22% in 1999/2000.

There is a *low level of household metering* in England and Wales; only 19% of domestic users are metered whereas 87% of non-domestic users are. Per capita household water consumption increased over the 1990s from 130 litres per day to 150. There is no metering in Northern Ireland and almost none in Scotland. In England and Wales the shift to metering had been held back by concern that low-income households with children would suffer financial hardship (Chapter 7, Section 1.2), but now the priority is to expand metering. New houses are generally metered and the 1999 Water Industry

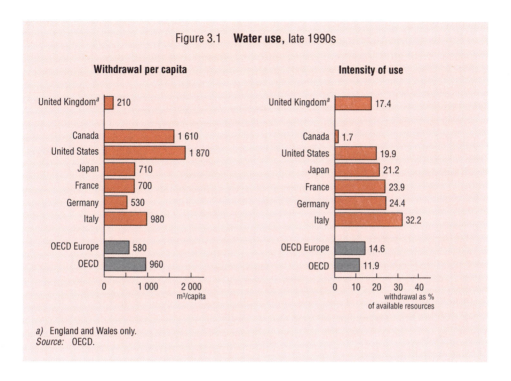

Figure 3.1 **Water use,** late 1990s

Withdrawal per capita

United Kingdom[a]	210
Canada	1 610
United States	1 870
Japan	710
France	700
Germany	530
Italy	980
OECD Europe	580
OECD	960

0   1 000   2 000
m³/capita

Intensity of use

United Kingdom[a]	17.4
Canada	1.7
United States	19.9
Japan	21.2
France	23.9
Germany	24.4
Italy	32.2
OECD Europe	14.6
OECD	11.9

0   10   20   30   40
withdrawal as %
of available resources

a) England and Wales only.
Source: OECD.

Act requires water companies to provide a meter free to domestic consumers who want one. However, unless they fall into certain high-usage categories, domestic consumers can choose to continue to pay a charge based on property value. Extending metering should be pursued, particularly in the south and east of England, which is much drier than the rest of the country. Water companies can ask the government to declare water scarcity areas where metering would be compulsory, but none so far has done so. Metering would also help in extending seasonal pricing (already introduced on a trial basis) and reducing peak demand in summer.

In England and Wales, most withdrawals above 5 m³ per day are subject to licensing. A pending Water Bill would raise the threshold to 20 m³ a day and withdraw most blanket exemptions. The Environment Agency sets withdrawal charges, on a regional basis, to cover its costs in administering the licensing system. Public consultations are planned on a *revised withdrawal charging regime* in which charges would better reflect water availability and environmental damage caused by withdrawals. Since 1976, the secretary of state (deputy minister) for environment has been able to issue local drought orders to temporarily restrict withdrawal. It was recently decided to introduce a system of tradable withdrawal permits. For that to work to best effect, the many permits issued "in perpetuity" in the 1960s need to be replaced with time-limited ones (usually 12 years). Various policy measures and legislative changes (in the Water Bill) will encourage a move to all licences being time limited. To prevent a monopoly over water availability, the Environment Agency was required to determine "reasonable needs" and guard against licence hoarding. In 2001 the agency introduced non-statutory Catchment Abstraction Management Strategies, to make information on water resource allocation publicly available. This process should be finalised in each of the 129 catchments in England and Wales by 2008. This will facilitate agency decisions on whether a new licence can be issued and on the terms attached to licences, and allow better management of water resources.

Flood management

The frequency and severity of river flooding have increased in recent years, particularly since 1998. Around 10% of the population and 12% of farmland are within flood risk areas in England. This translates to property worth over GBP 200 billion and land worth over GBP 7 billion. Britain spends relatively little on flood defence: 0.03% of GDP. Unlike in most other OECD countries, *responsibility for flood damage* has been allocated to the insurance industry (since 1961, through a "gentlemen's agreement"). All household insurance policies in Britain include flood insurance. However, with the recent rise in flood incidence, insurers are now request-ing a 50% increase in government spending on flood defence, along with tighter planning guidelines to discourage building on floodplains. If flood insurance were to be made optional, people living in flood-prone areas would face a drastic rise in premiums or perhaps simply be unable to get insurance at all.

As regards flood prevention, the Department of Environment, Food and Rural Affairs (DEFRA) issued a policy guideline in 2001 on *better integrating flood risk management into land use planning*. The document refers to several recent non-statutory planning initiatives that should be integrated, where appropriate, with the statutory development plans. The latter include the Catchment Flood Management Plans that the Environment Agency is developing and the Shoreline Management Plans already completed for all English coasts. Water Level Management Plans, prepared by flood defence authorities, allocate water to agriculture, flood defence and nature conservation, thereby co-ordinating flood and land drainage management within each river basin. These are not binding instruments, however, and the issuance of building permits is left to local authorities' discretion. There are no incentives for landowners to undertake flood relief measures (e.g. to reduce flash runoff problems or restrict cultivation), or allow their land to be flooded (washland).

River basin management

Statutory water quality objectives, setting mid-term targets, were originally due to be put in place in England and Wales immediately after the water industry privatisation in 1989. *Non-statutory river quality objectives* have been in place since the 1970s. They were consolidated into government targets only recently (in 1997), mostly because of official concerns about their potential impact on water prices. Set by DEFRA for each stretch of river, they reflect the use to which waters are put, and they are the basis for issuing permits for discharges to rivers and for controls on other sources of pollution. Implementation of the EU water framework directive (2000/60) will require the setting of *statutory quality objectives for all surface waters and groundwater*.

At the heart of the framework directive are mandatory, *comprehensive river basin management plans* describing how objectives are to be achieved for both surface waters and groundwater. By 2004, a detailed analysis of pressures is to be made, to help identify which waters are likely to fail to meet the objectives, and an economic analysis is to help identify the most cost-effective measures and water pricing policies required. By 2008, draft plans are required. By 2015, the objectives are to be met. In the process, surface water will have been classified according to its ecological status (biodiversity), and quantitative and chemical quality objectives will have been set for groundwater.

Much of the *implementation will be done by the Environment Agency* as successor of the National Rivers Authority. The agency also has a statutory duty to conserve and secure the efficient use of water under the Water Resources Act. This means there will be no need to change the roles and statutory bases of other bodies. Implementation in Scotland and Northern Ireland will be separate. Plans call for 11 river basin districts in England and Wales, including three stand-alone basins encompassing a single river each (Severn, Thames and Trent) and three basins shared with Scotland. Mechanisms to assure administrative co-ordination will be needed for the latter. The districts largely fit within the Environment Agency's current regional boundaries.

In Scotland, the Water Environment and Water Services (Scotland) Bill that came before Parliament in June 2002 proposes a framework for implementation of the EU water framework directive. Ministers would delineate one main Scotland-wide river basin district and set special arrangements for cross-border basins. The Scottish Environment Protection Agency (SEPA) would establish a network of consultative groups to give input on the main Scottish river basin plan and cross-border plans, such as those for Solway, Tweed and Tyne, that would be prepared and implemented jointly with the Environment Agency. SEPA would have the lead role in preparing the river basin plans. In the process it would acquire new responsibilities regarding social and economic considerations. It would have discretion on regulating discharges, either via water use licences or using general binding rules, implying a significant departure from the current system of permits for point source discharges. A similar approach would apply to withdrawal: notification would be triggered by thresholds set locally, then SEPA would decide what level of control is appropriate. The agency would also be able to serve many kinds of notices, including enforcement notices, suspension notices and project notices ordering work carried out to prevent or reverse serious environmental damage. Overall, these changes would give SEPA much broader powers than it now has.

1.3 Improving public health and safety as regards water

Overall, *water quality clearly improved* in the 1990s (Chapter 3, Section 2.1). Compliance with river quality objectives increased over 1998-2001 from 82% to 90%, mainly because of improvements by the water companies. Drinking water quality, basic chemical quality (oxygen and ammonia) in rivers and microbiological quality in coastal bathing waters have all improved (Table 3.1). Further improvements are expected through investment in sewage treatment and storm overflows planned up to 2005. These achievements need to be consolidated and extended, however, with measures such as controls on iron, manganese and lead in drinking water, and improved waste water treatment in large cities. In addition, nutrient and pesticide concentrations remain relatively high.

Point source pollution

In 1995, only 61% of treated sewage met requirements of the *EU urban waste water treatment directive* (91/271). The directive requires all towns in England and Wales above 15 000 p.e. to be served by secondary treatment by the end of 2001, and those above 2 000 p.e. to have secondary treatment by 2005. To this end, GBP 6.6 billion was invested in 1995-2000, and a further GBP 5.3 billion investment was planned for 2000-05. The share of population connected to public waste water treatment facilities (mostly secondary and tertiary) is 84% (Figure 3.2). The share of population connected to public sewerage is 96%. In the 1990s pollution loads (BOD, ammonia and phosphate) from all sewage treatment plants in England and Wales were reduced by approximately 40%.

In the past, the UK used only primary or preliminary treatment in areas of high natural dispersion, such as *estuaries and coastal areas*. Following pressure from the European Commission, in 1998 the government decided to move to a more precautionary approach in these areas and provide secondary treatment for significant coastal discharges. Eight British coastal towns with population of more than

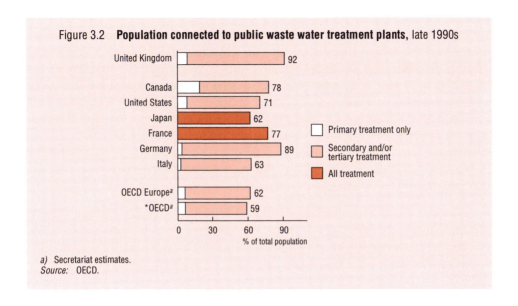

Figure 3.2 **Population connected to public waste water treatment plants,** late 1990s

Primary treatment only

Secondary and/or tertiary treatment

All treatment

a) Secretariat estimates.
Source: OECD.

Table 3.1 **Water quality**
(% of good or fair quality)

	England		Wales		Northern Ireland		Scotland	
	1990	2000	1990	2000	1990	2000	1990	2000
Rivers								
Chemical quality[a]	83	94	98	99	95	96	97	98
Biological quality[b]	86	94	97	98	100	97[j]	96	96
Phosphate[c]	33	40	..	..	74[k]	73	..	..
Nitrate[d]	70[k, l]	68[l]	..	..	..	..	..	..
Aesthetics[e]	..	67[l]	..	..	..	..	..	..
Estuaries[f]	91[k]	95	..	..	..	..	..	..
Bathing waters[g]	78[l]	95[l]	..	..	93	100	52	85
Drinking water supply zones[h]	98.4[l]	99.8[l]	..	..	..	..	98.0	98.5
Pesticides[i]	70[l]	87[l]	..	..	..	..	..	..

a) % of river length with little organic pollution.
b) % of river length with overall good health.
c) % of river length with a mean concentration less than 0.1 mg P/litre.
d) % of river length with concentration less than 30 mg NO_3/litre.
e) % of selected sites free of (or with little) litter, oil, scum, foam, sewage, fungus and ochreous deposits, and with fair colour and smell.
f) % of estuaries with good biological, aesthetic and chemical quality.
g) % of samples complying with mandatory EU standards (Directive 76/160).

h) % of samples complying with mandatory EU standards (Directive 75/440).
i) % of samples complying with mandatory EU standards for individual pesticides (Directive 75/440).
j) Monitored river length increased from 2 500 km in 1990 to 5 000 km in 2000.
k) 1995 data.
l) England and Wales.

Source: DEFRA.

150 000 are still without waste water treatment, however, and 22 others have levels of treatment below EU standards. In addition, the UK is behind in identifying sensitive areas: by 2000, it had designated only 62 rivers and canals (around 2 500 km), 13 lakes and reservoirs and five estuaries. For these reasons, the Commision decided in 2001 to send the UK a reasoned opinion (second written warning) for non-respect of Directive 91/271. Further designations of sensitive areas are expected in 2002. Provision of additional sewage treatment affecting the current and new sensitive areas is to be completed by 2004. The UK has not yet formally accepted the North Sea Conference targets regarding reduction of pollutant discharges to the North Sea (Chapter 9, Section 1.4). Nonetheless, the targets were largely met, except for that concerning nitrogen (Table 3.2).

The number of *water pollution incidents* reported to the Environment Agency remained high in the 1990s, at 80-100 per day (compared with 6-7 per day for SEPA). Nevertheless, the number of substantiated incidents has fallen by 27% since 1997, exceeding the 15% reduction target for 2005. In addition, the number of major incidents decreased over the decade (Table 3.3). Industry, agriculture and the sewage and water industry continue to be the main sources of major incidents. Measures to prevent the introduction of List I substances to groundwater were strengthened through the introduction of the 1998 Groundwater Regulations, though pesticides were still being recorded as having entered groundwater. A list of 79 List I substances was published in 2001 under Directive 80/68, though it is still provisional. The UK decided *not to proceed with water pollution charges*, but rather to use discharge permits and local river quality objectives as basic tools for maintaining and improving water quality. The continuing *low level of fines* for pollution incidents encourages firms to treat prosecution as an acceptable risk. Water companies are prominent among the poor performers, measured by the number of court appearances and offences.

Heightened standards of sewage treatment have meant an increase in the amount of *sewage sludge* produced. Some 55% of sludge is recycled to land, which translates to savings of GBP 21 million per year in fertiliser costs. The government supports this as the best practical environmental option in most circumstances. Disposal at sea has ceased, and landfilling of sludge is no longer considered a sustainable option. The regulations that control the application of sludge to agricultural land implement the EU sewage sludge directive (86/278). They set mandatory limits for heavy metals and restrictions on post-application use of soil (to protect against transfer of pathogens). In 1998 these regulations were supplemented by the Safe Sludge Matrix, a voluntary agreement between the UK water industry and the British Retail Consortium aiming to further reduce the potential for pathogen transfer by imposing higher standards. Another measure to better protect the environment and human health would be to

Table 3.2   **Pollutant discharges to UK coastal waters**[a]

	1985	1995	1985-95 (% change)[b]
Heavy metals (tonnes)			
Cadmium	80	31	−62
Mercury	27	6	−77
Copper	1 275	645	−49
Lead	1 660	419	−75
Zinc	3 630	2 805	−23
Nutrients (kt)			
Orthophosphates	58	32	−46
Total nitrogen	319	361	13
Organic substances (kg)			
Lindane	1 560	608	−61
PCBs	4 200[c]	1 870	−55[d]

a) Upper value estimates of direct inputs from land-based sources and riverine inputs.
b) Original North Sea Conference target was −50% over 1985-95; target date has since been extended to 2005.
c) 1990.
d) % change 1990-95.
Source: DEFRA.

Table 3.3   **Water pollution incidents**[a]

	1991	1995	1999	1991-99 (% change)
Reported incidents	29 372	35 890	36 623	25
Substantiated incidents[b]	22 469	23 463	14 374	−36
Major incidents from:[c]	386	199	90	−77
Agriculture	99	32	29	−71
Industry	83	62	20	−76
Sewage and water services	96	48	15	−84
Transport	. .	16	9	. .
Domestic/residential		. .	1	
Other	108	41	16	−85

a) England and Wales.
b) Reported incidents for which evidence was found. Substantiated incidents are classified as Category 1 (Major), 2 (Significant) or 3 (Minor).
c) By source of pollution.
Source: Environment Agency.

strengthen waste management licensing (sewage sludge is a controlled waste). The government is reviewing exemptions relating to the use of sludge in agriculture (storage and spreading). The use of sludge on agricultural land is generally not constrained by legal limits on heavy metal content. The EU directive (86/278) is likely to be revised in the near future, with more stringent standards for heavy metals and organic contaminants. To face these new challenges, a sewage sludge management strategy should be developed, based on economic and environmental analysis.

Diffuse pollution

UK fertiliser use decreased by 10% in the 1990s but remains fairly high by OECD standards (Figure 3.3). The national nitrogen surplus from agriculture, measured by the soil surface nitrogen balance, fell from 107 kg/ha of farmland in 1985-87 to 86 kg/ha in 1995-97, but this is well above the EU average of 58 kg/ha. Nitrate levels of more than 30 mg per litre are found in 32% of total UK river length, up from 30% in 1995. About 70-80% of the nitrate input to water comes from diffuse pollution, with *agriculture as the main contributor*. Agriculture also accounts for 40-50% of diffuse phosphate input. Around 78% of catchments are affected by eutrophication, and in 44% of them it was identified as a "specific environmental issue".

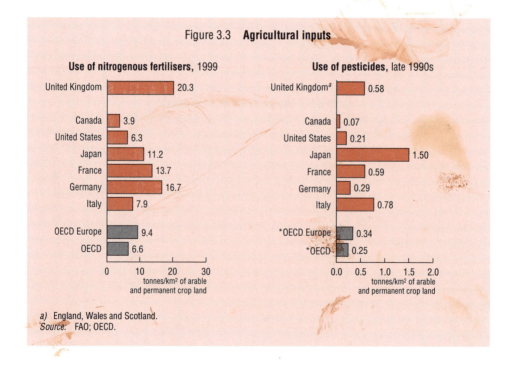

Figure 3.3   **Agricultural inputs**

Use of nitrogenous fertilisers, 1999

United Kingdom	20.3
Canada	3.9
United States	6.3
Japan	11.2
France	13.7
Germany	16.7
Italy	7.9
OECD Europe	9.4
OECD	6.6

0   10   20   30
tonnes/km² of arable
and permanent crop land

Use of pesticides, late 1990s

United Kingdom[a]	0.58
Canada	0.07
United States	0.21
Japan	1.50
France	0.59
Germany	0.29
Italy	0.78
*OECD Europe	0.34
*OECD	0.25

0.0   0.5   1.0   1.5   2.0
tonnes/km² of arable
and permanent crop land

a) England, Wales and Scotland.
Source: FAO; OECD.

The EU *nitrate directive* (91/676) requires the UK to establish an action programme of control measures and apply it in designated nitrate vulnerable zones (NVZs). In 1996, 66 NVZs, totalling 600 000 hectares or 8% of the English land area, were designated in England, but only in terms of protecting drinking water supplies. In Northern Ireland, NVZs were not designated until 1999, using the same restrictive criteria. In 1999, three years after the deadline in the directive, an action programme came into force. It involves nitrogen limits for fertiliser and manure (reducing the limit from 210 kg/ha to 170 kg/ha by 2003), manure spreading controls, and rules on slurry storage and farm record keeping. The Farm Waste Grant programme, introduced in 1996, can help farmers in existing NVZs by covering 40% of eligible expenditure. In December 2000, the European Court of Justice ruled that the UK had failed to comply with the nitrate directive. Full compliance will require designation of NVZs covering a substantial proportion of England's land area. The devolved administrations in Scotland and Wales also need to designate NVZs. In June 2002 the Scottish Executive announced that regulations had been laid before the Scottish Parliament designating 14% of Scotland as NVZs (mainly on the east coast). Compliance costs, expected to total GBP 21 million in England and Wales and GBP 7-10 million in Scotland, will mostly be for record keeping. Some farmers will face more substantial costs to construct additional slurry storage. In England and Wales, the government intends to extend the Farm Waste Grant programme to assist farmers with these costs. A similar plan is being introduced in Scotland.

Several *voluntary initiatives* have been taken in areas other than NVZs. One is England's code of good agricultural practice for water protection. DEFRA, the Environment Agency and farmers' federations are exploring a nutrient management initiative. The Environment Agency's eutrophication strategy, released in 2000, recommends local consultation at catchment level, and eutrophication control action plans have been initiated in 11 catchments, on a pilot basis. The area under organic farming has increased, but remains modest at 62 500 hectares in 2001.

Over the 1990s, with the introduction of herbicides requiring lower doses, farmers reduced *pesticide consumption* by 14% (in tonnes of active ingredients). The intensity of pesticide use remains high by OECD standards, however (Figure 3.3). Water pollution by agricultural herbicides such as isoproturon and mecoprop frequently occurs. In 1998 in England and Wales, 27% of groundwater samples and 11% of surface water samples contained mecoprop at levels above the drinking water limit of 0.1 µg/litre. Atrazine and simazine have declined since their ban in agriculture in 1993. In 2001, the government asked pesticide manufacturers and farmers' associations to take voluntary initiatives to reduce the environmental impact of pesticide use. Statutory codes of practice have been developed, such as the Green Code for safe pesticide use in agriculture and the Yellow Code for pesticide suppliers.

In Scotland, a proposal to enable SEPA to order farmers to prepare farm waste management plans was rejected in 2001. The Scottish Executive has also recently backed off from a suggestion that licensing of farming and forestry discharges might be required. The emphasis has been on general binding rules and statutory codes of practice, with notice powers available to SEPA as a backstop. The Water Environment and Water Services (Scotland) Bill would give Scottish ministers more powers to control diffuse agricultural pollution.

New measures are needed to stem diffuse pollution from agriculture. A review of diffuse pollution of water by agriculture in England is under way to identify such measures. It is considering all measures that could raise standards of agricultural practice, including economic instruments and voluntary actions alongside regulations. Among the possible measures are to link farm support with a test of environmental compliance, to decouple direct payments from agricultural production and to tie agri-environmental payments more directly to environmental results, though this last idea remains to a large extent within the domain of the EU Common Agricultural Policy. Although demand for inorganic fertiliser is relatively price-inelastic, a fertiliser tax could help discourage overuse. As the cost-effectiveness of economic instruments greatly depends on transaction costs, there is a need to balance the targeting of measures to environmental concerns with the public resources required to implement and enforce them.

In 1997 DEFRA issued a research report on the use of economic instruments for water pollution, modelling how *taxes on cereal grass weed herbicides* would encourage changes in farming practices. Two tax rates, 50% and 125%, would reduce consumption of herbicides by 20% and 31%, respectively, while gross farm income would decline by 2% and 6%, and annual revenue would amount to GBP 70-80 million and GBP 170-200 million. To keep farmers from switching to cheaper and often less specific and less environmentally benign pesticides, the tax would need to be differentiated, with more hazardous active ingredients carrying a higher tax rate. Although the design of such a tax has been challenged, the possibility of its introduction is being kept in reserve should voluntary initiatives fail to improve control of pesticide use.

Diffuse pollution in urban areas is also a major source of concern. Some pollutants can wash off soil and urban surfaces or seep into the ground from what may be a very large number of small sources. The cumulative effect can contribute to poor water quality. The significance of such pollution is becoming more apparent following progress in cleaning up large point sources. Sewage and waste water treatment charges make some provision for surface drainage (runoff from properties) and highway drainage (runoff from roads and pavements). If water companies are to get further involved in treating low-level contamination of urban runoff, the issue of funding will need to be addressed. In Scotland, a Sustainable Urban Drainage System manual was incorporated into policy guidance for urban planning in July 2001.

1.4 Promoting an efficient, competitive water industry

Water service privatisation

In England and Wales, when the water industry was privatised in 1989, one reason cited was a *lack of investment* by the ten regional water authorities (RWAs) that had been created in 1974. The RWAs had been responsible for integrated water management, including water and waste water services, along with pollution control and water resource management. The 1989 Water Act (consolidated into the 1991 Water Industry and Water Resources Acts) separated the provision of piped water (now privatised) from the enforcement function, now given to the Environment Agency. The RWAs' water and waste water infrastructure was transferred to ten *regional water companies* until 2014. In some areas of England and Wales, water supply continues to be provided by smaller private companies that existed prior to 1989. Mergers have reduced the number of these water-only providers from 39 to 15.

Because each water and sewerage company has a regional monopoly, it was decided to regulate water prices. The 1991 Water Industry Act assigned this task to the *Office of Water Services* (OFWAT). OFWAT is an economic regulator, monitoring water companies' results and charged with protecting water consumers' interests. With 150 staff members, it supervises the companies' accounts, investments and service quality, and carries out field surveys upon consumer request. OFWAT is financed by levies on the water companies, in proportion to their budget. Price regulation is by means of a limit on the average increase in charges in any year (Chapter 3, Section 2.2). In cases of conflict with OFWAT, companies may appeal to the Competition Commission, an independent public body established by the 1998 Competition Act. The government intends to introduce competition in water supply to large non-domestic users, though the present companies will retain their strategic water resource and environmental duties. Other companies will be given clearer rights to enter the water market, providing an opportunity for innovation and efficiency gains.

Water pricing and water infrastructure investment

The regulated *water pricing* regime, while aiming at "reasonable cost and benefit" rather than at providing incentives to increase efficiency, has allowed the water industry to invest GBP 38 billion in water infrastructure since privatisation, of which more than 60% has been for sewerage and waste water treatment (Figure 3.4). This investment has been financed almost exclusively by water price increases (Chapter 3, Section 2.2). Whether *OFWAT should also be given a duty to facilitate sustainable development* has long been debated. OFWAT could be given new

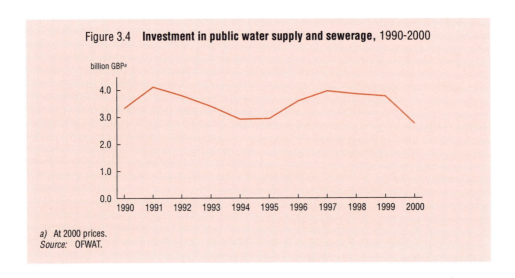

Figure 3.4   **Investment in public water supply and sewerage**, 1990-2000

a) At 2000 prices.
Source: OFWAT.

responsibility to ensure that water supplies and the environment are properly protected, while also protecting the consumer from rising bills. Such a move would
improve consistency in the efforts of OFWAT and the Environment Agency, as long
as the former's five-year economic focus did not compromise the latter's achievement
of long-term environmental targets.

Long-term environmental investment planning is particularly needed for water
resources, environmental quality and serviceability of water pipes and sewers. The
water industry has made commitments to reduce *leakage* (with GBP 4 billion allocated
for 1995-2005), replace *lead pipes* to comply with the 1998 drinking water quality
directive (GBP 2 billion by 2013), and deal with excess *iron and manganese* in drinking
water. Moreover, the planned introduction of tradable withdrawal permits and reforms
to withdrawal charges are likely to increase companies' *withdrawal costs*. More
stringent treatment will be needed to comply with the forthcoming *sewage sludge*
directive. The proposed *bathing water* directive would likely require another major
round of sewage treatment improvements and tighter controls on storm overflows. A
key element is to address diffuse pollution issues. Removal of *pesticides* is one of the
most expensive treatments the water companies have to carry out. Companies have
invested huge amounts in pesticide removal plants, which cost GBP 30-35 million per
year to run. Part of the revenue of a pesticide tax could be used to compensate water
companies for the cost of removing pesticides from water.

The total *cost of complying with the new water framework directive* in England and Wales, given river length and river habitat requiring improvement and river sites affected by low flows, is estimated at GBP 2 billion to 9 billion (in Scotland it is estimated at GBP 1 billion between now and 2040). Part of this is covered by planned investments by the water industry for 2000-05. The work involved is mainly to reduce loadings of BOD, ammonia, nitrogen and phosphorus from sewage treatment works (45%) and other industrial discharges (15%), and to reduce diffuse pollution, particularly by agriculture (30%). Water companies will probably have to install *phosphate* stripping equipment at many sewage works, so, on grounds of equity at least, farmers should make a contribution via a phosphate tax, part of whose revenue could be used for removal of phosphate from sediments and other measures to restore the value of aquatic wildlife conservation sites. Agricultural inputs of *nitrate* impose costs on water consumers as a result of the need to install nitrate removal equipment at some drinking water sources. The costs of this work, and of blending high-nitrate supplies with cleaner water, are considerably lower than for pesticides, but the same issues arise about using tax revenue to keep water bills down.

2. Focus on Selected Topics

2.1 Water quality

Drinking water

Drinking water quality improved in the 1990s. In 2000, only 0.2% of measurements in public water supplies in England and Wales did not comply with EU Directive 80/778, compared with 1.6% in 1991 (Table 3.4). Nevertheless, the *European Court of Justice* held the UK to be in breach of the directive. At issue is the implementation method in England and Wales, which relies on *voluntary commitments* ("undertakings") by water companies. Some undertakings were accepted without any reference to quality standards to be met, or with lax standards. Moreover, this method prevents consumers from going to court if they receive low-quality water.

The newest EU drinking water directive (98/83) establishes challenging targets for *lead concentration in drinking water*. The maximum admissible concentration is to be reduced from 50 μg/litre to 25 μg in 2003 and 10 μg in 2013. In recent years, performance relative to the 50 μg/litre standard has improved in England and Wales. Nonetheless, treating water to reduce its lead solvency will not allow compliance with the future limit of 10 μg/litre. The only way to meet the proposed limit is to replace lead pipes serving 8.2 million properties (though this is not required by the new directive). At the present rate it would take 50-60 years to replace all domestic lead plumbing. The use of lead solder in domestic water systems has been illegal since 1987 throughout the UK. Yet, plumbers often prefer lead because it is cheaper and easier to use than other solders. A survey commissioned by the Scottish Health Department in 2000 revealed that up to half of all new homes (which do not have lead pipes) showed lead levels in excess of 5 µg/litre in their water, possibly because of the use of lead solder. A publicity campaign should be launched to alert consumers to the health hazards of lead in drinking water, particularly for children, infants and foetuses.

Table 3.4   **Drinking water quality**[a]

Parameter	England and Wales			Scotland		Northern Ireland	
	1991	1995	2000	1995	2000	1995	2000
Coliforms	1.4	0.7	0.6	2.6	1.1	1.4	0.5
Faecal coliforms	0.2	0.1	< 0.1	1.0	0.2	1.3	0.2
Colour	< 0.1	< 0.1	< 0.1	2.2	0.7	0.4	0.1
Turbidity	0.2	0.2	0.1	0.5	0.1	0.7	0.3
Odour	0.2	0.1	< 0.1	..	..	0.2	0.0
Taste	0.2	0.2	< 0.1	..	..	0.2	0.0
PH	0.6	0.1	0.1	0.3	0.3	2.1	0.1
Nitrate	2.8	0.4	0.1	..	..	0.0	0.0
Nitrite	4.8	4.9	3.0	..	..	0.0	0.0
Aluminium	0.7	0.4	0.1	1.8	1.1	3.9	4.0
Iron	2.8	2.2	1.3	3.6	2.6	6.6	4.0
Manganese	1.0	0.7	0.3	1.1	0.6	0.2	0.0
Lead	3.0	3.4	0.9	1.1	1.1	3.1	3.1
Polycyclic aromatic hydrocarbons	2.0	4.9	3.0	..	..	4.7	2.5
Trihalomethanes	3.7	1.3	1.1	18.1	16.5	38.2	55.4
Total pesticides	9.2	3.2	< 0.1	..	..	0.0	0.0
Individual pesticides	2.8	0.8	< 0.1	..	..	0.2	0.0
Other parameters	0.1	< 0.1	< 0.1	0.4	0.2	0.1	0.3
All parameters	1.6	0.7	0.2	1.3	1.0	1.6	1.8

a) % of drinking water exceeding prescribed concentration values (PCVs), or relaxed PCVs. A relaxation of the water quality standards may be granted, subject to the completion of improvement work, as a result of exceptional meteorological conditions or because of the nature of the soil in the water supply area.
Source: Drinking Water Inspectorate; Scottish Executive; Department of the Environment (Northern Ireland).

Ambient water

In 1990 a new five-yearly monitoring survey, the General Quality Assessment, was introduced in England and Wales. It examines stretches of fresh water separately in terms of their chemical (organic pollutant), biological, nutrient and aesthetic qualities. Overall *river quality* has improved in the last ten years, mainly reflecting major investments in sewage treatment (Table 3.5). Otters, salmon and an abundance of fish and birds have returned to waterways. In north-western England, however, 16% of rivers are still classified as poor or bad, though this is down from 37% a decade ago. The latest survey, in 2000, includes new information on the aesthetic quality of rivers. It also shows that nitrate levels have marginally increased overall, despite a fall in fertiliser application. Levels of phosphates dropped substantially though the 1990s.

Bathing water quality has continuously improved in the last decade. In 2001, 97.7% of English coastal bathing waters (95.2% in the UK) met the microbiological standards of the bathing water directive (76/160), against 78% in 1990. Good results for both inland and coastal bathing waters in north-western England (the Blackpool-Fylde coast) in the 2001 season helped the government avoid prosecution under the directive. Despite bathing water improvements, prosecution did go ahead in November 2001 for failure to meet the standards in 1996 and 1997. Further improvements in bathing water quality are expected from investment in coastal sewage treatment and storm overflows. GBP 600 million is committed up to 2005 for England and Wales.

Table 3.5 **Chemical water quality in rivers**[a]

Class	England[b]			Wales[b]			Scotland			Northern Ireland[b]		
	1990	1995	2000	1990	1995	2000	1990[c]	1995[c]	2000[d]	1991	1995	2000
Good	43	55	64	86	94	94	97	97	91	44	45	59
Fair	40	35	29	11	5	5	2	2	7	51	43	37
Poor	14	9	6	2	1	1	1	1	2	4	12	4
Bad	3	1	1	1	0	0	–	–	–	1	–	–
Km[e]	30 646	35 932	36 027	3 512	4 561	4 561	49 050	50 260	50 250	1 680	2 350	2 400

a) % of river length in class; results are not fully comparable because of differences in survey techniques.
b) Good (A and B); Fair (C and D); Poor (E); Bad (F).
c) Good (Unpolluted); Fair (Fairly Good); Poor (Poor); Bad (Grossly Polluted).
d) Good (Excellent A1 and Good A2); Fair (B); Poor (C); Bad (Seriously Polluted D).
e) Length surveyed.
Source: Environment Agency; SEPA; Environment and Heritage Service.

In 1997, five out of 18 *shellfish waters* in England and Wales failed to meet quality standards of the directive on shellfish water quality (79/923). In 1998, 76 additional shellfish waters were designated and in 2000, of the 94 shellfish waters in England and Wales, 76 met the standards. Sewage and agricultural runoff remain threats to compliance. Further improvement is expected from the GBP 50 million being invested up to 2005 in coastal sewage discharges and sewer overflows to achieve at least category B of Directive 91/492 on the quality of shellfish flesh. There is uncertainty about the water quality standard needed to achieve category A status, and it is claimed that a more stringent standard would be expensive and difficult for the water industry to meet. The Environment Agency's standards for permitting discharges to meet requirements of the shellfish water directive state that for inter-mittent discharges from storm overflows, no more than ten significant independent spills (of more than 50 m³) per year are allowed. The shellfish industry fears that this norm is too lenient and that combined sewer overflow discharges should be directed away from the few remaining category A shellfish waters. In 2000, the UK was referred to the European Court of Justice for failure to comply with Directive 79/923, but its efforts to fully implement the directive have led the Commission to propose formally closing the case. In Scotland, 75 additional shellfish waters were designated in 2001, bringing the total to 108. SEPA's improvement programmes and permitting policy are directed at achieving category A status.

2.2   Water pricing

In England and Wales, *OFWAT sets water prices* so as to ensure that: i) the functions of a water or sewerage company are properly carried out; ii) companies can *finance* the proper fulfilment of their functions, in particular by securing reasonable returns on capital; and iii) the interests of the *customers* of regulated water and sewerage companies are protected.

An *annual price increase limit* (price cap) is applied to a "tariff basket" of charges for water and waste water services, covering both industry and households. Charges may be adjusted each year for inflation plus a factor "K", set every five years for each company. In the late 1990s, water prices in UK cities were relatively low in OECD Europe terms (Table 3.6). Unlike in other privatised public services, K factors have generally been positive, implying price increases in real terms, particularly to cover investment needed after a long period of underinvestment. The K factor can be revised before the end of the five-year period for companies with higher profit than expected. Water prices were reduced by around 12% in 2000 and have remained virtually unchanged since, and investment is still being made.

Each company is responsible for its charging structure, which depends on local circumstances and history. Charges must be broadly cost-reflective, and OFWAT must ensure that there is "no undue discrimination or preference" among consumers. This *non-discrimination principle* has meant that prices to industrial users have until recently been comparable with those for metered household consumers. Water companies are also obliged to try to maintain a balance between charges to metered and non-metered customers.

Water pricing for 20% of *household users* is metered; for the rest it is based on property value. Water supply charges for metered households and *industrial users* generally have two components: a fixed (standing) charge, which for industry is

Table 3.6   **Water prices in selected OECD countries,**[a] 1998

(USD/m^3)

		At current exchange rates	Adjusted for PPP[b]
United Kingdom	London	0.62	0.57
	Bristol	0.57	0.52
	Manchester	0.55	0.51
Canada	Ottawa	0.34	0.43
	Toronto	0.31	0.39
	Winnipeg	0.73	0.92
USA	New York	0.43	0.43
	Los Angeles	0.58	0.58
	Miami	0.36	0.36
Japan	Tokyo	0.92	0.74
	Osaka	0.68	0.54
	Sapporo	1.13	0.90
France	Paris (suburb)	1.46	1.28
	Bordeaux	1.16	1.02
	Lyon	1.45	1.27
Germany	Berlin	1.94	1.70
	Hamburg	1.74	1.53
	Munich	1.35	1.19
Italy	Rome	0.28	0.29
	Milan	0.13	0.13
	Naples	0.57	0.59

a) Prices calculated for water supply to a family of four (two adults and two children) living in a house with garden rather than an apartment. Price based on annual consumption of 200 m^3. VAT not included.
b) Purchasing power parities.
Source: International Water Supply Association.

based on the size of the supply pipe, and a variable (volumetric) charge, which depends on consumption. The standing charge for the smallest pipe size is the same for industry and households, as is the volumetric charge. Most water companies have introduced "large-user tariffs". OFWAT is proposing that large industrial users (those consuming more than 250 000 m^3 a year), and possibly new housing or industrial development as well, should be removed from the regulated tariff basket.

Sewerage and waste water treatment charges are calculated in the same way as water supply charges, either according to property value or based on the volume of water delivered, less a small allowance (typically 5%) for water not discharged to sewers. They are independent of the strength of the effluent, except for industrial discharges into public sewers, where charges are based on volume and quality (oxygen demand, suspended solids) according to the Mogden formula. Such charges are averaged across regions (with a minimum of GBP 75 to GBP 219 per year) and so are unlikely to reflect costs incurred at any one sewage treatment plant.

A consultation paper issued by DEFRA in 1997 reviewed proposals for *water pollution charges*. Several such charges exist in Europe (e.g. in France, Germany and the Netherlands). Given current monitoring constraints, at least interim thresholds below which charges are not imposed, or are set at a fixed rate, would likely have to be set. Rates would need to reflect the monetary value of pollution damage to the water environment or the marginal costs of pollution abatement. A charge of at least GBP 1/kg of BOD would be needed to stimulate investments in improved effluent treatment. This would raise an estimated GBP 220-355 million per year. Further income would accrue from charges on other pollutants (DEFRA has identified suspended solids, nutrients, ammonia and dangerous substances as candidates for charges). Questions remain: how would the incentive effect of a charging system be passed on to dischargers to sewers, which account for the vast bulk of industrial effluents? How could the programme be integrated into the water industry's price regulation system? What use would be made of the income and what would be the social and distributional consequences of water pollution charges? It was recently decided not to proceed with pollution charges in the UK, however, as it was felt there was a risk that local improvements in water quality, which are required to meet water quality objectives, might be sacrificed in the interest of improving cost-effectiveness in cleaning up water pollution.

In Scotland, three public water authorities were established in 1995 to take over water supply and waste water treatment from nine regional and three island councils. The water authorities were encouraged to seek private financing for capital invest-ments. In 1999, an economic regulator, the Water Industry Commissioner, was introduced to control price increases. Water prices have risen by 50% in the last two years. In the three years to March 2002, GBP 1.8 billion was spent to improve and renew infrastructure. The expenditure was shared equally between drinking water supply and sewage treatment. In February 2002, the Scottish Parliament passed the Water Industry (Scotland) Act, merging the three water authorities into a single public authority, Scottish Water. The aim is increase economic efficiency in the provison of water and waste water services. Scottish Water will also have a sustainable development duty, where this is not inconsistent with meeting its statutory functions. (Efforts by members of Parliament to give a similar duty to the Water Industry Commissioner were unsuccessful.) Scottish Water must report annually on how it has fulfilled this duty, and it must prepare a code of practice on consulting the public about the impact of its activities. The Act also established a drinking water quality regulator to take over a task previously carried out by the Scottish Executive.

WASTE MANAGEMENT*

Recommendations

The following recommendations are part of the overall conclusions and recommendations of the Environmental Performance Review of the United Kingdom:

- establish a systematic *data collection and information system* concerning the generation, recovery and disposal of non-municipal waste;
- introduce effective measures to encourage *waste minimisation* (e.g. waste charges for household waste, material resource efficiency standards) and accelerate efforts to increase *material recovery* rates;
- strengthen measures to prevent and discourage *illegal disposal of waste*, with emphasis on inspection and enforcement;
- review and revise *landfill-related measures* (e.g. landfill tax rates, exemptions; inspection and enforcement) so as to more effectively support objectives related to reduction of landfilling and diversion of waste to unlicensed sites;
- accelerate measures to ensure that treatment and disposal of *hazardous waste* are organised in an environmentally sound and economically efficient manner (e.g. eliminating "co-disposal"), and clearly identify infrastructure needs;
- assure implementation of new legislation on remediation of *contaminated land*.

---

* The present chapter reviews progress in the last ten years, and particularly since the previous OECD Environmental Performance Review of 1994. It also reviews progress with respect to the objective "maintaining the integrity of ecosystems" of the 2001 OECD Environmental Strategy.

Conclusions

In 1999 and 2000, the UK established *national waste management strategies* that, for the first time, included quantitative targets. It initiated data collection on municipal waste generation and management in the mid-1990s. Mechanisms to improve local authorities' performance on municipal waste management (e.g. "Best Value" duty) were introduced. The UK developed several *economic instruments* for waste management in the 1990s, including the landfill tax and the aggregates levy. A system of tradable permits for the landfilling of biodegradable municipal waste has been proposed. For some waste streams, recycling rates gradually increased over the decade. The UK transposed the EU packaging directive into national legislation, and progressed with preparations to implement EU directives on waste electrical and electronic equipment and on end-of-life vehicles. *Regulations* on hazardous waste were strengthened with, for instance, a broader definition of "special waste" and the obligatory attachment of consignment notes. A new regime for the identification and remediation of contaminated land was introduced.

The *rate of municipal waste generation* showed no sign of decoupling from GDP growth in the 1990s. Furthermore, given the relatively low cost of landfilling, there is little incentive to reduce waste generation or increase recycling. Measures to encourage waste minimisation remain very weak, and charges on household waste management have not been introduced despite a recommendation in the 1994 OECD review. An official *data collection system for non-municipal waste* is still lacking, rendering analysis of waste generation, management and disposal trends impossible, except for selected waste streams. The controversial practice of *"co-disposal"* (landfilling hazardous waste with other waste) continues, though it is supposed to be phased out by 2004 to comply with the EU landfill directive. Full compliance with EU legislation will require considerable investment to expand waste treatment capacity. Recycling rates continue to be among the lowest in OECD countries due to low public awareness and a lack of recycling infrastructure. *Regulatory inspection* of waste management sites should be made more systematic and consistent, and efforts to control illegal disposal should be further strengthened.

1.   Evaluation of Performance

1.1   *Objectives and institutional framework*

A range of primary and secondary environmental legislation (e.g. 1990 Environmental Protection Act, 1994 Waste Management Licensing Regulations) forms the regulatory framework for waste management in the UK. While the development of *waste legislation* in the 1990s was largely driven by the need to transpose EU directives into national legislation, the 1995 Environment Act introduced a holistic approach by obligating the central and devolved governments to prepare national strategies on waste. Separate legislation is applied in Northern Ireland. Physical planning and development legislation (e.g. 1990 Town and Country Planning Act) plays a dominant role in the planning and establishment of waste management facilities. The UK faces an enormous challenge as regards the EU directive on landfilling, a form of disposal on which the country has long relied heavily.

The *2000 waste strategy* was the first national plan for waste management in England and Wales. It sets out comprehensive views on the challenges to be tackled in the years to come, and proposes a variety of actions to be taken by each part of society. The strategy also sets *quantitative national targets*, partly replacing those that the central government set in 1990 and 1995 white papers. Both the central government and industry developed quite a number of quantitative targets in the 1990s (Table 4.1). However, no quantitative target for capping waste generation has so far been set, and the strategy does not adequately address measures for waste minimisation. Similar waste strategies were developed for Scotland and Northern Ireland in 1999 and 2000, respectively, and in June 2002 Wales got its own separate strategy.

Institutional arrangements for waste management are rather complex. In Scotland, Wales and parts of England, local authorities (i.e. "unitary" authorities, metropolitan authorities and London boroughs) are responsible for collection and disposal of municipal waste and for planning of waste management facilities. The rest of England has a two-tier system in which district councils are responsible for municipal waste collection while county councils are responsible for disposal and for planning of waste management facilities. In Northern Ireland, district councils are responsible for waste collection and disposal, while the Department of the Environment deals with land use planning. *Licensing and regulation* of waste management facilities are the responsibilities of the Environment Agency in England and Wales, and the Scottish Environment Protection Agency (SEPA) in Scotland (since 1996, when these responsibilities were transferred from local authorities). The Environment Agency and SEPA regulate waste from large-scale or complex polluting facilities through integrated pollution control (IPC) (Chapter 6, Section 2.1). In Northern Ireland, the Environment and Heritage Service is responsible for regulation of hazardous waste, control of producer responsibility on packaging and registration of waste carriers, and will soon take over Duty of Care control (Chapter 4, Section 1.4); all other waste-related responsibilities lie with districts and boroughs.

Table 4.1   **Selected quantitative targets in waste management policy**

Waste type	Targets[a]	Source
All controlled waste	Capping the proportion sent to landfill at 60% by 2005	1995 white paper[b]
Municipal waste	40% recovery by 2005	1995 white paper[b]
	40% recovery by 2005, 45% by 2010, 67% by 2015	Waste Strategy 2000[c]
	Reducing waste generation by 1% per year	National Waste Strategy: Scotland (1999)
	15% recycling and composting (minimum 5% recycling) by FY 2003, 25% (minimum 10% recycling) by FY 2006, 40% (minimum 15% recycling) by FY 2009	National Waste Strategy for Wales (2002)
Household waste	50% recycling and composting of recyclable content (*i.e.* about 25% of household waste) by 2000	1990 white paper[d]
	25% recycling or composting by 2000; 1 million tonnes per year to be composted by 2001	1995 white paper[b]
	25% recycling and composting by 2005, 30% by 2010, 33% by 2015	Waste Strategy 2000[c]
	Increasing recycling and composting at least two-fold by FY 2003, at least three-fold by FY 2005 (from FY 1998 level)	Local Government (Best Value) Performance Indicators and Performance Standards Order 2001[c]
	Capping generation per household at FY 1997 level by FY 2009; capping at 300kg per person per year by 2020	National Waste Strategy for Wales (2002)
Biodegradable municipal waste	Reducing amount sent to landfill to 75% of 1995 level by 2010, 50% by 2013, 35% by 2020	Waste Strategy 2000,[c] National Waste Strategy: Scotland (1999), in line with EU landfill directive
	Capping amount sent to landfill at 0.675 Mt by 2010, 0.450 Mt by 2013, 0.315 Mt by 2020	National Waste Strategy for Wales (2002)
Packaging waste	50-65% recovery including 25-45% material recovery of all packaging; minimum 15% material recovery for each material by end of 2001	Producer Responsibility Obligations (Packaging Waste) Regulations 1997,[c] in line with EU directive on packaging and packaging waste
Newsprint	60% recycled content by end of 2001, 65% by end of 2003, 70% by end of 2006	Voluntary agreement with Newspaper Publishers Association[e]
Glass	20 000 bottle banks by 2000	1995 white paper[b]
Paper	13 000 paper banks by 1996	1995 white paper[b]
Industrial and commercial waste	Reducing amount sent to landfill to 85% of 1998 level by 2005	Waste Strategy 2000[c]
	Reducing amount sent to landfill to 85% of 1998 level by 2005, 80% by 2010	National Waste Strategy for Wales (2002)

Table 4.1   **Selected quantitative targets in waste management policy** *(cont.)*

Waste type	Targets[a]	Source
Industrial waste	Reducing generation (excluding construction and demolition waste) by 3-5% by 2005, 6-9% by 2010, 10-12% by 2015	National Waste Strategy: Scotland (1999)
Hazardous waste	Reducing generation by 20% from 2000 level	National Waste Strategy for Wales (2002)
End-of-life vehicles	85% reuse or recycling by 2002, 95% by 2015	Voluntary commitment by Automotive Consortium on Recycling and Disposal[e]
	85% reuse or recovery, and 80% reuse or recycling by 2006; 95% reuse and recovery, and 85% reuse and recycling by 2015	EU directive on end-of-life vehicles[e]
Construction and demolition waste	Use of construction and demolition waste and secondary materials for aggregates: 40 Mt/year by 2001, 55 Mt/year by 2006	Minerals Planning Guidance Note 6 (1994)[c]
	75% reuse or recycling by 2005, 85% by 2010	National Waste Strategy for Wales (2002)

a) Percentages are expressed by weight. "Recycling" refers to material recovery. "Recovery" includes recycling, composting and energy recovery.
b) "Making Waste Work". Applicable to England and Wales. Superseded by Waste Strategy 2000 and National Waste Strategy for Wales (2002).
c) Applicable to England only. (Applied to Wales until June 2002, then was superseded by the National Waste Strategy for Wales.)
d) "This Common Inheritance". Applicable to England, Scotland and Wales.
e) Applicable to the whole UK.
Source: OECD.

The *1994 OECD Environmental Performance Review* of the UK recommended that:

– quantitative targets for waste reduction and recycling be developed;

– the central government encourage the inclusion of waste generation in IPC and draw up a long-term schedule of regulation, reflecting expected technological progress;

– economic instruments be used to encourage waste reduction and recycling;

– an inventory of the most contaminated sites, expansion of public funding for the worst problems and a comprehensive land clean-up system, including cost allocation measures, be established.

1.2   Waste generation trends

Municipal waste generation in the UK is estimated to have increased from 27 million tonnes (Mt) in 1990 to 33 Mt in 1999, a 23% rise. The increase closely tracked GDP growth; hence, decoupling was not achieved (Figure 4.1). The per capita waste generation rate (560 kg per year) is 22% higher than the OECD Europe average. About 80-90% of municipal waste is household waste. The rest is from commercial and industrial sites, public spaces (e.g. parks and beaches) and the clearance of illegal disposal. In the late 1990s, about 10% of municipal waste was collected for recycling (material recovery).

In the late 1990s, estimated annual generation of *non-municipal waste* totalled 400 Mt, comprising mining/quarrying waste (30%), agricultural waste (22%), construction and demolition waste (18%), dredged material (10%), industrial waste (13%) and commercial waste (6%). Sewage sludge accounted for less than 1% on a dry weight basis. Mining/quarrying waste and agricultural waste are not defined as "controlled waste" in UK waste legislation (unless they are moved to a licensed site or disposed of illegally), and thus are not regulated. About 190 Mt per year (48% of the total) of non-municipal waste is subject to regulation. Time-series information on non-municipal waste generation is so far limited to a few specific waste streams:

Figure 4.1   **Municipal waste generation**[a]

a) In interpreting national figures, it should be borne in mind that survey methods and definitions of municipal waste may vary from one country to another. According to the definition used by the OECD, municipal waste is waste collected by or for municipalities and includes household, bulky and commercial waste and similar waste handled at the same facilities.
b) Private final consumption.
Source: OECD.

mining/quarrying waste decreased by 35% between 1990 and 1998, mainly due to a sharp decline in deep-mined coal production, while *sewage sludge* generation was stable. Generation of *hazardous waste* (called "special waste" in the UK legislation) generally decreased until 1996, when the definition of special waste was extended (to include used oil, for instance) to conform with the EU Hazardous Waste List. This led to roughly doubled generation, statistically, to over 4.8 Mt per year since.

Quantitative information on waste management in the UK is generally poor and fragmented in terms of waste stream, geographical distribution and time coverage. Regular data collection has not yet been instituted for many waste streams. (One exception is municipal waste, for which regular monitoring was initiated in the mid-1990s in England and Wales. In Scotland and Northern Ireland, monitoring of municipal waste started in 1998/99.) Therefore, reliable data for the entire UK on long-term waste management trends are often not available. Since such information is ideally the basis for developing waste management policy, a comprehensive database should be urgently established, particularly as regards non-municipal waste.

1.3 Municipal waste management

Recovery and disposal trends

The overall *recycling and composting* rate for household waste in England and Wales increased from 3% to 10% between 1991 and 1999. This strongly suggests that the recycling/composting target for household waste set in the 1995 white paper (25% by 2000) was missed by a large margin. A two-fold increase in composting since the mid-1990s accounted for the bulk of the increase. Substantial rises in recycling rates were also recorded for some municipal waste streams. For example, between 1990 and 1998, the recycling rate for aluminium cans increased from 5% to 36%, and waste paper use in newsprint from 26% to 52%. Recycling of post-consumer plastics (about two-thirds of which are of household origin) doubled in tonnage between 1994 and 1999, raising the recycling rate to 7%; an additional 8% went to energy recovery. Collection of plastic bottles more than quadrupled between 1996 and 2000, to a total of 13 000 tonnes. For paper/board and glass containers, however, the trend was a relatively small rise or almost level (Table 4.2).

Landfilling continued to be the dominant disposal method for municipal waste in the 1990s. Although the proportion was gradually decreasing, more than 80% of municipal waste was still sent to landfill in the late 1990s, mostly without treatment. If municipal waste generation continues to grow at the average rate of the late 1990s (3% per year), some 33 Mt of biodegradable waste will have to be diverted from landfills each year by 2020 if the UK is to meet the EU landfill directive target. This represents a difficult challenge.

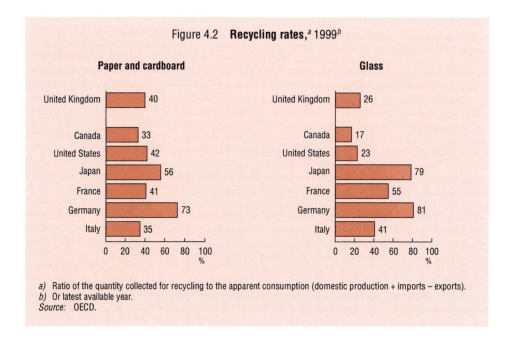

Figure 4.2   **Recycling rates,**[a] 1999[b]

Paper and cardboard

	%
United Kingdom	40
Canada	33
United States	42
Japan	56
France	41
Germany	73
Italy	35

Glass

	%
United Kingdom	26
Canada	17
United States	23
Japan	79
France	55
Germany	81
Italy	41

a) Ratio of the quantity collected for recycling to the apparent consumption (domestic production + imports – exports).
b) Or latest available year.
Source: OECD.

Table 4.2   **Recycling rates, selected municipal waste streams,** 1990-98

(%)

	1990	1991	1992	1993	1994	1995	1996	1997	1998
Paper/board[a]	32	34	34	32	34	37	38	38	38
Newsprint[a]	26	26	31	31	33	35	44	47	52
Glass containers[b]	15	17	20	22	22	22	22	21	22
Aluminium cans[c]	5	11	16	21	24	28	31	34	36

a) Waste material used as % of UK consumption.
b) Recycled glass container cullet as % of UK consumption.
c) Recycled aluminium as % of UK consumption. Includes recovery for processes other than can-to-can (e.g. deoxidants for steelmaking).
Source: British Paper and Board Industry Federation; Paper Federation of Great Britain; British Glass Manufacturers Confederation; Aluminium Can Recycling Association; Steel Can Recycling Information Bureau; DEFRA; Environment Agency.

The proportion of municipal waste that is *incinerated* has remained at about 8% since 1995. The overall *energy recovery* rate for municipal waste (i.e. electricity generation and/or heat recovery and manufacture of refuse-derived fuel) increased from 6% to 8% between 1995 and 1999. In compliance with the EU directive on air pollution from municipal waste incineration plants and the UK-wide dioxin controls, many municipal incinerators were closed, and a few retrofitted with emission reduction equipment, by the mid-1990s. Although some incinerators were built in the late 1990s, the net effect was a substantial drop in incineration capacity. Municipal waste incineration capacity in England and Wales now totals 2.7 Mt per year at 11 sites, and is almost fully utilised. Scotland has two municipal waste incineration sites, with total capacity of 145 kt per year. No municipal waste incineration site currently exists in Northern Ireland.

In all, *19% of municipal waste* was recycled, composted or used for energy recovery in 1999. Efforts will need to be accelerated to meet the national reuse/recovery targets of 40% by 2005, 45% by 2010 and 67% by 2015. Concerning *packaging waste*, the overall recycling rate of 28% in 1998 exceeded the minimum target established by the EU directive (25% by 2001) three years ahead of schedule. Material-specific recycling targets (15% minimum for each material by 2001) were also met, except for aluminium and plastic. On the other hand, the UK's overall recovery rate (including energy recovery) for packaging waste (33% in 1998) likely missed the EU target of at least 50% by 2001. In fact, the UK's overall recycling and recovery rates for packaging waste and glass remain among the lowest in the EU (Figure 4.2).

Policy measures: institutions and waste generation

Improving local authorities' performance on municipal waste management has become a priority in recent years. In 1999, waste management was designated one of the main local public services requiring improvement, and 19 local authorities in England and Wales (e.g. Reading) were subsequently selected under this theme in the Beacon Councils programme, designed to facilitate sharing of best practices among local governments. Since April 2000, household waste management services in England and Wales have been subject to the Best Value system under the 1999 Local Government Act, which means that local authorities must demonstrate that their public services are conducted efficiently and cost-effectively through quantitative target setting (e.g. for recycling rates, cost of waste collection and disposal) and regular performance monitoring. Local authorities in England and Wales are required to develop municipal waste strategies. In Scotland, local authorities are core members of 11 regional groups preparing area-wide waste plans. In Northern Ireland, district councils have formed three regional partnerships and are finalising their waste management plans.

Although the 1998 Waste Minimisation Act gave local authorities in England, Scotland and Wales *statutory power* to initiate efforts to minimise waste generation, little progress has been made so far in developing effective measures to this end. A comprehensive approach with strong measures would be necessary to reverse the current trend, which shows no sign of slowing. The introduction of concrete measures such as waste charges, material resource efficiency standards for consumer products and repair/maintenance service standards (to extend product life) could be considered. Also, public awareness-raising activities should be further strengthened.

Despite the recommendation of the 1994 OECD Environmental Performance Review, *waste charges* have not yet been introduced for household waste management (except for bulky refuse in some municipalities). The cost of collection and disposal (GBP 1.5 billion in England and Wales in 1999) continued to be financed almost fully by general budgets of local governments. Current legislation specifically prohibits local authorities from charging fees for their household waste management. To produce a strong incentive for consumers to reduce waste generation, and to incorporate the polluter pays principle into UK household waste management policy, the legislation as well as the local tax system should be reviewed, to enable local authorities to introduce such fees for households, preferably with differentiated rates (e.g. by weight, volume, material) at levels permitting appropriate cost recovery.

Separate collection of recyclable household waste primarily involves consumers taking materials to collection points or roadside recycling banks (about 70% of separately collected waste, by weight, is dealt with in this way in England and Wales). Kerbside collection accounts for a relatively small proportion of material recovery (28% in England and Wales). Increasing kerbside collection, where economically feasible in terms of location and frequency, could greatly accelerate the increase of recycling rates.

Policy measures: recycling and recovery

Where *responsibilities for collection and disposal of municipal waste* are shared by districts and counties (Chapter 4, Section 1.1), a lack of co-ordination between authorities could become a major obstacle to achieving waste-related targets. As the Audit Commission noted in 2001, this is sometimes the case in England. The situation particularly hampers efforts to increase recovery rates, since a county council's decisions over material priority, recovery methods and capacity building directly affect the investment and service provision planning of all the district councils in that county, and vice versa. In other words, co-ordinated planning between "two-tier" authorities and among different counties could lead to diseconomies of scale on recovered material. The allocation of responsibilities among local authorities and within regions should thus be re-examined with a view to promoting integration and pursuing economic efficiency in municipal waste management.

The *Recycling Credit programme* is a unique economic instrument, in place in England since 1992. Payments equal to avoided disposal costs are made from county councils to district councils in regions with the two-tier system (Chapter 4, Section 1.1). Although the basic purpose is to encourage and financially support district recycling/composting efforts, the revenue is sometimes used for other public services. In addition, the idea holds an intrinsic dilemma: the less waste going to final disposal, the higher the marginal disposal cost generally becomes. Hence, there is little incentive for district councils to increase recycling/composting or to promote waste minimisation. The effectiveness of the Recycling Credit programme may need to be re-examined and, where necessary, improved. The Recycling Credit programme also operates in Scotland, though because all local authorities there are unitary, there is no mandatory monetary transfer between collection and disposal authorities.

The UK stepped up efforts to *create stable markets for recovered materials* by establishing the Waste and Resources Action Programme (known as "WRAP") in 2000 (Chapter 4, Section 2.1). The programme is well designed, with clear quantitative targets, a combination of horizontal and material-specific projects, and an aim of avoiding duplication of efforts. Whereas the programme's research and information provision activities could be further extended, financial support for capital projects of private recycling businesses should be limited in scale and scope, to avoid major market distortion.

By transposing the EU directive on *packaging waste* into national legislation (the 1997 Producer Responsibility Obligations Regulations and the 1998 Packaging Regulations), the UK established a legal foundation for accelerating the recovery of packaging waste. This is the only UK legislation so far that incorporates the principle of *extended producer responsibility*. Although responsibility for collection and sorting remains with municipalities, responsibility for recovery is shared by the industries that produce or use the packaging, with a percentage of responsibility fixed for each part of the supply chain: raw material producers, packaging manufacturers, packers/fillers and sellers. The UK system is entirely market driven, with tradable certificates called packaging-waste recovery notes (PRNs) issued by reprocessors to the businesses covered by the regulations, to prove that a certain tonnage of reprocessing has taken place. Total revenue from selling PRNs was GBP 78 million in 1998. There is concern, however, that reprocessors might not be using as much of the revenue as expected to support recovered material prices or to invest in new recovery infrastructure. Since the PRN revenue is "windfall" profit for reprocessors, created by national waste management policy, some mechanism could be introduced to encourage reprocessors to use a certain proportion of the revenue to support development of the recovery market and infrastructure. Introduction of a deposit-refund system would also merit consideration for some types of bottles and other containers.

Preparation for transposition of the forthcoming EU directives on *waste electrical and electronic equipment* has progressed. Industry organisations have run or supported a number of trial collection/recycling projects for such waste. The Industry Council for Electronic Equipment Recycling, one such organisation, estimated the UK recycling rate for large household appliances to be 88% (by weight) in the late 1990s. The rates for telecommunication, information technology and video/audio equipment were 50%, 26% and 4%, respectively.

Policy measures: waste disposal

The UK has proposed a system of *tradable permits* to support progress towards limits on the landfilling of biodegradable municipal waste under the EU landfill directive. It is not yet confirmed whether Scotland and Northern Ireland will opt for the system. The system would start operating in 2003, with the traders being the local authorities in charge of municipal waste disposal (Chapter 4, Section 2.2). It is expected to create a strong economic incentive for local authorities to implement measures to reduce the generation and increase the recovery of municipal waste. The use of such economic instruments for waste management is pioneering, and could be extended to other waste streams if found to be cost-effective.

One major difficulty the UK will face in meeting the targets set by the EU landfill directive is that its *municipal waste incineration* capacity is relatively small in OECD terms. The former Department of Environment, Transport and the Regions estimated that, to meet the targets, the capacity would have to quadruple by 2020 at substantial costs (Chapter 4, Section 2.3), even assuming large increases in recycling. Strong public opposition to incineration, however, has slowed both the development of plants at new sites and the expansion of existing plants. Despite significant reductions in pollutant emissions (e.g. by 98% for dioxins between 1990 and 1997) and increased energy recovery from incineration (nearly all plants now incorporate energy recovery processes), public acceptance has not grown. Increased inspections and strict enforcement by the authorities, along with information disclosure by operators, could heighten public confidence. These issues should be addressed in the context of ongoing planning reform, with attention paid to increased accountability.

1.4   Management of non-municipal waste

Recovery and disposal trends

No information was available to evaluate overall trends for recovery and disposal of non-municipal waste in the 1990s. The new Department for Environment, Food and Rural Affairs (DEFRA) has estimated that, in England and Wales in the late 1990s, more than 40% (by weight) of the total 140-180 Mt per year of non-municipal controlled waste (commercial and industrial waste, excluding mining and quarrying waste) was recovered, with more than 30% recycled, while 55% (by weight) went directly to landfill. There are about 2 720 licensed landfill sites, including some 220 company-specific sites, in England and Wales. About 80% of the sites are operating and the rest have been closed. About two-thirds are large sites (with capacity exceeding 25 000 tonnes) subject to regulations under the IPC/IPPC system.

Of the 4.8 Mt of *hazardous waste* generated annually in England and Wales in the late 1990s, about half was landfilled. A significant proportion of the landfilling was at "co-disposal" sites, where hazardous waste is disposed of alongside household or similar waste, "to attenuate those constituents in hazardous wastes which are polluting and potentially hazardous". In the late 1990s, 230 co-disposal sites were in operation and 30 were closed in England and Wales. Hazardous waste was inciner-ated at three commercial hazardous waste incinerators with combined capacity of 134 000 tonnes per year, 14 in-house industrial incinerators, four drum reconditioning facilities and nine cement and lime kilns in England and Wales. Figures on the proportions of incineration and recovery of hazardous waste are not available.

Of about 70 Mt of *construction and demolition waste* generated annually in England and Wales in the 1990s, 63% was recycled or reused (including 30% used for landfill engineering: e.g. roads, containment cells and cover layers) and 30% was sent to landfill, according to the estimate generally accepted by DEFRA (Figure 8.2). There has been a gradual decrease in the amount sent to landfill since the introduction of the landfill tax (Figure 4.3), with much of the waste being diverted to sites where waste regulations are not applied (e.g. golf course development) (Chapter 4, Section 2.2). In Scotland, of the 6 Mt of construction and demolition waste generated annually in the late 1990s, 37% was recovered, 41% was landfilled and 22% was sent to sites exempted from regulations.

The average recycling rate for the more than 1.5 million *end-of-life vehicles* (ELVs) generated annually in the UK was 77% (by weight) in 1999. This figure mostly represents reuse of parts and recycling of metals; the rest was shredded and landfilled. More than 90% (by weight) of *automotive batteries* are recycled in the UK, thanks to the high value of lead plates, although fluctuation in world lead prices could undermine the economics of collection. The recovery rate for *used tyres* was more than 70% in the late 1990s. This included 16% energy recovery, a relatively small proportion compared to most OECD Europe countries.

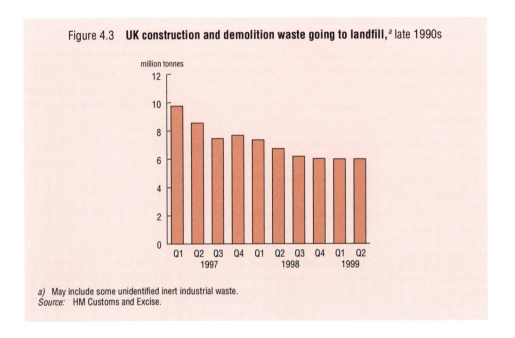

Figure 4.3   **UK construction and demolition waste going to landfill,**[a] late 1990s

million tonnes

a) May include some unidentified inert industrial waste.
Source: HM Customs and Excise.

Policy measures

Regulation of hazardous waste has been strengthened. The Duty of Care requirements, which entered into force in 1992, oblige holders of commercial or industrial waste to assure its appropriate storage and transfer. A consignment note system for hazardous waste has existed in England, Scotland and Wales since 1981. (Northern Ireland has not introduced a similar system yet but plans to do so shortly.) Under the Special Waste Regulations system, the Environment Agency or SEPA tracks hazardous waste from "cradle to grave" (generation to recovery/disposal). The agencies charge GBP 15 per note to cover the administrative costs of the tracking system. Annual revenue from this fee amounts to about GBP 8 million for the Environment Agency and about GBP 0.7 million for SEPA. The central government and the Scottish administration are considering lowering the fee for waste going to recovery, which would be a positive step.

The UK's widely criticised practice of *co-disposal* of hazardous and non-hazardous waste continued in the 1990s but is set to be phased out by July 2004 at existing sites. The opening of new co-disposal sites was banned in July 2001 in line with the EU landfill directive. Considering the potential risk posed by closed co-disposal sites, additional attention should be given to monitoring their emissions and leachate.

Industry intensified efforts to improve recovery of material from *ELVs* in the 1990s. In 1991, vehicle and material manufacturers, dismantlers and material recyclers set up the Automotive Consortium on Recycling and Disposal. Its members committed themselves in 1997 to increasing the recycling rate to 85% (by weight) by 2002 and 95% by 2015; the rate achieved in 1999 was 77%. UK vehicle manufacturers/importers and dismantlers have been collaboratively investing since the mid-1990s in R&D on technologies for reuse and recycling of materials from ELVs, and on developing markets for recycled materials via the CARE project. Nevertheless, meeting the long-term targets in the EU directive on ELVs (85% reuse or recycling and 95% reuse or recovery by the beginning of 2015) will be a challenge for the UK, especially given the rapid increase in fleet size in past decades. A substantial increase in recovery of non-metallic material such as plastic, rubber and glass, most of it now land-filled, will be necessary. Completely phasing out the landfilling of *used tyres* from 2003 (to be completed by 2006) as required by the EU landfill directive will be even more urgent and challenging, given that about 25% of used tyres (120 000 tonnes in 1999) are still sent to landfill.

The *landfill tax* introduced in 1996 aims to reduce the UK's heavy reliance on landfilling (Chapter 4, Section 2.2). Although information is limited, there are early signs of a decrease in the amount of construction and demolition waste sent to landfill (Figure 4.3). However, this is likely to have resulted from diversion to sites where the waste regulations are not applicable, or from illegal disposal. Exemptions from landfill licensing should be reviewed to close loopholes. Economic incentives for reducing waste generation rates remain weak for most sectors, as the landfill tax accounts for a minuscule proportion of turnover. The cost of landfilling, including the tax, is still much lower than in many OECD-Europe countries, even though the tax increased the per-tonne payment for landfilling by 30-100% for non-inert waste and by more than 100% for inert waste.

In April 2002, England, Scotland and Wales introduced an *aggregates levy* in an effort to increase recycling of construction/demolition waste and thus reduce land-filling (Chapter 4, Section 2.2). Although the impact of the tax may be limited, as the amount of recyclable contents that could substitute for new aggregates is far smaller than the overall demand for aggregates, the tax is expected to contribute to increased recycling and reduced landfilling. In Northern Ireland, the aggregates levy will be introduced in 2003, with rate increases over four years.

Integration of policies on recovery, landfill and incineration should be promoted. Although quantitative targets regarding increased recovery and reduced landfilling have been set and a range of initiatives is now in place for many waste streams, these were more or less independently developed. An overarching design, with co-ordinated sectoral targets and measures to achieve the overall recovery and disposal targets, is still lacking. Policy measures to encourage waste prevention are particularly weak.

The number of *illegal waste disposal cases* has mushroomed since the late 1990s. For example, over 1 000 incidents of mismanagement or illegal disposal of tyres were reported to the Environment Agency in 2000. Many less significant incidents, mostly fly-tipping (dumping), are dealt with by local authorities and are not reported to the agency. It is estimated that the costs of response and clearance of illegally disposed tyres alone, borne by the agency and local authorities in England and Wales, amounts to GBP 2 million per year. The agency is continuing its efforts to prevent illegal disposal, for example establishing a national strategy on waste tyre issues. It also piloted the use of enforcement teams, working with other enforcement agencies, such as the police, Customs and Excise, the Benefits Agency and local authorities, to target serious illegal waste activities. Considering the magnitude of illegal disposal cases, these efforts should continue to be strengthened.

The Environment Agency's *inspection and enforcement activities* on licensed waste operation sites fluctuated widely in the late 1990s. For example, the number of inspection visits decreased by 10% between 1997 and 1999 in England and Wales, while the issuance of waste-related enforcement and prohibition notices rose by 77%. It is not easy to compare numbers of inspection and enforcement cases as the activities are carried out on a risk and priority basis. Nevertheless, efforts should be made to ensure that the activities are consistent in terms of frequency and quality. An extension of the consignment note obligation to all non-municipal waste would be worth considering. As an additional benefit, this would facilitate systematic data collection concerning non-municipal waste, now sorely lacking in the UK.

Planning permission and licensing for the development of waste management facilities should be better integrated. The fact that separate authorisations are made by local authorities and the Environment Agency or SEPA leads to lengthy application procedures and, in some cases, conflicting decisions. Integration of development planning, land use planning and waste management planning should also be strengthened at national and regional levels to minimise the risk of decisions by local planning authorities being excessively influenced by local interests, as opposed to broader perspectives on the needs of waste management capacity in the longer term and in a wider regional context. Considering the UK's need to rapidly increase waste recovery capacity, priority should be put on streamlining permission and licensing processes to facilitate the development of waste recovery facilities. In Northern Ireland, waste management licensing should be urgently introduced.

The UK transposed the EU directive on PCB disposal into national legislation in 2000, two years after the deadline. An inventory of *residual stocks of PCBs or equipment* containing over 50 ppm of PCBs, completed in July 2000, revealed that the amount of PCB waste remaining (1 200 tonnes of PCBs or contaminated oil) was 85% smaller than the Environment Agency's 1995 estimate of 8 000 tonnes. The gap was partly due to the five-litre threshold for registration of PCBs, as well as progress in disposal. But differences in interpretation of the regulation's definition of "PCB waste" on the part of companies, plus illegal disposal, may have also contributed to the sharp decline, raising some concern. Although most disposal of registered PCB waste was completed by the end of 2000, as required by the regulation, sustained efforts will be necessary to assure the eventual safe disposal of items exempted from the deadline, notably transformers with PCB concentrations of less than 500 ppm, and cases individually authorised by the secretary of state.

Waste management accounted for around 40% of *pollution abatement and control (PAC) expenditure* in the late 1990s; 75% of this expenditure was borne by the public sector (Table 6.8). In 1999, the total figure came to GBP 2.8 billion, of which 70% was for investment and the rest for operations. The chemicals/rubber/plastic, metal products and food/beverage/tobacco industries accounted for about half of the UK's PAC expenditure for waste management by business.

1.5   *Transboundary movements of waste*

The UK's imports and exports of hazardous waste are *very small* compared to those of many OECD countries, reflecting a long-standing principle of self-sufficiency in waste disposal, embodied in the legally binding UK Management Plan for Exports and Imports of Waste. However, *imports of special (hazardous) waste* doubled from 1995 to 1996, to 90 000 tonnes, and have exceeded that amount every year since. The size of the increase is thought to have been due to better reporting and the Environment Agency's implementation of a quality assurance programme. The bulk of the imports originate in other EU countries, and most (90% by weight in 2000) are destined for recycling, including large proportions for metal recycling (31%) and solvent regeneration (12%). Energy recovery accounted for only 4%. Almost all special waste imported for disposal was incinerated. The trend in *exports of special waste* is similar to that for imports, but at a level well below that of imports (one-seventh in 1998).

The UK ratified the *Basel Convention* in 1992, and in 1994 transposed the EU directive on transboundary movements of waste, which implements the Basel Convention and the *OECD Council Decision* on control of transfrontier movements of waste destined for recovery. In 1997, the UK ratified the amendment of the Basel

Convention banning the export of hazardous waste from OECD countries to non-OECD countries, and has complied with the rule ever since, in line with the relevant EU regulation.

1.6   *Remediation of contaminated sites*

The Environment Agency recently estimated that there are *between 5 000 and 20 000 contaminated sites, covering some 300 000 hectares*, in England and Wales. Remediation of most contaminated sites in the UK is carried out through land use development and planning controls. Detailed risk assessments and remediation requirements can be stipulated in individual planning approvals for new developments. Remediation of contaminated sites having waste management licences or subject to IPC/IPPC is regulated by legislation. In England, when it is not possible to recover clean-up costs from the liable party, national funding for cleaning up contaminated land has been available to local authorities since 1990 in the Supplementary Credit Approval programme. In the late 1990s, GBP 13-14 million was granted annually under the programme. In Scotland, local authorities receive capital allocations (totalling about GBP 10 million in 2000-02) to allow them to undertake similar work. Where a contaminated site is part of a development project by one of the national urban regeneration programmes (which were integrated as the English Partnerships in 1999), remediation costs can be supported by the programme. In addition, a public-private partnership, called CLAIRE, was set up in 1999 to develop cost-effective technologies for remediating contaminated land. These efforts notwithstanding, policy measures on contaminated land were fragmented until recently.

Major legislative progress was made when a new *regulatory framework on land contamination* came into force in 2000-01 with the establishment of regulations (e.g. the 2000 Contaminated Land [England] Regulations) under the 1990 Environmental Protection Act. While planning controls are expected to continue to play a principal role in the remediation of contaminated land, the new regime fills a legislative gap by providing a way to remediate sites that would not otherwise come under legislation. The significance of the new regime also lies in its statutory definition of contaminated land and its establishment of the principle of liability based on the polluter pays principle. Moreover, the new regime enables *systematic and comprehensive identification and remediation of contaminated land* by requiring local authorities to identify contaminated sites, establish responsibilities for remediation and ensure that remediation takes place. Progress in identifying sites has so far been much slower than expected due to technical difficulties (e.g. in gathering historical and geographical data and in prioritising suspected sites for inspection) as well as limited financial resources of local authorities. The capacity of local authorities to address the issue varies greatly. For some, it takes several years to complete identification before remediation actually starts. Stronger guidance by, and financial support from, the central government may be needed.

2.   Focus on Selected Topics

2.1   *Facilitating recycling markets: Waste and Resources Action Programme*

Created under the auspices of the 2000 waste strategy, the *Waste and Resources Action Programme* for England, Scotland and Wales was established in December 2000. WRAP's objective is to create stable and efficient markets for recovered materials and products, and to remove barriers to waste minimisation, reuse and recycling. WRAP is operated by a non-profit company limited by guarantee, with substantial government funding (over GBP 40 million for 2001-03). It also receives some funding from the waste industry under the Landfill Tax Credit programme (Chapter 4, Section 2.2). It currently focuses on industrial, commercial and municipal waste, but may at some point extend its scope to include construction and demolition waste. It does not deal with mining waste or sewage sludge.

WRAP comprises *seven major programmes*: three general (financial mechanisms, procurement, and standards and specifications) and four on specific material streams (paper, glass, plastic and wood). The programmes provide funding to companies and academia for R&D and capital investment projects, market research and studies, training programmes, seminars and other forms of information provision and awareness raising. Financial support for recycling businesses (e.g. a loan guarantee fund or equipment lease guarantees) and price stabilisation mechanisms for recovered materials/products are under study as an eventual part of the financial mechanism programme. A range of targets, including many quantitative ones, is set for each programme.

In its first fiscal year of operation, WRAP contributed GBP 3.6 million to *21 R&D projects* (expected to cost GBP 5.6 million in all) on glass, plastic and wood recycling, and GBP 4 million to *capital investment projects* (increasing newsprint reprocessing capacity, setting up an automated plastic bottle sorting plant and increasing wood reprocessing capacity).

2.2   *Increased use of economic instruments in waste management*

Landfill tax

The UK introduced a landfill tax in October 1996 with the aim of internalising environmental costs of landfills and thereby *encouraging waste prevention and recovery* and reducing the amount of waste going to landfill. The initial tax rate was set at GBP 7 per tonne for non-inert waste, rising by GBP 1 per tonne per year (i.e. to GBP 13 per tonne in 2002) until April 2004. The rate is fixed at GBP 2 per tonne for inert waste. The tax is revenue-neutral, with taxed companies compensated by reduced national insurance contributions for their workers. Before the introduction of the tax, typical per-tonne fees for non-inert waste were GBP 7-25 and for inert waste no more than GBP 2. Thus, introduction of the tax brought about a significant increase in fees. *The Landfill Tax Credit programme* authorises operators to set aside 20% of tax liabilities for funding environmental projects meeting criteria set by the central government and carried out by registered environmental bodies.

The *amount of waste sent to landfill seems to have fallen since the introduction of the tax*. The reduction mainly involves inert waste (Figure 4.3). The figure for non-inert waste has been stable, with increased waste generation being offset by increased recovery. Some 36 Mt per year of inert waste may have been diverted away from landfills since 1996: one-third by recovery and the rest by diversion to regulation-exempted activities (e.g. landscaping, including golf courses and levelling of fields). The possible abuse of such exemptions at sites where policing is insufficient has been a source of concern.

Aggregates levy

Taxation on newly quarried, mined, dredged and imported aggregates (sand, gravel and crushed rock) came into force in April 2002 in England, Scotland and Wales. Increasing recycling of construction materials and reduction of environmental impacts associated with quarrying are among the main rationales for the tax. Around 600 companies are subject to the levy. At the rate of GBP 1.6 per tonne of aggregates (about 30% of the average aggregate price), the levy is expected to raise GBP 380 million per year. One argument challenging the need for the levy was that demand for aggregates was decreasing. Indeed, demand was about 20% less in the early 1990s than in the 1980s, and it stabilised in the late 1990s at an even lower level (around 220 Mt per year). The drop may be due to more efficient building practices and waste minimisation, as well as increased recycling of construction/demolition waste spurred by the introduction of the landfill tax in 1996 (Chapter 8, Section 1.4). The government estimates that the tax will reduce demand for primary aggregates by a further 10%.

Tradable permits for biodegradable waste

The EU landfill directive sets reduction targets for *biodegradable municipal waste going to landfill*, to reduce methane emissions from landfill sites. To support progress towards the targets, the UK has proposed a *tradable permit system* for such waste, to start in 2003 and be based on the reduction targets set in the directive (with derogations for the UK): 75% of the 1995 level by 2010, 50% by 2013 and 35% by 2020. Northern Ireland has not yet consulted on the matter. It is proposed that permits will be allocated at no charge to local authorities responsible for municipal waste disposal, possibly in proportion to population size and number of households. Other possible bases for calculating the allocations in Scotland include waste generated in 1994, waste generated in 1998 and waste landfilled in 1998. It is proposed that unlimited banking of permits be allowed, except during the three target years, but no borrowing of permits will be allowed. Ownership and transfers of permits will be recorded electronically on a central registry to be maintained by the Environment Agency. In Scotland, SEPA will likely monitor compliance, although the central registry would remain with the Environment Agency.

Providing permits to local authorities, rather than to landfill operators, is expected to lower the administrative costs of the system, as fewer and more homogeneous participants would be involved. Also, the provision of permits free of charge to local authorities, rather than by auction, is meant to minimise the transfer of wealth into or outside the local authority. These are the *main benefits of the UK's system* by design, in addition to the general benefits of tradable permits (e.g. minimising compliance costs).

2.3   *Cost estimation of increased municipal waste recovery*

In 2000, national environment authorities estimated the total *cost of meeting the EU landfill directive targets* for municipal waste over 2000-20; they predicted that the UK's costs for municipal waste management would increase by 10-33% during the period, depending on the policy approach taken and assumptions made (Table 4.3). However, the study said, if the external environmental costs were taken into account, the net environmental benefit would be GBP 0.7-13.8 billion for the period. Increasing incineration (with energy recovery) would be a cheaper means of meeting the targets than increasing recycling, but would mean building more than 100 additional incineration plants. This may not be feasible, considering the public resistance to incineration.

More importantly, the estimate indicates that reducing municipal waste generation would be more *cost-effective* than increasing treatment and disposal capacity. For example, the cost increase is estimated to be only 10-22% if waste generation stabilises at its 2000 level, compared to 21-33% if generation continues to increase by 3% per year. This study provides support for the general waste management hierarchy in UK policy (reduction, reuse, recovery, disposal).

Table 4.3   **Estimated costs of meeting EU landfill directive targets on municipal waste,**[a]
2000-20

Scenarios	Assumptions for 2000-20	Costs for 2000-20[b] (GBP billion)		Required number of new waste management facilities		
		Total costs	Total costs over base case	Recycling facilities	Composting stations	Incinerators
Base case	– Current levels (in absolute terms) of composting and recycling[c] – All other waste going to landfill	17.3-23.2	–	0	0	0
Case 1	– Current levels (in absolute terms) of composting and recycling[c] – All waste diversion by incineration with energy recovery	19.1-28.8	1.8-4.9	0	0	60-166
Case 2	– Increased composting and recycling of waste paper – Other waste diversion by incineration with energy recovery	20.1-29.4	2.7-6.2	0	99-196	41-128
Case 3	– Increased composting and recycling of all dry recyclables – Other waste diversion by incineration with energy recovery	20.8-30.3	3.4-7.1	113-223	59-116	33-112
Case 4	– As in Case 3, except higher level of composting and recycling	21.3-30.9	3.9-7.7	160-316	84-164	21-89

a) EU landfill directive targets for the UK: reduce landfilling of biodegradable municipal waste to 75% of 1995 level by 2010, 50% by 2013, 35% by 2020 (four-year derogations for the UK allowed by the directive).
b) Highest and lowest figures resulting from the different combinations of assumptions concerning the annual growth rate of municipal waste generation (0-3%) and of household participation rate in provided composting/recycling services (55%-75%). Excludes landfill tax.
c) Assumed patterns of generation, treatment and disposal are based on 1998 data for England and Wales.
Source: DEFRA.

NATURE CONSERVATION AND BIODIVERSITY*

Recommendations

The following recommendations are part of the overall conclusions and recommendations of the Environmental Performance Feview of the United Kingdom:

- extend and strengthen the use of *management agreements* for protected areas;
- fully implement the *biodiversity action plan* through local action plans, and improve monitoring of the condition of individual species and habitats;
- continue to encourage the expansion of *woodland and forest cover* and to promote sustainable forestry in line with the UK forestry standard;
- further promote *agri-environmental programmes*, as allowed for under the EU Common Agricultural Policy (CAP);
- develop and implement comprehensive legislative and institutional mechanisms for *marine nature conservation*, fully implementing the EU habitat directive in the 200-mile exclusive economic zone;
- continue to promote measures to conserve *wildlife species* that are in decline, and regularly monitor their status as a basis for establishing related conservation measures.

---

* The present chapter reviews progress in the 1990s, and particularly since the previous OECD Environmental Performance Review of 1994. It also reviews progress with respect to the objective "maintaining the integrity of ecosystems" of the 2001 OECD Environmental Strategy.

Conclusions

Since the 1994 OECD review, the UK has steadily strengthened *protection of special sites* by increasing their area (e.g. a 22% increase in areas and sites of special scientific interest between 1993 and 2001), enacting new legislation (e.g. the 2000 Countryside and Rights of Way Act) and promoting positive, rather than compensatory, management agreements with landowners/occupiers. Some trends of *habitat loss* seen before 1990 have been slowed, halted or reversed, including those affecting plant diversity in arable fields, area of fen/marsh/swamp and biological condition of small rivers. Forest cover increased by 16% between 1990 and 2000. A framework for implementing *"Biodiversity: The UK Action Plan"* was established with the preparation of individual action plans for 45 priority habitats and 391 species, as well as for 160 local areas, under highly successful voluntary public-private partnerships. The first five-year progress report was published in 2001. Incorporation of biodiversity concerns into other policy fields was further advanced through national initiatives such as sustainable development indicators and the UK forestry standard, although there is still need for improvement. Land area subject to agri-environmental programmes continued to increase, as did related public expenditure (from GBP 9 million in 1990 to GBP 150 million in 2000). Environmental NGOs play a major and influential role in managing nature and biodiversity in the UK.

Nevertheless, the UK still faces significant challenges concerning biodiversity and nature conservation. It is uncertain whether nature and biodiversity protection efforts are sufficient to balance the multiple pressures from densely clustered economic activities. There is still considerable room for improvement in the *condition of protected areas*, as only 60% are in either "favourable" or "unfavourable but recovering" condition (the national target is 95% by 2010). The deterioration of some habitats and species has continued (e.g. plant diversity in grasslands, population of farmland birds, number of shrubs and bogs), largely because of intensive agriculture. Runoff from agricultural sources still causes *eutrophication* of sensitive habitats (e.g. over 80% of riverine habitats). *Fertiliser and pesticide application intensities* for the UK are higher than OECD Europe averages by 100% and 70%, respectively. Intensive grazing causes major habitat deterioration, especially in uplands. Statutory mechanisms for *marine nature conservation* are patchy, and an overall policy framework is lacking. Information is still insufficient to allow the recent biodiversity status of some animal species to be known.

1.   Evaluation of Performance

1.1   Objectives

The UK's legal framework provides the means to comply with its international and regional commitments, and sets *additional objectives and measures* tailored to domestic circumstances. These include objectives on protecting specific wildlife species, protecting landscapes and assuring public access to the countryside (Chapter 5, Section 2.1).

A number of the UK's nature and biodiversity conservation objectives derive from *international commitments*. In the EU context, the habitat and bird directives play a particularly important role in inland ecosystem conservation, and will play an increasingly important role in marine ecosystem conservation (Chapter 9, Section 1.5). The UK is a party to a range of global and regional environmental agreements; hence, internationally agreed objectives also play an important role concerning wetlands (Ramsar Convention), international trade in endangered species (Washington Convention), migratory species (Bonn Convention) and biodiversity (UN Convention on Biological Diversity).

The UK's national objectives for biodiversity conservation were consolidated in *1994 in "Biodiversity: The UK Action Plan"*. Published in response to the Convention on Biological Diversity, the plan sets specific objectives for the government and its agencies for the period up to 2015, the overall goal being "to conserve and enhance biological diversity within the UK and to contribute to the conservation of global biodiversity". The 1999 *sustainable development strategy* also identifies objectives concerning protection of wildlife/habitats and landscape, including stronger protection for special sites and improved public access to the countryside, as well as monitoring of progress through indicators.

The *1994 OECD Environmental Performance Review* recommended:

– strengthening co-operation and integration between government bodies dealing with nature protection and landscapes and those dealing with other sectors;

– continuing integration of environmental objectives and management principles into agricultural support policies under the CAP;

– setting precise targets, broken down by type of measure and management responsibility, for species and habitats, and monitoring progress towards them;

– using stricter protection measures or the extension of special areas to achieve targets for species and habitats;

– more effectively safeguarding protected areas against development;

– strengthening and accelerating protection of coastal and marine environments, while increasing the number of marine nature reserves;

– considering financial measures to strengthen nature conservation policy.

1.2   Biodiversity

Some 88 000 *known species* (including marine species) exist in the UK. They include over 70 mammal species, 500 bird species, 50 freshwater fish species and 2 000 vascular plant species. About 20% of the mammal species and 30-40% of the reptile and amphibian species are categorised as *threatened*, compared with fewer than 10% of the bird, freshwater fish, invertebrate and vascular plant species (Table 5.1). These proportions are fairly low relative to those of other OECD countries (Figure 5.1).

Terrestrial species

Bird populations have been in general decline since the mid-1970s. In particular, the population of farmland birds (one of the 15 "headline" indicators in the UK sustainable development initiative) has nearly halved since 1970 (Figure 5.2). The number of *mammal* species with declining populations has exceeded that of species with growing populations over the last 30 years, particularly for endemic species. The declining trend is most evident for bats and rodents (e.g. squirrels, mice), whereas for larger mammals such as carnivores (e.g. fox, otter) and ungulates (e.g. deer, feral goat) the opposite trend is seen. An *insect* monitoring programme has shown that populations of butterflies and moths stopped declining and began increasing in the mid-1990s.

Similarly, *plant diversity* began to increase in arable fields in the 1990s, although it continued to decline in grasslands (so-called infertile grasslands, in particular). Meadow species of butterfly were particularly affected. Plant diversity of streamside vegetation also continued to decline (Chapter 5, Section 2.1).

Aquatic species

In the 1990s, improvements in water quality in many rivers in the UK generally resulted in growing *fish populations*. However, the continued deterioration of many reedy, clear-water lakes may be leading to reduced diversity of freshwater species. While catches of trout were generally stable, a long-term decrease in reported salmon catches continued in the 1990s, particularly in Scotland, reflecting the decline in numbers of *wild salmon* returning to UK rivers (Figure 5.3). In an attempt to halt and

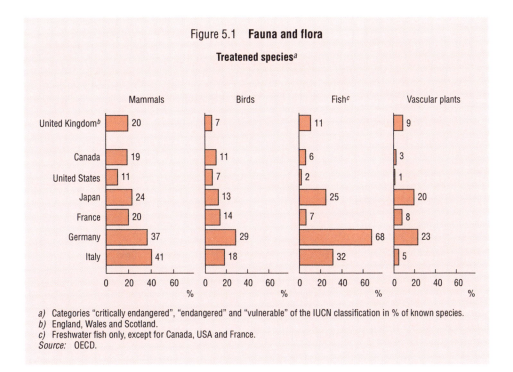

Figure 5.1 **Fauna and flora**

Treatened species[a]

a) Categories "critically endangered", "endangered" and "vulnerable" of the IUCN classification in % of known species.
b) England, Wales and Scotland.
c) Freshwater fish only, except for Canada, USA and France.
Source: OECD.

Table 5.1 **State of selected fauna and flora,**[a] late 1990s

	Number of known species	Number of threatened species			
		Critically endangered	Endangered	Vulnerable	Total
Mammals[b]	70	–	2	12	14
Birds[b]	517	3	24	8	35
Freshwater fish[b]	54	–	3	3	6
Reptiles[c]	7	–	1	2	3
Amphibians[c]	7	–	–	2	2
Invertebrates[c]	22 778	. .	573	403	976
Vascular plants[c]	2 230	25	43	132	200

a) England, Wales and Scotland.
b) Includes non-native species.
c) Endemic species only.
Source: OECD.

Figure 5.2 **Trends in bird populations,**[a] 1970-2000

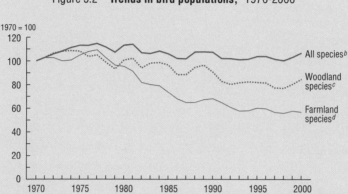

a) Index based on population estimates for native bird species in the UK. Rare (fewer than 500 breeding pairs in Britain) and extinct species are excluded.
b) Tracks 105 endemic species.
c) Tracks 33 woodland species.
d) Tracks 19 farmland species.
Source: DEFRA; RSPB; British Trust for Ornithology.

Figure 5.3 **Nominal catches of salmon**[a] **in UK fisheries,** 1986-2000

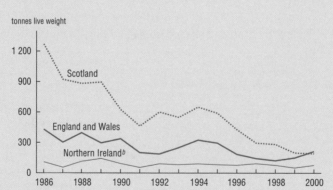

a) Includes grilse (young Atlantic salmon).
b) Includes 50% of catches in the River Foyle; excludes angling catch (mainly grilse).
Source: ICES.

reverse the trend, individual salmon action plans, including quantitative targets and restoration measures, were prepared for all major salmonid rivers in England and Wales by 2002. In Scotland, preventive and contingency measures against salmon escapes from fish farms, believed to be a threat to wild salmon stocks, were recently tightened. A comprehensive policy review on anadromous and freshwater fish and fisheries is under way both for Scotland and for England and Wales, examining how present policy affects species conservation, fishery economy and recreation. In addition, a review of the regulations on aquaculture was recently completed, as a result of which the regulations will be amended soon, in particular concerning licensing and inspection to minimise the environmental impact of this expanding industry.

Over the past decade, stocks of most economically important *marine fish species* in the seas surrounding the UK were below biologically sustainable levels due to over-fishing by the UK and other North Sea countries. For example, the stock levels of cod, haddock, plaice, saithe and whiting in 2000 fell short of biologically sustainable levels by 56%, 21%, 10%, 33% and 29%, respectively (Table 9.3). The country carried out a series of fishing vessel decommissioning programmes in the 1990s, but the capacity reduction effects were in large part eroded by a shift towards larger vessels (Chapter 9, Section 1.5). Capture fisheries landed nearly 750 000 tonnes of marine fish in 2000, largely from stocks classified as "outside biologically sustainable limits" (Chapter 9, Section 1.5). Fish farms, numbering nearly 400 in 2000, occupy space in inshore waters and exert pressures on marine biodiversity (e.g. nutrient input, use of veterinary medicines and "genetic interference" from escaped fish). Extensive offshore oil and gas development and high-volume maritime traffic also generate significant environmental pressures in the form of pollution discharges, oil spills and infrastructure development (Chapter 9, Section 1.4).

Policy measures

In October 1999, the UK Biodiversity Group, which the government formed to coordinate implementation of the biodiversity action plan, completed publication of individual *habitat- and species-specific action plans*, bringing the totals to 45 and 391, respectively. In addition, 160 *local biodiversity action plans*, covering Scotland, Wales and most of England, were prepared. These are notable achievements, not only because they improved understanding of the state of individual species and habitats and identified necessary actions with clear targets for better conservation, but also because they helped build co-operative relationships among public authorities, businesses, NGOs and academia. These relationships should be further nurtured during implementation, as the planned actions will require long-term involvement by the community for real improvement to take place. Conservation measures for widespread species should be reviewed and geographically broadened, with stronger measures (e.g. agri-environmental programmes, land use planning measures) to be taken outside protected areas.

The first five-year progress report under the biodiversity action plan, published in 2001, shows mixed results on the *biological status of priority habitats and species* for which action plans were prepared. Of seven habitat types assessed by 1999, five were showing signs of recovery, one was stable and one in decline. Of 135 species assessed, 33 were recovering, 58 stable and 44 in decline. There was a clear tendency for widespread species to be declining, while species with limited ranges were often recovering or stable. It is encouraging that species for which conservation plans were longer-established tended to show signs of recovery more than those with more recent plans. The report revealed large information gaps, which made it impossible to assess the status of 71% of priority habitats and 55% of priority species. A framework for biodiversity surveillance and monitoring is being developed by the Joint Nature Conservation Committee, a multi-agency coordinating body, and the National Biodiversity Network, a public-private information initiative.

Strong role of environmental NGOs

Non-governmental organisations (NGOs) play a strong role in nature conservation in the UK, carrying on a long tradition of extensive action and policy influence. They are deeply involved in *policy formulation* on nature conservation at both central and local levels. For example, under the biodiversity action plan, over 200 separate organisations are involved in habitat- and species-specific action plan steering groups. Membership in the ten leading conservation NGOs rose by 18% between 1995 and 2000, to a total of 5 million.

The *National Trust*, founded in 1895, privately owns more than 248 000 hectares of land, nearly 965 km of coastline and over 200 historic buildings and gardens in England, Wales and Northern Ireland. The Trust aims to protect sites of ecological importance or great natural beauty from development. It is supported by 8 000 regular and seasonal staff, 40 000 volunteers each year and 2.8 million members. About 28% of its land area is designated as sites of special scientific interest (SSSIs) or, in Northern Ireland, areas of special scientific interest (ASSIs). These together account for 6% of the total special sites in England, Wales and Northern Ireland. The rest of the Trust's land is mostly ordinary countryside, including over 140 000 hectares of land managed by tenant farmers. Backed by the 1907 National Trust Act, the Trust has long been a role model for NGOs worldwide interested in similar approaches to the preservation of nature sites and historic buildings.

The *Royal Society for the Protection of Birds (RSPB)* also has a long history. Founded in 1889, it now has more than a million members, making it Europe's largest wildlife conservation organisation. The RSPB manages over 160 nature reserves, covering more than 110 000 hectares across the UK, for the protection of birds and other species. It also plays a leading role in the preparation for and implementation of the biodiversity action plan. The RSPB is the lead partner in co-ordinating actions for 36 species-specific action plans, including some for non-bird species.

Launched in 1961, the UK branch of WWF was the first national organisation in the WWF network. It has funded more than 3 000 projects in the UK and spent some GBP 64 million on conservation work overseas.

1.3   Pressures on habitats

Major sources of environmental pressure on biodiversity and habitats include land use change, pollution and natural resource exploitation. Overall land use patterns were fairly positive throughout the 1990s, with some conversion of land from cultivation to permanent grassland (a 1-3% change overall since 1990), and a significant expansion of forest cover (a 16% increase from 1990 to 2000). Conversion of greenfield sites near major cities began attracting increased concern in the late 1990s, leading to recent efforts to stimulate reuse of brownfield sites (Chapter 8, Section 1.1). Overall, pollution pressures have also been decreasing since 1990, with ambient measures of many pollutants showing significant declines (Figure 2.2, Table 3.1). However, the use of nitrogenous fertilisers and pesticides in agriculture remains relatively intense (Figure 3.3), leading to eutrophication of nearly 80% of riverine habitats (Chapter 3, Section 1.3) and to high levels of bioaccumulative chemicals in some wildlife. About 70% of the UK land surface is agricultural, and this is the largest single source of pressure on the country's biodiversity. Use of land or of surface waters for recreation, hunting, forestry and transport also generates significant pressures, as does exploitation of offshore oil and gas and fishery resources. As economic activity and the population continue to grow, additional demand for transport infrastructure, housing and recreational facilities will further intensify pressures.

The UK ranked fifth for *population density* among OECD countries in 2000, exceeding the OECD average seven-fold and the OECD Europe average two-fold. Thus, human activities, including construction, industry and agriculture, have a major impact on nature and biodiversity. Pressures on coastal areas are generally even greater. *Urban development* is constantly putting pressure on UK nature habitats. In the 1990s, some 60 000 hectares in England (0.4% of England's total area) were converted from rural to urban use. While efforts to limit urban sprawl are being made via such measures as redevelopment in urban areas, it is estimated that development of rural areas will continue and that an additional 169 000 hectares will be converted from rural to urban use before 2020. In the same period, the number of households, a major driving force of urban development, is projected to increase by 23%.

Agricultural activity is the biggest threat to priority species and habitats, according to the first five-year progress report of the biodiversity action plan. A recent assessment of SSSIs in unfavourable condition also showed agricultural practices (related to livestock farming, in particular) to be the predominant source of pressure. Between 1990 and 2000, total agricultural land area gradually decreased by 3% and crop area fell by 7%. Livestock grazing intensity (animals per hectare) increased in the 1990s, reflecting a trend towards fewer but larger farms. Livestock numbers, expressed as the sum of cattle and sheep, decreased in the late 1990s by 4%, partly due to slaughtering of animals affected by "mad cow" disease. More recently, 200 000 cattle were slaughtered to prevent the spread of mad cow disease and 6.5 million cattle, sheep and pigs were killed in measures related to foot and mouth disease. Even so, livestock density remains high by OECD standards (Figure 5.4). The outbreak of foot and mouth disease in early 2001 also restricted public access to rural land for much of the year. Fertiliser application intensity (kilogrammes per hectare) in the 1990s was lower than in the 1980s, and on a declining trend. Pesticide consumption, however, has been increasing since the early 1990s. Application intensities for nitrogenous fertilisers and pesticides were higher than the OECD Europe averages by over 100% and 70%, respectively, in the late 1990s (Figure 3.3).

1.4   Protection of special sites

Terrestrial sites

The *land area protected for wildlife/habitat conservation* rose steadily during the 1990s (Table 5.2). The total area of SSSIs and ASSIs, which are the primary protection categories and must precede designation for other national or international protection status, increased by 22% between 1993 and 2001 to more than 2.3 million hectares. These 6 800 sites now represent about 10% of the UK's total land area. In particular, the extent of protected areas under the EU bird directive nearly quintupled during the period and that of Ramsar Convention wetlands more than doubled. By mid-2001, more than 500 sites totalling over 2 million hectares had been submitted as candidates for protected area status under the habitat directive.

In contrast, there was little increase in the 1990s in the *area protected primarily for landscape protection and recreational purposes* (i.e. national parks, areas of outstanding natural beauty and national scenic areas) (Table 5.2). However, in England the authorities recently initiated a designation process for two new national parks

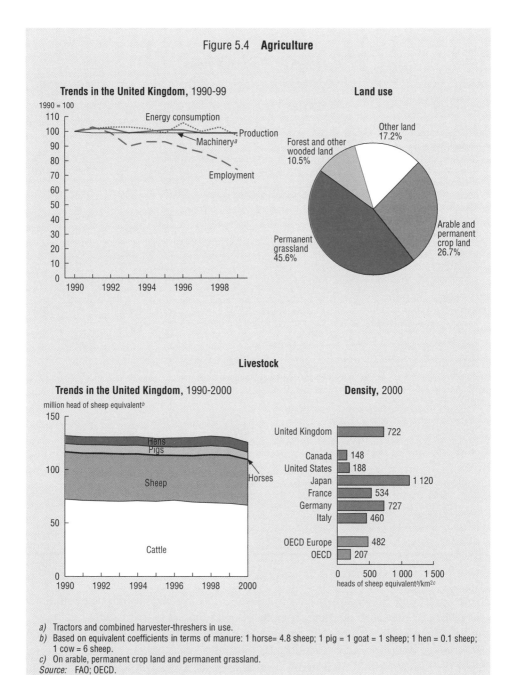

Figure 5.4 **Agriculture**

Trends in the United Kingdom, 1990-99

1990 = 100

Energy consumption
Production
Machinery[a]
Employment

Land use

Other land
17.2%

Forest and other
wooded land
10.5%

Arable and
permanent
crop land
26.7%

Permanent
grassland
45.6%

Livestock

Trends in the United Kingdom, 1990-2000

million head of sheep equivalent[b]

Hens
Pigs
Sheep
Horses
Cattle

Density, 2000

United Kingdom	722
Canada	148
United States	188
Japan	1 120
France	534
Germany	727
Italy	460
OECD Europe	482
OECD	207

heads of sheep equivalent[b]/km[2c]

a) Tractors and combined harvester-threshers in use.
b) Based on equivalent coefficients in terms of manure: 1 horse= 4.8 sheep; 1 pig = 1 goat = 1 sheep; 1 hen = 0.1 sheep;
1 cow = 6 sheep.
c) On arable, permanent crop land and permanent grassland.
Source: FAO; OECD.

Table 5.2   **Protected areas**

Purpose/Status[a]	Location	1993[b] Number	1993[b] Area (1 000 ha)	2001[c] Number	2001[c] Area (1 000 ha)
For wildlife/habitat protection					
Sites of special scientific interests	England, Scotland and Wales	5 964	1 892	6 573	2 280
Areas of special scientific interests	Northern Ireland	48	48	182	89
National nature reserves[d]	UK	304	190	392	226
Local nature reserves	England, Scotland and Wales	371	21	759	45
Marine nature reserves	UK	2	4	3	21
Special protection areas[d, e]	UK	77	264	219	1 249
Ramsar wetlands[d, f]	UK	70	309	138	735
Special conservation areas[d, g]	UK	–	–	546	2 232
Biosphere reserves[d, h]	UK	13	44	13	44
Biogenetic reserves[d]	UK	18	8	18	8
Environmentally sensitive areas[d, i]	UK	33	2 721	43	3 377
For landscape protection					
National parks[k]	England, Wales	11	1 405	11	1 405
Areas of outstanding natural beauty	England, Wales and Northern Ireland	49	2 328	50	2 433
National scenic areas	Scotland	40	1 017	40	1 002

a) Some areas may be included in more than one category.
b) As of December 1993, except for national nature reserves and local nature reserves, for which the data are as of March 1993.
c) As of March 2001.
d) Included in SSSIs or ASSIs.
e) Designation under the EU bird directive (79/409/EEC).
f) Designation under the Ramsar Convention.
g) Candidates for designation under the EU habitat directive (92/43/EEC).
h) Designation under UNESCO's Man and the Biosphere Programme.
i) Designation under the programme based on the recommendation by the 1973 European Ministerial Conference on the Environment.
j) Designation under the EU Council Regulation (85/797/EEC) on improving the efficiency of agricultural structures.
k) Includes the East Anglia Broads, which is not a national park but is given a similar status by law.
Source: DEFRA; Environment and Heritage Service (Northern Ireland); Scottish Office of Agriculture, Environment and Fisheries; Welsh Office; English Nature; Countryside Council for Wales; Scottish Nature Heritage; Joint Nature Conservation Committee.

(New Forest and South Downs). In Scotland, a law for establishing national parks was passed in 2000, and the first two parks (Loch Lomond and Trossachs, and Cairngorms) are being designated. Nevertheless, UK national parks do not meet the IUCN definition of national parks (Category II), but rather come under that of "protected landscape" (Category IV). All in all, over 25% of the UK's land currently has some form of protection (Figure 5.5).

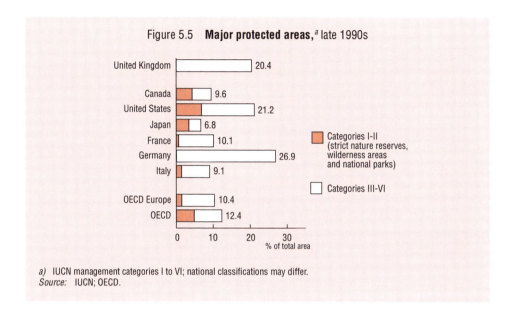

Figure 5.5   **Major protected areas,**^a late 1990s

a) IUCN management categories I to VI; national classifications may differ.
Source: IUCN; OECD.

Regular monitoring of the *condition of SSSIs* by the nature conservation agencies was initiated in the late 1990s. In England, assessments had been completed for two-thirds of SSSIs by March 2001. Only 40% were found to be in favourable condition, though 16% were rated as unfavourable but recovering. In Scotland, where the corresponding figures were 45% and 10%, bogs, calcareous grasslands and acid grasslands in uplands were among the worst affected, predominantly by over- or undergrazing. Considering the central government's target to bring 95% of SSSIs in England into favourable or unfavourable but recovering condition by 2010, measures to improve their condition should be accelerated, with a particular focus on the impact of livestock farming.

As SSSIs and ASSIs are mostly privately owned, *management agreements* between the nature conservation agencies and landowners/-occupiers are a key mechanism. In England, by March 2001, English Nature had concluded about 2 500 agreements with 26 000 owners or occupiers, covering 160 000 hectares (70% in number, 15% by area, of all SSSIs). In Scotland, the proportion of SSSIs under such agreements was 42% by number and 11% by area, while in Wales the corresponding figures were 54% and 21%. Efforts to increase the coverage of SSSI areas by management agreements should be continued. Although the rate of non-compliance with the agreements has been small (e.g. 7% of monitored agreements in Scotland in 2000), compliance checking should be continued and made more systematic.

From 1993 to 2001, *national nature reserves*, which include some of the most important SSSIs/ASSIs and are managed mostly by the nature conservation agencies either directly or through approved bodies, increased by 29% in number and 19% in area. Designation of *local nature reserves*, which represent wildlife or geological features of local interest (mostly outside SSSIs), was also accelerated in the 1990s: both the number and area doubled between 1993 and 2001 (Table 5.2).

The *2000 Countryside and Rights of Way Act* significantly strengthened the legal basis for the conservation of SSSIs in England and Wales. Although in practice conservation still largely relies upon voluntary management agreements between owners/occupiers and the nature conservation agencies, the agencies can now exercise regulatory and enforcement power over damaging activities in SSSIs. A fine of up to GBP 20 000 (or unlimited fines upon conviction on indictment in crown court) and a site restoration duty may be imposed, not only on owners/occupiers but also on any individual carrying out such activities. The agencies also have new powers to extend, modify, delete and even compulsorily purchase SSSIs. The Act gives all ministers and government departments a general duty to respect biodiversity conservation, and obliges all public bodies to further the conservation and enhancement of SSSIs in carrying out their functions. The former duty reflects an obligation under the Convention on Biological Diversity. The Act has some shortcomings, however. Detailed measures for marine conservation are lacking. Damaging activities authorised by planning permission are exempt from penalties. Enforcement against individuals (i.e. proving "intentionally or recklessly" caused damage) is difficult. The legal right to stand in court on behalf of nature is restricted to the agencies and not extended to NGOs or individuals, although they may take legal action under the general rules of judicial reviews (Chapter 7, Section 1.6). Efforts to further integrate policies on habitat protection and on land use or development planning, and to carry out enforcement actions systematically and rigorously, should be continued.

The 2000 Countryside and Rights of Way Act strengthened the protection of *areas of outstanding natural beauty* by recognizing that their landscape qualities are equivalent to those of national parks and thus they should be accorded equivalent protection. Local authorities are now required to prepare management plans for such areas and assume responsibility for their implementation. A conservation board can be established to take over this duty from local authorities, particularly where an area crosses local authority boundaries.

Public expenditure for the management of protected areas increased in the 1990s. In England, payments by English Nature under management agreements with owners/occupiers of SSSIs increased by more than 40% between 1991 and 2000, with a gradual shift from compensatory to positive payments (e.g. for habitat restoration). Various grant programmes available to NGOs and local authorities for conservation projects in protected areas were restructured and strengthened. In particular, financial support for local nature reserves in England was substantially boosted in 2000 when a new grant programme, totalling more than GBP 6 million over 2001-06, was launched with national lottery funding.

Marine and coastal sites

In contrast to terrestrial habitat conservation, UK policy development for marine habitat conservation was slow in the 1990s. Only one site was designated as a protected *marine nature reserve* between 1993 and 2001, bringing the total to a mere three sites covering 21 000 hectares. This lack is partly due to difficulty in co-ordinating the interests of the parties concerned, such as fishers, recreational divers and local authorities. The situation can be expected to improve as implementation of the EU habitat directive progresses. Already, 36 marine sites have been selected as candidates for protection under the directive, and management programmes have been established for 12 of them. Following a High Court ruling in October 1999, the geographical scope of the UK's application of the directive is being extended to the entire 200-mile exclusive economic zone (Chapter 9, Section 1.5). In line with this move, the government has decided to extend application of the bird directive to the same zone. Nature conservation agencies have begun identifying potential areas for protection under both directives. Furthermore, by late 1999, the biodiversity action plan had resulted in individual action plans for 14 marine habitat types. Nevertheless, there is a need to make the overall *policy framework* for marine nature conservation more coherent, and the UK's review of marine nature conservation ought to aim for this. Statutory measures have been developed in a rather piecemeal manner, and are currently limited to the protection of selected areas and species (e.g. marine nature reserves, species specified under the 1981 Wildlife and Countryside Act). Legislative and institutional arrangements for marine protection should be systematised and co-ordinated.

Concerning *coastal zones*, individual action plans for nine coastal habitat types have been prepared under the biodiversity action plan. Although not legally protected, 45 coastal areas of scenic beauty, covering 1 525 km of the English and Welsh coastlines, have been designated as heritage coasts. This designation is to be taken into consideration when local authorities exercise planning control. Coastal habitat management plans had been prepared by late 2001 for seven areas where there was a potential threat to areas protected under the bird directive, the habitat directive or the Ramsar Convention. These plans are to provide for greater integration of coastal habitat protection and storm/tide defence works.

1.5   Integration of nature conservation into sectoral policies

Agriculture

The UK accelerated its efforts to integrate nature/biodiversity concerns into *agricultural policy* in the 1990s. In its 1995 white paper on rural affairs, the government reiterated that nature conservation is an integral part of agricultural policy. A set of 35 indicators for sustainable agriculture, published in 2000 as part of the sustainable development strategy, includes indicators related to wildlife (e.g. wild bird populations) and to environmental pressures on nature (e.g. pesticide use, nutrient inputs).

The modulation mechanism under the Common Agricultural Policy has expanded the opportunity to encourage environmentally friendly agriculture through public funding, and the UK has been a pioneer in the use of *agri-environmental programmes* to create economic incentives for more sustainable farming. Since the mid-1980s, the UK has developed a range of such programmes, many of which have nature conservation as a central objective. Total annual public expenditure on agri-environmental programmes increased rapidly over the last decade, from GBP 9 million in 1990 to GBP 150 million in 2000. The government announced plans in early 2000 to further increase annual expenditure to more than GBP 200 million by 2006 (Chapter 6, Section 1.3). The first such programme in the UK, designating *environmentally sensitive areas* (launched in 1987), continued to grow in the 1990s. It now involves 11 000 agreements covering 532 000 hectares in 22 areas of high landscape, wildlife or historic value in England (e.g. the Lake District). Another key agri-environmental programme is *Countryside Stewardship*, begun in 1991 in England and applicable to all land not in an environmentally sensitive area. By 2000, 11 900 agreements covered 263 000 hectares, 22 000 kilometres of arable margins and 17 800 kilometres of linear features (e.g. hedges, stone walls). Similar stewardship programmes were established in Wales in 1994 and in Scotland in 1998. Countryside Stewardship and the environmentally sensitive areas account for more than 80% of total public expenditure for agri-environmental programmes. In England, 13% of farm holdings are under one or the other. Another positive development in agricultural funding since 2001 is a shift in funding for livestock farming in hilly areas from head-based to area-based payments, discouraging overstocking in environmentally vulnerable uplands.

There are *encouraging trends* in areas subject to agri-environmental pro- grammes. For example, the Countryside Survey, a national monitoring programme, found that grasslands covered by Countryside Stewardship in England were of better average quality than those in the wider countryside (though this may reflect the programme's success in attracting higher quality grasslands). *Organic farming* has gained momentum: grants for conversion to organic farming rose from

GBP 0.2 million in 1995 to GBP 20.5 million in 2000. Registered organic farms now cover 573 000 hectares in the UK. Nevertheless, room for improvement remains. For example, both the involvement of farmers and the area under agri-environmental programmes could be substantially increased by further boosting expenditure (Chapter 6, Section 1.3). Also, grouping like programmes into a single one would streamline application and other procedures. Grant conditions and rates could be made more flexible to better reflect priorities set in local biodiversity action plans.

Forestry

Forest cover accounts for 11% (2.8 million hectares) of the UK's total land area, which is one of the lowest shares in Europe. It increased by 16% between 1990 and 2000, largely through expansion of broadleaved forests to 40% of total forest cover in 2000. While many broadleaved trees were planted in the 1990s, expansion of coniferous forests was small. Replanting in existing forests was constant in the 1990s, both for coniferous and broadleaved forests. About 20% by area of the UK's forests are of ancient origin. About 5% of the forest area enjoys some form of statutory protection (e.g. SSSIs or ASSIs), and 11% is non-statutorily protected through "protective ownership" by public bodies or NGOs such as the National Trust. A further 33% is under protective management through state grants. The UK's *wood production* supplies only 15% by volume of its annual apparent consumption. Production gradually increased in the 1990s, and in Great Britain is expected to increase by a further 60% between 2000 and 2020.

Development of initiatives and standards for *sustainable forestry practice* was accelerated in the 1990s to promote integration of nature/biodiversity concerns into forestry. The commitments and principles set out in the 1994 sustainable forestry programme were translated into the 1998 UK forestry standard, comprising a range of criteria, indicators and good management practices. The standard is compatible with guidelines adopted at European level (the 1993 Helsinki Guidelines, the 1994 Pan-European Criteria). It sets criteria for new planting, management and felling controls. Sustainable forestry certification systems (the 1993 Forest Stewardship Council programme and the 1999 UK Woodland Assurance Programme) were also developed, and forestry businesses have increasingly applied them. In early 2002, more than 35% of total forest cover (65% of commercial forestry) in the UK was certified by the *Forestry Stewardship Council*. In the 1998 England Forestry Strategy, "environment and nature conservation" was one of the four major areas listed for action.

About 70% by area of UK forest land is privately owned, so public financial support to influence *private landowners* to increase forest area or carry out sustainable forestry management practices is an important policy integration mechanism. State grants to private forest owners have been in place since 1988, paralleling the phase-out of tax relief measures. Most private forests are now supported by such grants for new planting, replanting and forest management. In 2000, of the total GBP 37 million in grants provided to the forestry sector in Great Britain, 64% was for new planting, 10% for replanting in existing forests and 22% for sustainable management. Farmers received an additional GBP 16 million for planting new woodlands on farms. In recent years, to reflect the 1998 UK forestry standard, conditions related to nature/biodiversity conservation attached to these grants have been strengthened and made more detailed.

1.6   International agreements

The UK ratified the 1971 *Ramsar Convention* on the protection of wetlands in 1976. By early 2002 it had designated 168 Ramsar sites covering over 858 000 hectares (including overseas territories). The UK became a party to the *Convention on Biological Diversity* in 1994. Its biodiversity action plan, published as its national strategy on the subject in the same year, has been actively implemented. The UK signed the 2000 *Cartagena Protocol on Biosafety* under the biodiversity convention in 2000, but has not yet ratified it. The UK is a party to the 1979 *Bonn Convention* on the Conservation of Migratory Species of Wild Animals, and was one of the driving forces behind the 1991 Agreement on the Conservation of Bats in Europe, for which it acted as interim secretariat until 1995.

Other regional agreements to which the UK is a party include the 1979 *Bern Convention* on the Conservation of European Wildlife and Natural Habitats, the 1982 Convention for the Conservation of Salmon in the North Atlantic Ocean and the 1992 *OSPAR Convention* for the Protection of the Marine Environment of the North-East Atlantic.

The UK has been a party to the 1973 *Washington Convention* on International Trade in Endangered Species (CITES) since 1976. In 1995, the Partnership for Action against Wildlife Crime, grouping police and customs officials and related government departments, was launched to strengthen enforcement against illegal wildlife trade. Nevertheless, such trade is still extensive in the UK: over one million illegally imported items were seized at customs in about 2 200 separate incidents between 1996 and 2000, including about 14 000 mammal bodies or products, over 1 000 (mostly live) birds and 545 000 plants. Enforcement has been very rare: customs officials have undertaken just one prosecution for every 130 800 items seized, court fines are low and the maximum custodial sentence has never been imposed. The National Wildlife Crime Intelligence Unit was set up in 2002 to strengthen enforcement by collecting and analysing intelligence about wildlife criminals.

2.   Focus on Selected Topics

2.1   *Legislative and institutional framework for nature conservation*

Legislation

Since the late 1940s the UK *policy framework* for nature and biodiversity conservation has established a clear distinction between wildlife/habitat conservation (mainly for scientific interest) and landscape protection (mainly for recreational interest). Because almost all UK land has been affected by human influences and a great majority of it is privately owned, site protection has traditionally relied heavily on voluntary measures (i.e. influencing landowners/-occupiers to manage sites appropriately), and on land use planning control by local authorities. For wildlife species protection, on the other hand, the UK has a long history of applying strict regulations, dating back to the 1880 Protection of Wild Birds Act.

The *1949 National Parks and Access to the Countryside Act* and the *1981 Wildlife and Countryside Act* are the principal frameworks for legislative protection of wildlife/habitats and landscapes in England and Wales. Complemented by similar legislation elsewhere in the UK, as well as accompanying regulations, they implement the EU bird and habitat directives, provide statutory status for protected areas and define measures to prevent damaging activities in protected areas. The Wildlife and Countryside Act, along with a series of specific laws for wildlife protection such as the 1991 Deer Act, also prohibits the killing, injuring or taking of certain species. The *2000 Countryside and Rights of Way Act* significantly strengthened habitat and landscape protection by enhancing regulatory powers of nature conservation agencies (Chapter 5, Section 1.2). In line with the approach of the biodiversity action plan, it also requires the central government and the National Assembly of Wales to maintain and publish lists of species and habitat types of principal importance for biodiversity conservation. Similar legislation is being considered in Scotland and Northern Ireland. Other nature conservation legislation that was developed in the 1990s includes the *1996 Wild Mammals (Protection) Act*, which prohibits certain cruel acts against wild mammals.

Institutional framework

The Department for Environment, Food and Rural Affairs (DEFRA) and the environmental protection departments in the *devolved administrations* have overall responsibility for nature conservation in their respective juridictions. In Great Britain (England, Scotland and Wales) the departments are also responsible for rural affairs. Non-ministerial agencies in those areas designate protected areas and implement policy. In England, the responsibilities are divided between English Nature for nature conservation and the Countryside Agency (Countryside Commission before April 1999) for landscape protection. Elsewhere, a single agency (Scottish Natural Heritage, the Countryside Commission for Wales, the Environment and Heritage Service for Northern Ireland) carries out both duties. The three nature conservation agencies in Great Britain co-ordinate their work (e.g. on site monitoring) and, through the Joint Nature Conservation Committee, collectively advise the central government and the devolved administrations on the development of nature conservation policies. Every national park has a body exercising authority for land use planning in the park area. *Local authorities* also have an important role in nature conservation through land use planning.

Monitoring habitats and landscape trends: Countryside Survey

The Countryside Survey, a national monitoring programme for habitats and landscape in the countryside, has been carried out since 1978 in Great Britain. In Northern Ireland, a similar programme has been in place since 1990. The surveys are based on field observations in randomly sampled, one square kilometre grids: 569 grids for field survey and 404 for freshwater survey, for example, in 1998. Combined with satellite imagery, they provide comprehensive data sets. The survey has been conducted so far in 1978, 1984, 1990 and 1998/99 for Great Britain and in 1990 and 1998 in Northern Ireland.

The broad *conclusion of the latest surveys* is that some trends of habitat loss seen before 1990 have been slowed, halted or reversed, partly through policy measures such as hedgerow management incentives and farm woodland grants. However, some land cover types continued to decline in the 1990s, in part because of eutrophication and land conversion. Positive trends detected in the surveys in the 1990s include increased plant diversity in arable fields, especially in field margins; a halt to the decline of hedgerows; increased area of broadleaved woodland and of fen, marsh and swamp; more lowland ponds; and improved biological condition of streams and small rivers. Negative trends included continuing declines in area and plant diversity in the least agriculturally improved grasslands (those classified as neutral, acid and calcareous); decline in quality of bogs and dwarf shrub heaths; and decline in species richness of some hedges, roadside verges and streamsides, which are being dominated by tall, competitive plants associated with nutrient-rich conditions (Table 5.3).

Table 5.3   **Area of various land cover types,** 1990-98

	Great Britain[a]		Northern Ireland		UK total	
	Area in 1998 (10^3 ha)	Change 1990-98 (%)	Area in 1998 (10^3 ha)	Change 1990-98 (%)	Area in 1998 (10^3 ha)	Change 1990-98 (%)
Improved grassland	5 482	−1.9	568	32.9	6 050	0.6
Acid grassland	1 295	−10.5	28	−8.0	1 324	−10.4
Neutral grassland	613	1.6	254	−31.7	867	−11.6
Calcareous grassland	65	−18.0	1	−7.2	66	−17.8
Arable and horticultural land	5 249	1.7	59	−25.0	5 307	1.3
Bog	2 218	−0.8	148	−8.3	2 367	−1.3
Broadleaved and mixed forests	1 471	4.9	51	8.5	1 522	5.1
Coniferous woodland	1 374	−0.7	61	11.6	1 435	−0.2
Dwarf shrub heath	1 487	−3.9	13	−7.6	1 500	−3.9
Bracken	439	6.2	4	4.6	443	6.2
Fen, marsh and swamp	547	21.6	53	−18.6	600	16.6

a) England, Wales and Scotland.
Source: DEFRA.

2.2   *Protecting wild Atlantic salmon*

There has been a sharp *downward trend in reported catches* of wild Atlantic salmon in UK rivers and coastal areas over the past 25 years (Figure 5.3), reflecting both a decline in the stocks and a substantial reduction in fishing effort. In the late 1990s, WWF rated just 33% of salmon stocks in rivers in England and Wales as in healthy condition, the rest being vulnerable (14%), endangered (25%), in critical condition (14%) or even extinct (9%). The situation is much better in Scotland (63% healthy, 37% endangered), but the declining trend in catches over the past 25 years is even more evident there than in the rest of the UK. Factors that may be contributing to the decline include degradation of freshwater habitats and water quality, impared access to spawning areas, changes in natural environmental conditions in the sea, overfishing, the spread of parasites (e.g. sea lice) and disease from salmon farming.

In England and Wales, the National Rivers Authority established policy objectives for salmon stock conservation in the *National Salmon Management Strategy* of 1996. The Environment Agency as the successor to the river authority is developing salmon action plans to implement the strategy, including "conservation limits" (minimum conservation levels). Individual plans are being prepared for the 68 main salmon-bearing rivers and these should be completed in 2003. Progress regarding actions in the plans is reviewed annually at both regional and national levels. The 1975 Salmon and Freshwater Fisheries Act provides for *regulation of salmon fishing*, including a ban on taking of juvenile salmon, closed seasons for fishing and restrictions on fishing gear. Both rod and net fishing require a licence, and about 20% of the Environment Agency's administrative costs related to salmon and sea trout fisheries are recovered via licence fees. In contrast, income from coarse and trout licences funds 100% of the agency's expenditure on these fisheries. An expert group reviewed the policy and legislation relating to salmon and freshwater fish in 2000, and proposed a major restructuring. The aim is to better manage stocks and improve economic and social aspects of the fisheries. As an EU country the UK is committed to the conservation of North Atlantic salmon under the 1982 Convention for the Conservation of Salmon in the North Atlantic Ocean, under which it actively participates in the North Atlantic Salmon Conservation Organisation.

Environmental pressures from *salmon farming* grew in the 1990s, particularly off western Scotland, where marine farms are concentrated. The output of Scottish salmon farms quadrupled between 1990 and 2000. The number of farmed salmon escapes reported increased from 95 000 in 1998 to 440 000 in 2000, leading to major concerns about the *genetic impact* on wild salmon as well as the spread of *parasites/disease*. Several studies have concluded that sea lice associated with salmon farming are probably the main cause of the decline in stocks of wild salmon in Scottish rivers. As a response, the Scottish Executive has started requiring site-specific containment and contingency plans in support of all fish farm applications. Also, fish farming organisations have produced voluntary codes of practice on containment. The *discharge of nutrients and chemicals* from salmon farms into coastal waters is another source of environmental concern and is therefore regulated. In the summer of 2000, 57 out of 60 closures of areas to scallop fishing were in salmon farming areas, prompted by high levels of shellfish poisoning due to toxic algal blooms.

2.3   *Assisting biodiversity conservation in developing countries: the Darwin Initiative*

The UK has long supported biodiversity conservation in developing countries. In addition to a range of projects funded by official development assistance, the UK launched a new funding mechanism at the 1992 Rio summit called the *Darwin Initiative for the Survival of Species*. It provides grants to UK organisations and individuals for collaborative projects with partners from public or private organisations or individuals in developing countries. One important function of the initiative is to help developing countries implement their commitments under the biodiversity convention. It also supports institutional capacity building, training, research, environmental education and awareness raising. The initiative currently has a budget of GBP 3 million to fund 20-30 projects per year.

By 2001, the initiative had committed GBP 24 million to 200-some projects in over 80 countries, involving more than 80 UK institutions, universities and NGOs. Some 28% of the projects have been in Africa, followed by South-east Asia with 16%. The initiative also funded projects in the UK's overseas territories and in Central and Eastern Europe. An evaluation of the initiative up to 2000 recorded 14 200 person-training weeks provided, 119 management or conservation plans and 157 databases produced, resources worth GBP 506 000 left in the host countries and 439 permanent field plots established. In addition, participating organisations and other donors have provided a GBP 2.9 million research fund. The future aims of the initiative will be more closely tied to those of the biodiversity convention.

Part II
SUSTAINABLE DEVELOPMENT

6

ENVIRONMENTAL – ECONOMIC INTERFACE*

Recommendations

The following recommendations are part of the overall conclusions and recommendations of the Environmental Performance Review of the United Kingdom:

• reflect sustainable development objectives more systematically in *public service agreements* and through integrated analysis (e.g. extended cost-benefit analysis) of policy measures;

• ensure that central government initiatives for improved environmental integration and sustainable development are effectively translated into *regional development priorities and local action*;

• strengthen the incentive role of economic instruments in inducing targeted *modal shifts in transport*, with appropriate phasing and consultation;

• further extend the shift of Common Agricultural Policy (CAP) resources towards integrated rural development programmes, including through *agri-environmental measures*;

• study and develop the extension of the *climate change levy* into a broader based tax on greenhouse gas (GHG) emissions;

---

* The present chapter reviews progress in the last ten years, and particularly since the previous OECD Environmental Performance Review of 1994. It also reviews progress with respect to the objective "decoupling environmental pressures from economic growth" of the 2001 OECD Environmental Strategy. It takes into account the latest OECD Economic Surveys of the United Kingdom.

Recommendations (cont.)

- strengthen *inspection and enforcement* and related monitoring efforts, as necessary to implement revised environmental regulations;

- review present *systems of charging users* for waste and waste water services, identifying opportunities to strengthen economic incentives for resource conservation and efficiency;

- review *environmental expenditure* and increase investment in environmental infrastructure (e.g. waste and waste water treatment facilities);

- develop and apply *economic and regulatory instruments* so as to meet reduction targets for diffuse pollution, particularly from agriculture and transport;

- continue to integrate environmental concerns into *land use planning*.

Conclusions

Integrating environmental concerns in economic decisions

The UK economy has grown by almost 2.5% per year since the early 1990s. *Strong decoupling* from GDP growth has been achieved for emissions of major air pollutants and CO_2, as well as for water withdrawals and application of agrochemicals. A sustainable development strategy is in place. Progress towards sustainable development has been aided by institutional and market-based integration in several sectors. *Institutional integration* of sustainable development has been fostered by a range of high-level co-ordination committees (e.g. Green Ministers Committee, Environmental Audit Committee) and advisory bodies (e.g. Sustainable Development Commission). Strengthened procedures for taking environmental issues into account have been built into policy-making processes. The traditional filtering of policy measures through cost-benefit analysis has been extended, with a stronger focus on objective setting and monitoring of progress through indicators. Substantial progress in policy integration has been achieved with respect to energy, transport, construction and agriculture. The UK has begun to use the modulation mechanism of the CAP, strengthening integrated rural development approaches, including through targeted support for environmental management and biodiversity. A number of *market-based instruments* have been introduced, such as the climate change levy, that apply the principle of taxing "bads" and using the revenue to support "goods". In transport, the fuel duty escalator influenced the modal split, shifting the trend back towards rail and water, and thus helped the UK reduce air pollutant emissions. At project level, environmental impact assessments are carried out for large projects, and recent legislative changes are expanding their scope, in compliance with EU legislation.

On the other hand, many UK indicators of environmental pressure intensity are still in the OECD middle range. Changes in consumption patterns are generating and/or accentuating environmental concerns. For instance, traffic volumes continue to grow, and municipal waste generation closely tracks GDP growth. Decoupling of diffuse pollution from economic growth will require continued efforts. Much remains to be done to translate sustainable development orientations into practice and to achieve full integration of economic, social and environmental considerations in important *sectoral policies*. Although such efforts have been fairly comprehensive on the part of the central government, translation of general intentions into *regional development priorities* and local action is patchy. The integration of environmental objectives into the policies of *economic regulators* such as OFGEM should be improved. The guidance function of important environment-related *energy and transport taxes* should be reviewed. Progress toward national goals concerning renewable forms of energy, waste management and agri-environmental concerns remains slower than what is needed to reach them.

Implementing environmental policies

Since the 1994 review, the UK has made noteworthy progress in achieving a number of its *environmental objectives* and in expanding its *environmental infrastructure*, although at the pace allowed by relatively limited pollution abatement and control expenditure. Targets related to emissions of conventional air pollutants, persistent organic pollutants and heavy metals, and to quality of drinking and surface water, were reached. Large-scale investment in waste water treatment infrastructure has accompanied privatisation of water services in England and Wales. The UK has extended the range of its environmental objectives, partly in response to EU and other international commitments, and partly as a consequence of its own sustainable development commitments. The mix of policy measures used has become more balanced, with more use of economic instruments in recent years, and continued effective use of regulation and land use planning. Regulation of significant point sources of industrial pollution has been carried out in an *integrated pollution control* (IPC) framework since 1990, with cost-effectiveness as a guiding principle (BATNEEC). Lesser industrial point sources and urban waste water treatment are subject to media-specific regulatory regimes. Modifications to the pollution control system, initiated to conform with provisions of the EU directive on integrated pollution prevention and control (IPPC), are encompassing previously excluded installations and introducing additional objectives of pollution prevention and resource efficiency. For water supply and waste water treatment, the *polluter pays and user pays principles* are applied fairly consistently in England and Wales, although less so in Scotland. The UK has developed and begun to apply new economic instruments such as a landfill tax, an aggregates levy, a climate change levy and emission trading systems. A reform is under way to enhance integration of environmental objectives with land use planning.

Notwithstanding the revival of environmental management in the late 1980s and the real progress just described, there is considerable *margin for further environmental progress*, as the UK is in the middle range of EU or OECD countries for many environmental indicators, has not yet achieved a number of its environmental objectives and still presents a deficit of environmental infrastructure (e.g. waste and waste water treatment infrastructure). Municipal waste generation has continued to parallel GDP growth, with recycling and recovery rates trailing those of comparable EU countries and landfilling rates remaining high. Developing the infrastructure necessary to implement best practices concerning *hazardous waste disposal* will require considerable investment. There is a need to further develop policy instruments to address *diffuse pollution concerns*, particularly as regards agriculture and urban runoff; the nitrogen surplus of the UK, although reduced, still exceeds the EU average by nearly 50% and the number of declared nitrate vulnerable zones is still insufficient to comply with the nitrate directive. Measures to conserve marine habitats and biodiversity should be reinforced. Significant expansion in *inspection and enforcement* will be required to accommodate the extended scope of IPPC regulation. Pollution abatement and control expenditure continues to represent 0.8% of GDP, and will probably need to be increased to meet future infrastructure investment requirements. The use of cost-benefit analysis to support decision making is part of the administrative culture in the UK, but limited information on costs and benefits makes it difficult to assess the cost-effectiveness of the IPC system. Also, the extended efficiency criteria have to be made compatible with the international and sustainable development objectives that are increasingly shaping the UK's environmental policies. In summary, considerable effort and investment will be necessary for the UK to consolidate and extend implementation of environmental policies.

1.   Progress Towards Sustainable Development

1.1   *Decoupling of economic growth and environmental pressures*

Economic growth and structures

Over the last decade, the UK has experienced continuous *economic growth*. GDP rose by 26% from 1990 to 2001 (averaging 2.4% per year in real terms) and GDP per capita increased by 20% (Figure 6.1). Most of this growth has come from the service

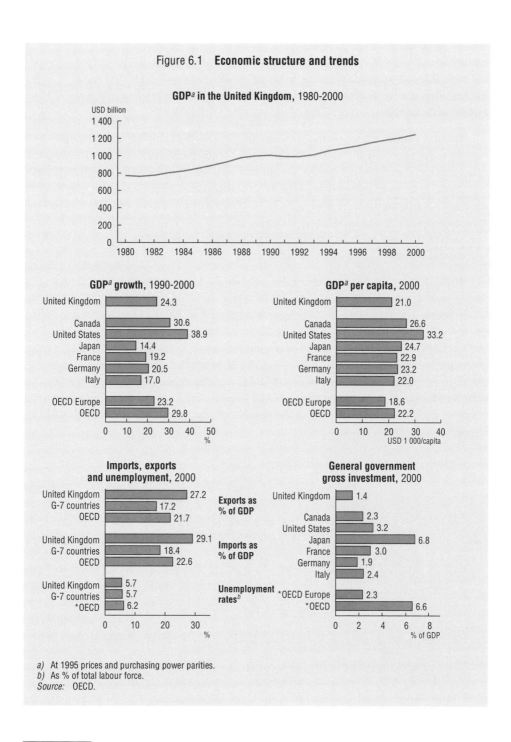

Figure 6.1 **Economic structure and trends**

GDP[a] in the United Kingdom, 1980-2000

USD billion

GDP[a] growth, 1990-2000

United Kingdom	24.3
Canada	30.6
United States	38.9
Japan	14.4
France	19.2
Germany	20.5
Italy	17.0
OECD Europe	23.2
OECD	29.8

%

GDP[a] per capita, 2000

United Kingdom	21.0
Canada	26.6
United States	33.2
Japan	24.7
France	22.9
Germany	23.2
Italy	22.0
OECD Europe	18.6
OECD	22.2

USD 1 000/capita

Imports, exports and unemployment, 2000

United Kingdom	27.2	Exports as % of GDP
G-7 countries	17.2	
OECD	21.7	
United Kingdom	29.1	Imports as % of GDP
G-7 countries	18.4	
OECD	22.6	
United Kingdom	5.7	Unemployment rates[b]
G-7 countries	5.7	
*OECD	6.2	

%

General government gross investment, 2000

United Kingdom	1.4
Canada	2.3
United States	3.2
Japan	6.8
France	3.0
Germany	1.9
Italy	2.4
*OECD Europe	2.3
*OECD	6.6

% of GDP

a) At 1995 prices and purchasing power parities.
b) As % of total labour force.
Source: OECD.

sector (particularly banking, insurance and business services), which now accounts for more than 70% of GDP (Chapter 6, Section 3.1). Although industrial output increased by more than 10%, manufacturing industry's contribution to GDP fell by 25%. Agriculture accounts for less than 1% of GDP, but its environmental significance is much higher, since farmland covers 70% of the country's land area.

In the 1990s, the growth of *road traffic volume* slowed significantly from previous decades. Still, road freight traffic and passenger car traffic together increased by about 15%. The UK's road traffic intensity (distance travelled divided by length of the road network) is OECD's third highest. There has been only limited success in decoupling growth from CO_2 emissions. Transport CO_2 emissions increased by 3% while total CO_2 emissions fell 9% over the decade. Fuel efficiency improvements have been largely offset by factors such as increases in road transport and a trend towards larger-engined vehicles.

From 1990 to 2000, the *energy intensity* of the UK economy decreased by 10%, and is now at the OECD average of 0.19 tonne of oil equivalent per USD 1 000 of GDP. Growing energy demand in the transport and residential sectors largely offset energy efficiency gains in industry. Still, while economic output increased by 26% between 1990 and 2001, energy consumption rose by only 8%. Thus, energy consumption per unit of GDP fell by 1.3% per year (Figure 9.2). Household energy use did not change much over the period. Houses have become better insulated, but householders may have taken some of the benefits in keeping their homes warmer (Chapter 8, Section 1.4). Growth in the number of electrical appliances per household has also increased residential energy use.

Trends in environmental pressures

Emissions of air pollutants such as PM_{10}, NO_x, SO_x, NMVOCs and CO have shown strong decoupling over the last decade. SO_x emissions declined in the 1990s by almost 70%, NO_x emissions by over 40% and NMVOC emissions by nearly 35%. Emission intensities of SO_x and NO_x per unit of GDP are about equal to EU averages (Figure 2.1). Major improvements in vehicle and fuel technologies have resulted in reduced emissions of air pollutants from road vehicles. Reductions in SO_x emissions associated with electricity production have also been significant, reflecting a switch from coal to gas and, to a lesser extent, an increase in nuclear energy (Figure 9.2). Although CO_2 *emissions*, largely from energy use, fell by 8% between 1990 and 2000, the UK ranks 14th among the 30 OECD countries in CO_2 emissions per unit of GDP.

On average, *municipal waste generation* has grown at about the rate of GDP, and is now growing faster (Figure 4.1). In 1999, it reached 560 kg per person, up by 23% from 1990 in real terms, and by 18% per capita. This increase reflects several factors, including a rise in the number of households and changes in consumption patterns. Only 10% of municipal waste is recycled or composted (Chapter 4, Section 1.4).

On agricultural land, the *nitrogen surplus* fell by roughly 20% to 86 kg N/ha, but remains some 50% above the EU average (Chapter 3, Section 1.3). Pesticide use (in tonnes of active ingredients), after falling by 10%, has now climbed back to its 1990 level. Total *water withdrawals* fell by 18% during the 1990s; in 1999, withdrawals represented about 17% of resources (Figure 3.1). While water use by the electricity industry has fluctuated, other industries show signs of increased efficiency.

Overall assessment

The UK has made significant *progress in decoupling* economic growth from environmental pressures. It achieved strong decoupling from GDP growth in the 1990s for major air pollutants and CO_2, as well as for water withdrawals and agro-chemical consumption (Table 6.1). Yet, further efforts are warranted. The UK could still improve its ranking among OECD countries with respect to most indicators of pressure intensity. Decoupling of *diffuse pollution* from economic growth requires particular attention. Strong implementation of EU fuel quality, vehicle emission and fuel efficiency standards has served only to moderate the effects of strong volume growth in road transport. Furthermore, regulation of pollution and of environmental risks from agriculture and aquaculture has so far been insufficient to deal with the magnitude of environmental pressure generated by these sectors.

1.2   Institutional integration

The UK's approach to developing and reviewing environmental policies evolved significantly in the 1990s. The traditional *efficiency approach*, with economic and environmental assessment of new environmental measures and projects (including a strong focus on cost-benefit and risk assessment analysis), has become more and more linked to an *objective-oriented strategic approach* (Chapter 6, Section 3.2). In part, this development comes in response to the UK's increasing number of European and worldwide environmental commitments, and to its sustainable development priorities. Overall, the approach has evolved from a budget and project/measure assessment focus (which is still present) towards an extended strategic and objective-oriented administrative culture.

Sustainable development strategy

The UK adopted its first *sustainable development strategy* in 1994 and its second in 1999. The latter, entitled "A Better Quality of Life", lists four key objectives: social progress that recognises everyone's needs; effective environmental protection;

prudent use of natural resources; and maintenance of high and stable levels of economic growth. It defines mechanisms and measures for integrating environmental and social concerns into economic and sectoral policies. It also recognises the need for new forms of dialogue and institutional responses to increase participation by communities and other stakeholders.

The sustainable development strategy is informing the *national budget process* through public service agreements for each government ministry or agency. These

Table 6.1   **Economic trends and environmental pressures**, 1980-2000

(% change)

	1980-90	1990-2000
Selected economic trends		
GDP[a]	30	24
Population	2	4
GDP[a]/capita	28	20
Agricultural production	8	−1
Industrial production[b]	23	11
Total primary energy supply	6	85[e]
Energy intensity	−19	−10[e]
Road freight traffic volumes[c]	46	16
Passenger car traffic volumes[d]	56	13
Selected environmental pressures[e]		
CO_2 emissions from energy use[f]	−2	−6
SO_x emissions	−23	−68
NO_x emissions	7	−42
NMVOC emissions	13	−37
Water withdrawals[g]	−11	−18
Nitrogenous fertiliser consumption	22	−14
Pesticide use[h]	7	−1
Municipal waste	. .	23

a) At 1995 prices and purchasing power parities.
b) Includes mining and quarrying, manufacturing, gas, electricity and water.
c) Based on values expressed in tonne-kilometres.
d) Based on values expressed in vehicle-kilometres.
e) Latest data available are from 1999.
f) Excluding marine and aviation bunkers.
g) England and Wales only (1990-98).
h) England, Wales and Scotland only (1990-97).
Source: OECD; IEA-OECD.

agreements set out objectives and performance targets. Ministries (departments) report annually on their progress in meeting the targets. In 2001 the government began issuing annual reports summarising progress in implementing the strategy, using a *set of 15 "headline" indicators*. This has helped raise the profile of sustainable development thinking in policy considerations.

All ministries are required to consider the *environmental costs and benefits* of new and revised policies. With the help of Cabinet and Treasury guidelines, ministries have developed procedures for screening their policies in terms of sustainable development implications and environmental impacts (Chapter 6, Section 3.2). New policy initiatives are open to extensive public consultation, and a large amount of information is made available to the public.

Institutional structures and procedures

The Cabinet Office's *Performance and Innovation Unit* (recently renamed the Strategy Unit) considers strategic policy questions, including issues that have a major effect on sustainable development, taking into account detailed analyses and feedback from stakeholders. Also within the Cabinet Office, the *Regulatory Impact Unit* ensures that new regulations and policies are submitted to a regulatory impact assessment, of which cost-benefit analysis constitutes the major part.

Policy integration is fostered by a range of high-level *co-ordination committees and consultative bodies* (Chapter 6, Section 3.3). The Cabinet Environment Committee has formal responsibility for sustainable development policy. The Green Ministers, a Cabinet subcommittee, promote awareness raising on sustainable development, along with integration of environmental considerations into policy making. Consultative bodies such as the Royal Commission on Environmental Pollution and the Sustainable Development Commission, both of which include representatives from civil society, provide strategic advice on environmental and sustainable development issues. In the House of Commons, the Environmental Audit Committee (EAC) assesses the government's performance in integrating sustainable development concerns into policy and decision making.

Despite this extensive institutional framework, and numerous inter-agency policy initiatives, work remains to be done to achieve integration of sustainability concerns into policy, especially beyond the central government level. For example, *economic regulators* focus almost entirely on economic and competition objectives, regardless of their announced intention to implement sustainable development policies. An EAC review concluded that there is a risk that environmental objectives may receive less priority in the framework of integrated sustainable development policies. It also said that weak integration between central government initiatives and regional/local priorities could constitute a practical barrier to integrating sustainability issues into procedures and programmes.

Most *regional development strategies*, recently established by the decentralised development agencies for the English regions, show a lack of integration of environmental concerns. For example, while Best Value Performance measurement has helped encourage more value for money, it has not always led to better environmental outcomes. In a growing number of cases, however, local authorities (e.g. in Reading and Newcastle) are beginning to see environmental management and rehabilitation and natural resource management not as economic burdens but as investments in the local asset base, important for attracting people and companies.

1.3   Sectoral integration

Energy

During the 1990s, total energy consumption in the UK increased by 10%, but *energy intensity* (energy supply per unit of GDP) decreased by 10% and is now in line with the OECD Europe average (Chapter 9, Section 1.2). Energy-related emissions dropped significantly, in part as a result of *fuel switching* in electricity generation. UK energy policy is partly driven by climate protection considerations. So far, the accent has been on improving the efficiency of energy use rather than on moderating energy demand. The Energy Saving Trust, set up in 1992 by the government and major energy suppliers, works to promote sustainable, efficient energy use through partnerships.

The government's 2000 *Climate Change Programme* requires electricity suppliers to generate 10% of the UK's power from renewable sources by 2010. It also provides for new funding for energy efficiency programmes and establishes a target of doubling the capacity of combined heat and power facilities by 2010. Other policy measures in this package include a climate change levy, negotiated agreements with energy-intensive sectors, voluntary agreements with car manufacturers to cut vehicles' CO_2 emissions, and integrated transport policies (Chapter 9, Section 2.1).

Mechanisms are in place to enable interministerial co-ordination and implementation of this package. Beyond central government agencies, further steps may be needed. Economic regulators such as the *Office of Gas and Electricity Markets (OFGEM)* have a primarily economic mandate. That of OFGEM, set out in the 2000 Utilities Act, is to promote competition in the gas and electricity markets, as well as value for money and reliable service. OFGEM has achieved a significant reduction in electricity prices, but it is not required to integrate environmental considerations into its policies and decision making.

The *New Electricity Trading Arrangements* penalise generators that do not honour advance contract commitments. This creates particular difficulties for renewable-based providers with their typically highly fluctuating supply. Despite special assistance to such providers, their earnings and output have fallen considerably under this system. OFGEM has suggested that the government should review the need for additional support for green energy. Broadening OFGEM's mandate so that it takes greater account of its policies' environmental impacts should also be considered.

Transport

Despite some *weak decoupling of road traffic growth* from GDP growth, problems related to increasing traffic persist, particularly in highly urbanised regions. Though technological improvements in fuel and vehicle quality have led to strong decoupling of transport-related air emissions (Chapter 2, Section 1.4), developing a sustainable transport system remains a major challenge. Transport accounts for about one-third of UK energy consumption and one-quarter of CO_2 emissions (Figure 9.2).

In terms of *modal split*, domestic transport is dominated by road traffic (93%), with rail accounting for only 6%. Although rail transport has stopped declining in recent years (in rail-kilometres, both passenger and freight traffic have begun to increase again) this has had only a marginal effect on the overall road/rail balance (Figure 6.2). The rail system suffered a long period of underinvestment. Many tracks need repair, and passenger trains are prone to delays. *Prices for public transport* have increased more rapidly than those for private transport, making public transport even less attractive.

The 1998 white paper "A New Deal for Transport" presented a framework for an integrated policy encouraging sustainable transport, with attention to environmental objectives. In July 2000, *Transport 2010: The 10 Year Plan* set out a medium-term strategy for a quicker, safer, more reliable transport system having less impact on the environment. This plan includes a substantial increase in investment (GBP 180 billion over ten years) combined with active demand management. The aim is to bring about a 50% increase in passenger rail traffic and an 80% increase in rail freight transport, and to enable greenhouse gas (GHG) reduction targets to be met. Even if these objectives were realised, this would mean a relatively small increase in the share of rail freight, from 7% to 10%, and a limited modal shift in passenger traffic.

Concerning road investment proposals, the government issued a *New Approach to Appraisal* in 2000. It evaluates proposals in terms of environmental impact, safety, economic implications, accessibility and integration. The environmental dimension

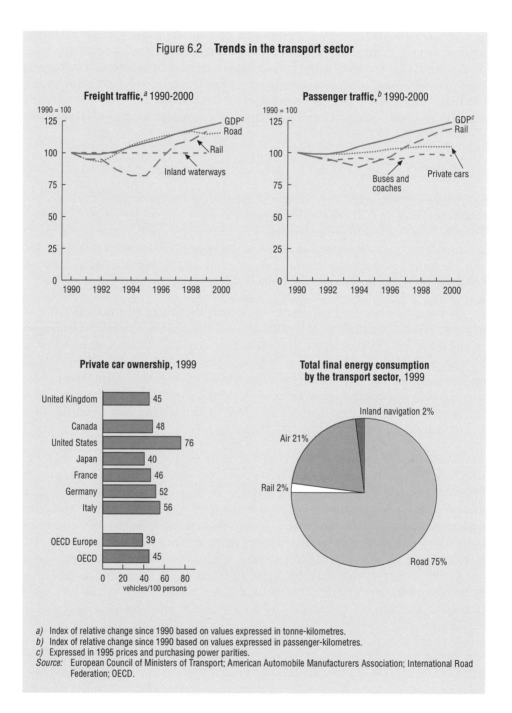

Figure 6.2   **Trends in the transport sector**

Freight traffic, [a] 1990-2000

Passenger traffic, [b] 1990-2000

Private car ownership, 1999

Total final energy consumption by the transport sector, 1999

a) Index of relative change since 1990 based on values expressed in tonne-kilometres.
b) Index of relative change since 1990 based on values expressed in passenger-kilometres.
c) Expressed in 1995 prices and purchasing power parities.
Source: European Council of Ministers of Transport; American Automobile Manufacturers Association; International Road
         Federation; OECD.

© OECD 2002

covers noise, vibration, local air quality, water, landscape and biodiversity, as well as geological and historical heritage. The full integration of the environmental appraisal component is a step forward from previous practice, where environmental assessment was often considered an add-on formality.

To promote sustainable transport through *market-oriented programmes*, the Transport Action Initiative was established under the Energy Saving Trust. It features two primarily government-financed programmes: PowerShift and CleanUp. *Power-Shift* seeks to stimulate markets for vehicles using cleaner fuels such as LPG and fuel cells, and has an annual budget of about GBP 10 million. *CleanUp* promotes retro-fitting of emission control equipment on the most polluting vehicles, particularly buses, taxis and delivery trucks operating in pollution "hot spots"; its budget is projected to double to GBP 12 million by 2004 (Chapter 2, Section 2.4).

Agriculture

Agriculture has a *strong impact* on the UK environment, both positive and negative. While its contribution to GDP is less than 1%, farming occupies over 70% of the countryside. Agriculture generates some 10% of total GHG emissions in the UK, 33% of methane and 50% of N_2O. Despite modest decoupling, the nutrient balance shows an annual surplus of about 1.5 million tonnes of nitrogen, some 86 kg per hectare of agricultural area. Half the nutrient input is not taken up in agricultural production but rather contributes to diffuse pollution (Chapter 3, Section 1.3). In 2000, agriculture accounted for 27% of serious or significant water pollution accidents (compared to industry at 17%). The population of farmland birds is declining much more rapidly than bird populations in general, by nearly half since the early 1970s (Figure 5.2). This biodiversity indicator is one of the four "headline indicators" that showed "significant change away from meeting the objective" during the 1990s.

Consumer confidence has been seriously undermined by a series of agricultural crises including bovine spongiform encephalopathy *("mad cow disease"), swine fever and foot and mouth disease*. Despite annual budget expenditure of GBP 3.2 billion on agriculture (over 75% of it EU funded), real farm income is now as low as in the early 1970s. Employment in the sector continues to fall. All major stakeholders recognize that a fundamental reorientation is needed to put UK agriculture and rural economies on a sustainable development path.

The policy context for UK agriculture is to a large extent defined by the EU Common Agricultural Policy (CAP). The UK has long argued for more ambitious, *market-oriented CAP reform*, moving towards direct payments decoupled from output, introducing environmental cross-compliance mechanisms, targeting remuner-ation to provision of environmental services and broadening rural development support beyond the farming sector. Progress at the EU level has been limited, however. In response to the EU's reform Agenda 2000, the UK Government announced "A New Direction for Agriculture" (1999) and published a white paper called "Our Countryside: The Future" (2000), sketching out an integrated deve-lopment approach for rural England. By 2006, the England Rural Development Programme is to spend GBP 1.6 billion. Scotland, Wales and Northern Ireland have similar programmes. A high-level policy commission reporting to the Cabinet Office presented a report called "Farming and Food: A Sustainable Future" in early 2002, again outlining the need for policy reform and proposing options.

While the CAP establishes the framework, EU countries do have some latitude when it comes to implementation. The UK was one of the first to establish a major programme of management agreements in environmentally sensitive areas. The UK uses the CAP's *cross-compliance provisions* making commodity-related support conditional on compliance with basic environmental standards. It is also one of the few EU countries already using the "*modulation*" *option*, which permits the reduction of commodity-related direct payments if the money is used to promote other rural development and environment measures. The CAP sets the upper limit for modu-lation at 20%; the UK is at 2.5% and plans to raise the rate to 4.5% by 2006.

Of the annual agricultural budget, which exceeds GBP 3 billion, only about 5% is spent on targeted *agri-environmental programmes*, such as the Environmentally Sensitive Areas and Countryside Stewardship programmes. Since 1990 such funding has increased rapidly, from GBP 10 million to almost GBP 200 million. Yet, this is insufficient even to neutralise the negative environmental effects stemming from distorted incentives under mainstream agricultural support measures. Resources for agri-environmental programmes should be increased and the various programmes better integrated. Area coverage should be broadened and greater flexibility provided so that responses can be tailored to local circumstances.

1.4   *Market-based integration*

Since the early 1990s, the UK Government has shown growing interest in using economic instruments to provide signals to producers and consumers about the true costs of using natural resources and depleting ecosystem buffering capacities. In practice it has taken time, however, for economic instruments to be more widely used to help achieve market-based integration. The 1997 *Government Statement of Intent on Environmental Taxation* affirmed the aim of reforming the tax system so as to increase incentives to reduce environmental damage. The idea is to shift the tax burden from "goods" such as jobs to "bads" such as pollution, all the while encou-raging innovation in meeting the higher environmental standards. The statement set out test criteria for good environmental tax design, such as consideration of side-effects, dead-weight compliance costs, distributive impacts and international competitiveness issues. In 2001 the government announced further steps to ensure that taxation and public spending priorities contribute to sustainable development and environmental protection, including initiatives in energy and transport taxation and support for technological innovation.

Energy taxation

While the UK's prices for transport fuel are among the highest for OECD countries (Figure 2.3), its fuel oil and natural gas prices are considerably lower than the OECD and EU averages (Table 2.2). Electricity prices are also well below the EU average. *Taxation of fuels used by households* is low or non-existent. For example, coal, natural gas and electricity are not subject to excise duties. Only a small levy, earmarked for the promotion of electricity generation from renewable sources, is charged on electricity, corresponding to less than 1% of the market price. Kerosene and LPG used for heating are exempt from fuel duty. The VAT rate applied to heating fuels is set at the EU minimum, 5%, rather than the standard UK rate of 17.5%. Overall, economic incentives to increase energy efficiency in households are weak. Households are also unaffected by the climate change levy introduced as part of the Climate Change Programme (2000).

The *climate change levy* is administered on all forms of energy (except renewable sources and fuel oil) consumed by the business and public sectors. It is designed to be broadly neutral between the manufacturing and service sectors, with no net gain for the Treasury. Thus, levy payments are partly offset by a 0.3 percentage point cut in employers' national insurance contributions. Also, from 2001 to 2004, the Carbon Trust, a non-profit company, is "recycling" GBP 100 million in levy revenue as grants to businesses that install low-carbon technologies. The Carbon Trust also administers an enhanced capital allowance programme for businesses, under which approved energy saving investments are eligible for 100% first-year capital allowance deductions (at an estimated cost of GBP 200 million, depending on rate of uptake). Energy-intensive industries participating in voluntary agreements with the government (which specify quantitative targets for reducing operational energy intensity and GHG emissions) are granted an 80% discount in the levy rates. Firms that more than meet their commitments can be allocated allowances for the extra reductions, which can then be traded in the UK Emissions Trading Scheme (Chapter 6, Section 2.2).

Transport taxation

Fuel duties were first introduced in the UK as a revenue-raising measure in 1928. In 1993, with the announcement that the government intended to increase fuel duties

Table 6.2   **Selected environment-related taxes on energy and transport**

			GBP/litre 1998	GBP/litre 1999	GBP/litre 2000
Energy products	*Excise tax*				
		Gas oil	0.0282	0.0303	0.0313
		Heavy fuel oil	0.0222	0.0269	0.0313
		LPG	–	–	–
		Kerosene (individual/commercial use)	0.0251	0.0303	0.0313
		Kerosene (heating)	–	–	–
	Exemption	For heating: VAT 5% instead of 17.5%			
	Revenue 1998/99	*GBP 253 million (gas oil only)*			

				GBP/kWh
Climate change levy	*Tax on energy use by business (from April 2001). Recycled to usiness through cut in NICs[a] (0.3% points), capital allowance reductions and Climate Trust funds.*			
		Electricity		0.0043
		Natural gas		0.0015
		Coal		0.0015
		LPG		0.0007
	Exemptions	No levy for energy from renewable resources or CHP; 80% discount for energy intensive sectors; 50% discount (up to 5 years) for horticulture		
	Revenue 2001/02[b]	*GBP 1.0 billion*		

			GBP/litre 1998	GBP/litre 1999	GBP/litre 2000
Transport fuels	*Excise tax*				
		Leaded gasoline	0.493	0.529	0.547
		Super-unleaded gasoline	. .	0.523	0.492
		Unleaded gasoline	0.440	0.472	0.488
		Ultra-low-sulphur gasoline	. .	. .	0.478
		Super-unleaded gasoline	. .	0.523	0.492
		Diesel/gas oil	0.450	0.502	0.478
		Ultra-low-sulphur diesel	0.440	0.472	0.472
		Kerosene (propellant)	0.403	0.529	0.549
		LPG (propellant)	0.211	0.150	0.150
	Exemption	Fuel for use on ships other than on inland waters			
	Revenue 1998/99	*GBP 21.6 billion*			

Table 6.2   **Selected environment-related taxes on energy and transport** *(cont.)*

			GBP/year
Vehicle excise duty	*Programme changed in 2001: for all new cars, differentiated depending on CO_2 emissions. Annual lump sum collected by Driver and Vehicle Licensing Agency.*		
		Private car (engine capacity > 1 100 cc)	155
		Private car (engine capacity 1 100 cc or less)	100
		Motorcycles and tricycles (depending on engine capacity)	15-60
		Goods vehicles < 3 500 kg	155
		Goods vehicles > 3 500 kg	Max. 9 250
		Reduced-emission goods vehicles	155-8 250
		Agricultural machines, electric vehicles	40
	Exemptions	Vehicles in private use constructed before 1 January 1973, vehicles used by persons in receipt of certain disability living allowances	
	Revenue 1998/99	*GBP 4.6 billion*	
Air passenger duty	*Paid by passengers*		GBP/ passenger
		Flights to EEA[c] (economy class) from April 2001	5
		Flights to EEA[c] (other classes) from April 2001	10
		Flights to rest of world (economy class) from April 2001	20
		Flights to rest of world (other classes) from April 2001	40
	Revenue 1998/99	*GBP 837 million*	

a) National insurance contributions.
b) Estimated.
c) European Economic Area.
Source: DEFRA; EU; OECD.

annually by at least 3% in real terms, their environmental guidance function was accentuated. After 1994, the new administration increased the commitment to 5% annually, then 6%. This automatic *fuel duty escalator* was stopped in 1999 after hauliers, farmers and others protested against a spike in fuel prices resulting from a major increase in crude oil prices. There is evidence that the fuel duties, by reducing energy use in the transport sector, helped the UK reduce CO_2 emissions. There are also indications that the escalator affected the modal split, shifting the trend back towards rail and water transport (Figure 6.2). It was concluded, however, that "the environmental benefits of higher fuel prices must be balanced with the Government's social and economic objectives". Consequently, decisions on fuel duties are now made from budget to budget, and any real-term increases go directly into an earmarked fund for the modernisation of roads and public transport. In 2000 and 2001, fuel duties were unchanged in nominal terms, or reduced in real terms, so their environmental guidance function has effectively been weakened.

During the 1990s, the UK encouraged technological innovation and guided consumer behaviour by taxing both ownership and use of cars, with a gradual shift towards the latter. However, since 1999, emphasis in transport taxation has been shifting back towards *taxing vehicle ownership*, with tax differentiation to encourage technological innovation (Table 6.2). As in the 1990s with leaded and unleaded gasoline, *tax differentiation* is now used to promote the use of diesel and gasoline that have ultra-low sulphur content. The duty differential with conventional diesel was increased from GBP 0.01 to 0.03 per litre in 1999. Even though ultra-low-sulphur diesel made up 100% of UK diesel use by 2000, further duty cuts were made in 2000 and 2001 (by GBP 0.03 per litre). In 2000 and 2001, duties were also reduced for ultra-low-sulphur gasoline, which, similarly, already accounted for 100% of the market. The initial environmental incentive thus has effectively turned into a general reduction in fuel tax burden. To further stimulate interest in developing and producing profitable alternative fuels offering environmental advantages, in 2000 the government launched the *Green Fuels Challenge*. Duties were cut for bio-diesel (GBP 0.20 below the ultra-low-sulphur rate) and road fuel gases (for CNG and LPG the duty was cut from GBP 0.15 to 0.09 per kg). These duties will be frozen in real terms until at least 2004.

The *vehicle excise duty* was reformed in 2000. For all new cars purchased from 2001, a four-band graduated system was introduced, whereby vehicles are taxed based on their CO_2 emission potential (Table 6.2). The difference is rather small; owners of the least polluting vehicles now pay up to GBP 70 less. However, reductions in the excise duty for small cars have decreased taxation for nearly one-third of UK car owners since 1999. The duty on goods vehicles was reformed in December 2001, with rate differentiation in favour of more environmentally friendly vehicles. While these reforms are a step in the right direction, the overall reduction in the level of duties charged (up to 50% since 1999) is not. Tax differentials should be increased to improve the incentive for buying less polluting vehicles.

From 2002, *income tax charges* for company cars are calculated as a percentage of the vehicle's list price, graduated according to its theoretical CO_2 emission intensity. Both giving and receiving free fuel for private use in company cars is also discouraged fiscally (Chapter 2, Section 1.4). In tandem with these measures, income tax incentives have been introduced to encourage car-pooling and green commuting.

Despite a number of attempts, *road use charging* has so far not been used except in limited locations (e.g. bridges). However, local authorities in England and Wales were recently given the legislative power to introduce such charges. Several local authorities have proposed road use charges for city centres, including London, where a congestion charge will take effect in late 2002. Also, in the most recent budget, the government announced a distance-related road user charge on haulage vehicles for 2005/06. Use of such economic instruments should be fully explored as means of combatting persistent urban air quality and congestion problems.

2. Efficiency and Cost-effectiveness of Environmental Management

The UK's approach to environmental management (air pollution, waste, water resources and biodiversity) was previously driven largely by the results of *cost-benefit analyses* carried out instrument by instrument. It has now evolved to include a range of *media-specific objectives and targets* (Chapters 2, 3, 4 and 5). This evolution towards the establishment of explicit objectives and more strategic planning is an important and positive shift. One factor behind it is the influence of the UK's international commitments concerning environmental management. In particular, EU legislation has driven the setting of national targets (Table 2.1), as have international agreements concerning climate change, transboundary air pollution and the North Sea (Chapter 9). Another element has been the UK's sustainable development strategy, which includes "prudent use of natural resources" and "effective protection of the environment" as two of its four overarching objectives and commits the government to an indicator-based, result-oriented approach (Chapter 6, Section 1.2).

The late 1990s saw a *shift in the UK's environmental policy logic* towards greater integration with the social and economic facets of sustainable development. Policy-making and review processes have become more transparent, with enhanced public consultation and systematic use of quantified targets and indicators to monitor implementation. Regular publishing of indicators has heightened the policy focus on outcomes. These changes have been paralleled by important institutional trends towards devolution and decentralisation of regulatory power (Chapter 6, Section 3.4).

Overall, the *mix of instruments* used to implement environmental policy in the UK has become more balanced, with a greater role given to economic instruments in recent years, and continued effective use of regulation and land use planning. The use of environmental impact assessment (EIA) has increased while that of voluntary agreements remains limited. The application of economic analysis to support decision making is deeply rooted in the UK, but its application ex post should be further developed to support efforts to adjust instruments so they are more cost-effective.

2.1 Regulatory instruments

Historically, most UK *environmental laws and regulations* were each designed to deal with a particular environmental concern (Table 6.3), although some recent laws

Table 6.3   **Major environmental legislation**

1897	Public Health (Scotland) Act
1908	Alkali and Works Regulation Act
1956	Clean Air Act
1971	Prevention of Oil Pollution Act
1972	Water Act (Northern Ireland)
1973	Diseases of Fish Act
1974	Control of Pollution Act
	Health and Safety at Work Act
1978	Pollution Control and Local Government (Northern Ireland) Order
1981	Wildlife and Countryside Act (amended in 1991)
1983	Radioactive Substances (Carriage by Road) Regulations (Northern Ireland)
1985	Food and Environment Protection Act
1989	Water Act (superseded by 1991 Water Resources Act)
	Water Supply (Water Quality) Regulations
1990	Environmental Protection Act
	Town and Country Planning Act
	Water Supply (Water Quality) (Scotland) Regulations
1991	Water Industry Act (amended in 1999)
	Water Resources Act
	Planning and Compensation Act
	Natural Heritage (Scotland) Act
	Genetically Modified Organisms (Northern Ireland) Order
1992	Genetically Modified Organisms (Deliberate Release) Regulations
	Controlled Waste Regulations
1993	Radioactive Substances Act
1995	Environment Act
	Home Energy Conservation Act
1996	Wild Mammals (Protection) Act
	Energy Conservation Act
	Noise Act
1997	Road Traffic Reduction Act
	Industrial Pollution Control (Northern Ireland) Order
	Merchant Shipping (Port Waste Reception Facilities) Regulations
	Producer Responsibility Obligations Regulations
1998	Waste Minimisation Act
	Industrial Pollution Control Regulations (Northern Ireland)
	Packaging Regulations
1999	Pollution Prevention and Control Act
	Water Industry Act
	Local Government Act
	Town and Country Planning (Environmental Impact Assessment) (England and Wales) Regulations
2000	Countryside and Rights of Way Act
	Transport Act
	National Parks (Scotland) Act
	Control of Major Accident Hazard Regulations (Northern Ireland)
	Contaminated Land (England) Regulations

Source: DEFRA.

have addressed several kinds of pollution (e.g. 1990 Environmental Protection Act, 1995 Environment Act). Regulatory measures have been used to achieve large reductions in emissions of criteria air pollutants, persistent organic pollutants and heavy metals (Chapter 2, Section 1.2). They have also stimulated major improvements in the quality of drinking, bathing and surface waters (Chapter 3, Section 2.1). Attempts to control illegal waste disposal through regulation have not yet affected the increasing trend in dumping (Chapter 4, Section 1.4).

Regulatory approaches have changed markedly since the 1994 OECD Environmental Performance Review. The 1996 EU directive on integrated pollution prevention and control (IPPC) sparked an overhaul and expansion of the UK's system of integrated pollution control (IPC). A significant expansion in the capacity of regulatory institutions for inspection and enforcement will be required to accommodate the extended scope of IPPC regulation. Responsibility for inspection and enforcement of environmental regulations was devolved to sub-national regulatory agencies in mid-1996 (Chapter 6, Section 3.5).

Integrated pollution control

Since 1990, regulation of pollution from large point sources in the UK has been carried out in an IPC framework. The 1990 Environmental Protection Act established a *two-tier regulatory regime* comprising the IPC system and the local air pollution control (LAPC) system. The most polluting industrial processes, categorised as "Part A", were subject to integrated permitting for air, water and waste discharges under the IPC system. That system covered some 2 100 installations, about half of them in the chemical industry. In England and Wales, integrated permits were issued by Her Majesty's Inspectorate for Pollution until 1996 and by the Environment Agency thereafter. In Scotland, they were issued by Her Majesty's Industrial Pollution Inspectorate until 1996 and by the Scottish Environment Protection Agency (SEPA) thereafter. In Northern Ireland, they were and are issued by the Industrial Pollution and Radiochemical Inspectorate.

Industries regulated under IPC have been required to provide an evaluation of the environmental impact of their gaseous, liquid and solid releases, and to determine the "*best practicable environmental option*" for control. In the LAPC system, minor ("Part B") polluters have been required to obtain permits for air emissions only, under supervision of local authorities (counties/county boroughs in Wales, districts/boroughs elsewhere). Both the IPC and LAPC systems required the use of "best available techniques not entailing excessive cost" (BATNEEC) to limit pollutant discharges. A survey in the mid-1990s showed that fewer than half of IPC applicants provided proof of BATNEEC use as required.

Industries complained of much *uncertainty* during the early years of the IPC system. The 1990 Act did not clearly designate processes subject to IPC, and the regulatory agencies had considerable difficulty, in practice, defining what constituted a "process". Although, in principle, *BATNEEC* for one process is likely the same for a comparable process, individual inspectors had to define BATNEEC case by case. Guidance documents issued by the government to help select best practicable environmental options were criticised for their complexity and their attempts to compare different environmental impacts in different environmental media. For industry, advantages such as streamlined permitting processes were tempered by considerable *regional variability* in requirements for process information and technological improvements. With time, the system became clearer and more understandable, and industries became more positive, though they still complained that control costs had increased. From a regulatory point of view, the IPC system was rather narrow in scope, dealing only with emissions and not considering product life cycles.

The UK was a pioneer in implementation of an IPC approach, and its experiences influenced the development of the *1996 EU directive on IPPC*, which in turn is stimulating wide-ranging regulatory adjustments in the UK. Regulations under the 1999 Pollution Prevention and Control Act transposed the directive into UK law. From 2001 to 2007, the IPPC system is being phased in, gradually superseding the IPC system (Figure 6.3). While maintaining the basic principles of the previous system, the new one goes beyond the traditional focus on emissions, also promoting energy efficiency, waste prevention and site restoration. A range of sectors and installations not subject to IPC are being brought under IPPC. Thus, more processes (around 7 000 installations in England and Wales, 2 000 in Scotland) will be covered. In general, the industries that are new to integrated permitting, such as landfilling, intensive farming and the food and drink sectors, previously had to seek separate waste management licences, issued under Part II of the Environmental Protection Act, and/or water discharge consents under the Water Resources Act or the Water Industry Act. The main provisions of IPPC apply equally to industries that have been covered by IPC and to some (notably the intensive livestock-rearing industry and the food and drink industry) new to integrated permitting.

A common argument in favour of IPC systems is that they can help achieve results *more cost-effectively* for both regulator and regulatee. Whether the UK's first decade of experience with IPC bears this argument out has not been assessed. However, a survey carried out in the mid-1990s by the environmental consultancy ENDS concluded that only 8% of the relevant installations found that IPC had led to cost savings, and only 9% expected the licensing to lead to significant improvements in their environmental performance. In 2001, a joint survey by DEFRA and the Environment Agency of 40 industries already subject to the IPPC system concluded that the average cost of

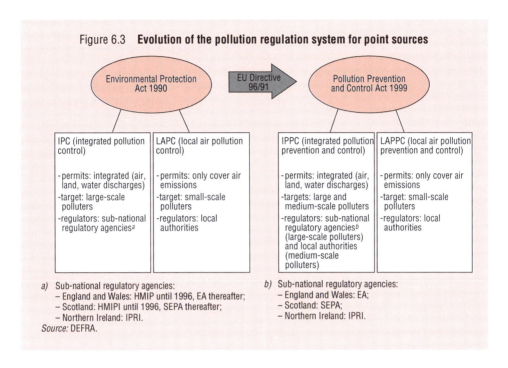

Figure 6.3   **Evolution of the pollution regulation system for point sources**

IPC (integrated pollution control)	LAPC (local air pollution control)	IPPC (integrated pollution prevention and control)	LAPPC (local air pollution prevention and control)
- permits: integrated (air, land, water discharges) - target: large-scale polluters - regulators: sub-national regulatory agencies*a*	- permits: only cover air emissions - target: small-scale polluters - regulators: local authorities	- permits: integrated (air, land, water discharges) - targets: large and medium-scale polluters - regulators: sub-national regulatory agencies*b* (large-scale polluters) and local authorities (medium-scale polluters)	- permits: only cover air emissions - target: small-scale polluters - regulators: local authorities

Environmental Protection Act 1990 → EU Directive 96/91 → Pollution Prevention and Control Act 1999

a) Sub-national regulatory agencies:
  – England and Wales: HMIP until 1996, EA thereafter;
  – Scotland: HMIPI until 1996, SEPA thereafter;
  – Northern Ireland: IPRI.
Source: DEFRA.

b) Sub-national regulatory agencies:
  – England and Wales: EA;
  – Scotland: SEPA;
  – Northern Ireland: IPRI.

preparing an IPPC application was GBP 32 000 to 43 000 (not including application fees), depending on the sector. Most companies said they needed six months to prepare an application.

Enforcement and prosecution

During the first five years of the Environment Agency's existence, the effectiveness of its *enforcement and prosecution* activities has been roundly criticised, particularly by the House of Commons' Environmental Audit Committee. In 1996, the agency inherited diverse approaches to enforcement from its predecessor organisations (Chapter 6, Section 3.5). It introduced an integrated Enforcement and Prosecution Policy in 1998, developed following extensive public consultation. An internal audit of the policy's effectiveness was carried out in 2000, following the first full year of implementation. While the audit revealed a high level of staff commitment when dealing with pollution incidents and breaches of environmental permits, various compliance issues were identified. For example, the agency had prosecuted only 23% of the most severe environmental incidents ("Category I" incidents), despite the policy's stipulation that prosecution should be the normal response to such incidents. The review concluded that major gaps and shortcomings in data management compromised the prosecution policy's effectiveness.

The agency has taken steps to *strengthen enforcement policy implementation* in response to the issues highlighted in the audit. In particular, it introduced a new warrant procedure and a competency assessment programme, which requires all new officers to undergo training and demonstrate competency in areas such as application of the policy, investigative techniques and dealing with threatening or hostile situations. Existing enforcement staff (3 500 in all) have also been required to participate in the training programme, and periodic competency reassessments are scheduled. For key compliance issues, specialised enforcement teams are being developed, and targeted audits to assess progress are scheduled. To improve record keeping, the Environment Agency has reinforced its national incident reporting system and developed a compliance classification system. Progress has been measurable, with rises in numbers of successful prosecutions (33% greater in 2002 than in 1997/98), formal cautions (up more than 100%) and enforcement notices. Meanwhile the total number of substantiated environmental incidents has fallen by 10%; water pollution incident alone are down by 23%.

The *number of inspections* has declined by over 20% in recent years (Table 6.4), in part because the agency has reprioritised its inspection programme to take account

Table 6.4   **Trends in inspections by the Environment Agency, 1998-2001**[a]

	1998	1999	2000	2001	Change 1998-2001 (%)
Discharges to water	115 540	95 725	85 769	87 912	*−24*
IPC processes	5 583	5 231	5 943	4 245	*−24*
Licensed waste sites	140 210	149 022	126 237	119 899	*−15*
Waste broker checks	424	60	. .	2 376	*460*
Waste carriers	6 738	5 658	3 042	. .	*−55*
Waste producers	1 662	1 026	1 551	1 743	*5*
Transboundary waste	287	532	343	320	*+11*
Exempt waste facilities	5 325	4 443	. .	1 972	*−63*
Exempt metal recycling facilities	1 775	1 312	2 023	1 361	*−23*
RSR[b] sites	1 458	1 588	2 021	1 534	*5*
COMAH[c] sites	−	−	66	297	. .
Farms in NVZs[d]	−	−	1 212	1 688	. .
Total	281 964	265 944	228 207	223 347	*−21*

a)   Reported for fiscal years ending in year indicated.
b)   Radioactive Substance Regulations.
c)   Control of Major Accident Hazards Regulations.
d)   Nitrate vulnerable zones.
Source: Environment Agency.

of risk, thus reducing inspection frequency for minor discharges and focusing more attention on "problem sites". For example, for licensed waste sites, a risk-based inspection programme launched in 2000 has increased inspection frequency of hazardous waste sites. For large industrial sources, effort has been refocused on higher-risk discharges and installations of high public concern.

The *limited data on regulatory enforcement* by the Environment Agency made available for this review is inadequate for overall performance assessment. But it appears that a review of resources available for inspection and enforcement may be necessary given the agency's recently introduced responsibility for expanded enforcement under IPPC.

SEPA is responsible for inspection and enforcement in *Scotland*. In the late 1990s it carried out some 200 inspections annually of major industrial plants regulated under IPC, and some 15 000 inspections of sites having permits to discharge to water. With the phase-in of the IPPC system, SEPA's inspection and enforcement activities will need to be further expanded. Regarding water discharges, the rate of compliance with permit conditions has improved significantly in recent years, from 73% to 82% overall (Table 6.5). SEPA ascribes 46% of polluted river lengths to diffuse sources, including runoff and leaching from agriculture and forestry, along with urban drainage.

Table 6.5   **Effluent compliance with discharge consents in Scotland,** 1997-2000[a]

Type of discharge consent	Samples complying with relevant standards (%)			
	1997	1998	1999	2000
Industrial effluent	74	83	78	80
Public sewage	78	82	86	86
Private sewage	51	64	75	70
Other discharges	87	89	91	93
Total	73	80	82	82

a) Reported for fiscal years ending in year indicated.
Source: SEPA.

Energy efficiency and fuel quality standards

At EU level, *vehicle emission and fuel quality standards* are set by various programmes and legislation. Since 1990, emission standards for new vehicles have been made 50-100% tighter, depending on vehicle and pollutant types. Further tightening (Euro IV) is planned for 2006. In 2001, a large majority of cars in the UK fleet complied with Euro I, II or III standards (Chapter 2, Section 1.4). The UK has also upgraded its motor vehicle fuel quality standards, in conformance with EU legislation. In 2000, all transport fuels sold in the UK conformed with the EU's 2005 standards for ultra-low-sulphur fuels (< 50 ppm sulphur), five years ahead of schedule.

Regulation of *energy efficiency in buildings* has been significantly strengthened since 1994. Through repeated revision of building regulations, commendable progress has been made in upgrading the energy efficiency of new buildings. Even so, the UK's energy efficiency standards are not yet on a par with those of some other EU countries, leaving room for improvement (Chapter 8, Section 1.3). Moreover, further effort is needed to upgrade the performance of the existing building stock, which holds the greatest potential for energy efficiency gains.

2.2   Economic instruments

The UK has a long-established and highly developed tradition of *economic analysis* during policy development. The BATNEEC principle has been applied under the IPC system and elsewhere. Furthermore, the Best Value system requires local authorities to ensure that environmental services are delivered in the most cost-effective way (Chapter 7, Section 1.7). Until recently, emphasis on cost-effectiveness analysis applied particularly to regulatory programmes and the country used a relatively limited array of economic instruments to help internalise environmental costs. Since 1997 the UK has put much greater emphasis on development of economic instruments to address specific environmental issues, particularly those related to consumption patterns.

The UK's expressed *interest in using economic instruments* as environmental policy tools dates from the early 1990s (Chapter 6, Section 1.4). In 1997, the government indicated that it would seek to increase taxation of "bads" such as pollution, and use part of the revenue to support "goods" such as jobs, following five principles: i) polluters should face the true costs that their actions impose on society; ii) the social consequences of environmental taxation must be acceptable; iii) economic instruments must deliver real environmental gains cost-effectively; iv) environmental policies must be based on sound evidence, but uncertainty cannot justify inaction; and v) environmental policies must not threaten the competitiveness of UK business.

Polluter and user charges

A range of polluter and user charges are applied to recover the costs of providing environmental services (Table 6.6). *Sewerage and waste water treatment charges* help cover the costs of related services, for example. They contain some provisions for

Table 6.6   Taxes and charges for water and waste

Water supply charge	*Cost-covering charge on drinking water supply Households pay either according to actual measurement or a flat rate Industry tariff structure has 3 elements: connection, fixed (pipe size) and volume-based*	GBP/household/year
	Average household bill (metered)	87
	Average household bill (non-metered)	106
	Revenue 1998/99 GBP 3.1 billion	
Waste water treatment charge (households)	*Cost-recovery charge based on actual measurement or flat rate (related to property value); includes surface and highway drainage*	
	Average household bill for water use	116
	Average household bill (metered)	102
	Average household bill (unmetered)	119
	Revenue 1998/99 GBP 3.2 billion	
Waste water treatment charge (industry)	*Cost-recovery charge for indirect discharges: effluent charge based on volume and strength of effluent*	GBP/unit
	Average charges	71-230
	Revenue 1998/99 GBP 190 million	
Charge on water discharge	*Levied on direct discharges to surface and groundwater, two components*	GBP/unit
	Application charge: standard one-off rate	505
	Annual charge: based on volume and content of discharge and type of receiving water	389
	Revenue 1998/99 GBP 39.8 million	
Water withdrawal charge	*Depends on criteria such as area, water source and season*	GBP/1 000 m^3
	Minimum rate (1995/96)	6.3
	Maximum rate (1995/96)	16.2
Landfill tax	*Levied on disposal of waste to landfill*	GBP/t
	Standard rate for non-inert waste (1999)[a]	10
	Reduced rate for inert or frozen waste	2
	Exemption From the reduced rate: waste used in restoration of landfill sites and quarries	
	Revenue 1998/99 GBP 340 million	
Charge on municipal waste management	*Cost-recovery user charge on waste collection and disposal*	GBP/t
	For households: part of the council tax	18-33
	For industry: actual measurement	

a) The standard rate was raised in 1999 from GBP 7 to GBP 10 and a 5-year escalator was introduced, raising the tax by GBP 1 each
   year until 2004, when the standard rate will be GBP 16 per tonne.
Source: Inventory of Taxes in the Member States of the European Union, 17th edition; OECD/EU database on environment-related
   taxes.

surface drainage (runoff from properties) and highway drainage (runoff from roads and pavements). Overall, application of the polluter pays and user pays principles to *water services* is fairly comprehensive except as regards pollution from fertilisers and pesticides. Particular progress has been made since 1994 concerning municipal and industrial waste water management. For *waste management*, higher priority should be given to raising user charges to achieve full cost recovery and to encourage waste prevention. There is a particular need to develop instruments to internalise the costs of pollution from diffuse sources, especially agriculture and transport.

Under the new IPPC system, the Environment Agency has begun *charging regulated parties* on the basis of the time its experts spend advising them or carrying out inspections. While this is a valid application of the user pays principle, regulated industries complain that the time-based charges polarise the relationship between regulator and regulatee and hinders communication with the agency. Under a proposed new charging system, permit charges would be calculated as a function of an installation's "risk rating". The agency would estimate the installation's risk, based on complexity, emissions, location and operator performance. Such a system would provide incentives by lowering regulatory costs for the cleanest operators in a given industrial branch.

Green taxes

A number of *green taxes* have been introduced in recent years, notably the landfill tax, the aggregates levy and the climate change levy. The *landfill tax* (1996) aims to reduce the UK's heavy reliance on landfilling (Chapter 4, Section 2.2). Although information is limited, there are early signs of a decrease in inert waste sent to landfill since the introduction of the tax, though this likely involves considerable diversion of construction and demolition waste to sites where the waste regulations are not applicable (Chapter 8, Section 1.4). Exemptions from landfill licensing should be reviewed to close such loopholes. As the landfill tax is equivalent to a minuscule proportion of turnover for most industrial sectors, it has not yet created a real incentive for waste prevention. Even with the tax, landfilling costs are much lower in the UK than in many other OECD Europe countries. The *aggregates levy* (April 2002) seeks to increase recycling of construction and demolition waste and thus reduce landfilling (Chapter 8, Section 1.4). The *climate change levy* (2002) is a revenue-neutral levy applying to all energy consumed by business and the public sector, except renewables and fuel oil (Chapter 6, Section 1.4).

It is too early to assess the *cost-effectiveness* of these economic instruments, but in theory they should help lead to market internalisation of environmental concerns. Critics have suggested that the tax rates will need to be gradually raised to create effective economic signals that encourage more sustainable consumption patterns. It may also be necessary to better inform the public about the benefits of such approaches and to explain that they are revenue-neutral. Public acceptance of the use of fiscal instruments to implement environmental policy has reportedly waned in recent years. Opinion surveys show that this is partly because "green taxes" are widely perceived as fulfilling a revenue-raising, rather than incentive-creating, function (Chapter 7, Section 1.2). A high priority should be regular follow-up analysis and serious review of the effectiveness and role of these instruments.

The UK is implementing a combination of fiscal measures intended to give market signals in favour of *low CO_2 emitting* passenger cars (Chapter 2, Section 1.3). In 2001, the annual *vehicle excise duty* was differentiated in favour of more fuel-efficient vehicles. *Company car taxation* has also been differentiated in favour of such vehicles, and other fiscal measures discourage the use of company cars. The UK overhauled the *vehicle excise duties* applied to cars and light goods vehicles in 2001, differentiating the tax in proportion to engine capacity. This reform introduced higher duty rates for diesel cars and lower rates for low-emission vehicles. The maximum differentiation, however, is 10% above or below the rates applied to gasoline cars, and the strength of the resulting incentive to buy less-polluting cars is likely to be correspondingly low.

Transferable permits

The UK is pioneering the establishment of national *emission trading* for GHGs. The voluntary Emissions Trading Scheme, which began operating in April 2002, is the world's first economy-wide trading system of its kind. Participants can buy or sell emission allowances to achieve emission reductions at least costs. A mechanism has been established to connect the markets for relative and absolute reductions. To "kick-start" the trading system, the government made GBP 215 million available for the first five years. An important consideration has been the aspiration to establish London as an eventual centre for international GHG emission trading.

The UK has also proposed introducing a system of *tradable waste permits* to help limit landfilling of biodegradable municipal waste as required by the EU landfill directive. The system would start operating in 2003, with municipal waste management authorities acting as traders (Chapter 4, Section 2.2). The system would create strong economic incentives for local authorities to take measures to reduce municipal waste generation and increase recovery. The Environment Agency is also reviewing the scope for *sulphur and NO_x trading* in the electricity supply industry.

2.3   Other instruments

Spatial planning

Land use planning has existed in the UK since 1947, and has worked effectively to separate incompatible land uses, preserve historic areas and, at least to some extent, rein in urban sprawl. The 1990 Town and Country Planning Act consolidated the legislation for England and Wales, and further precision regarding compensation was set out in the 1991 Planning and Compensation Act. Scottish legislation was consolidated in the 1997 Town and Country Planning (Scotland) Act. Land use planning in the UK is carried out through two complementary approaches: development control (through regulation of building, engineering and changes in land use) and development planning (through county structure plans and local development plans). Almost any development of consequence requires planning permission, granted by local authorities guided by national policies. In recent years, as concerns have been raised about the rate of land conversion for new development, the number of permits granted for construction of large peri-urban retail developments has tapered off. At the same time, planning guidance notes have been issued recommending the avoidance of unnecessary development of greenfield sites, the protection and further creation of urban green spaces, the integration of environmental concerns into traffic planning and the adoption of a precautionary approach to development in flood-prone areas.

Wide public consultation on plans and on applications for development permission is a traditional strength of the UK's land use planning system. For example, all components of a development plan are subject to extensive consultation and scrutiny. Objectors to a proposed plan may be individuals or organisations with an interest in the land in question, or those with a more general interest in planning policy (e.g. amenity groups, business groups). Statutory environmental agencies and government departments may also participate. If objections are made, a public inquiry is carried out by an inspector (England and Wales) or an inquiry reporter (Scotland). All structure plans are considered at public hearings conducted by a panel chaired by a ministerial appointee. The local authority then considers whether to modify the plan.

In recent years, there have been calls for *reform* of the land use planning system from many camps. Criticism has been directed both at the complexities of the system and at delays in producing development plans and decisions on applications. In the 2001 UK election, all three of the main political parties featured reform of the planning system in their manifestos. The UK's sustainable development strategy, "A Better Quality of Life", declared that the reform should be aimed at promoting "more sustainable patterns of development", in particular by: i) concentrating new development in existing urban areas; ii) seeking to reduce travel needs when siting new developments; iii) using previously developed land and bringing empty homes/buildings back into use; iv) extending existing urban areas rather than building isolated new settlements; and v) providing enough urban green spaces to create high-quality living environments.

In December 2001, a government *green paper* on the planning system in England proposed that regional spatial strategies should replace regional planning guidance, that structure plans should be abolished and that local plans should be replaced by local development frameworks, which would be updated annually and supplemented by community action plans. Other proposals concern amending the system of development control. In March 2002, the *Royal Commission on Environmental Pollution* issued a report ("Environmental Planning") evaluating the ability of the UK's land use planning system to help achieve environmental policy objectives, as well as the environmental implications of certain aspects of the proposed reforms. The report concurred that there was a need for reform, finding that the present system does not provide an integrated and transparent way of setting and achieving environmental goals at different levels, in particular because it is based on a complex array of legislation that clearly defines neither environmental priorities nor administrative responsibilities. However, the report expresses concern that, in its present form, the proposals for "streamlining" processes and plans could undermine the effectiveness of spatial planning as an instrument for public dialogue and for integration of broader environmental sustainability concerns.

Environmental impact assessment

Environmental assessment of infrastructure and development projects has long been part of the land use planning system. In the 1990s, following the formal enactment of EIA legislation in line with EU legislation, full-fledged EIA began being used for large projects (Table 6.7). In 1999, new regulations for England and Wales

Table 6.7   **EIAs by major project type,** 1991-2000

	Total EIAs[a]	Urban development[b] (non-transport)[c]	Transport[b] (roads, railways, ports)	Agriculture, forestry, fisheries[b]	Energy, industry[b]
1991	326	214	43	8	29
1992	330	225	40	9	23
1993	398	226	58	30	12
1994	402	229	69	18	23
1995	345	208	35	15	19
1996	286	174	30	12	17
1997	326	185	30	14	25
1998	296	190	17	15	12
1999	418	303	20	21	21
2000	639	549	23	20	42

a) UK total.
b) England, Scotland and Wales.
c) Includes environmental statements received under Town and Country Planning Regulations.
Source: DEFRA.

extended the range of projects subject to EIA and made some procedural changes. In particular, developers can now obtain a formal (scoping) opinion from the relevant planning authority on what should be included in the environmental statement. Developers must outline in the statement the main alternatives considered and the reasons for the final choice. After reviewing a project application, the local planning authority or the DEFRA secretary of state (deputy minister) must inform the public of the decision taken and the main reasons for it, regardless of whether the application is approved. Following a threat of legal action from the European Commission, the UK began taking steps in 2001 to apply EIA to *intensive agriculture*, in compliance with the EU directive on EIA. For example, EIA requirements will be extended to projects that involve conversion of uncultivated and semi-natural land to intensive agriculture.

Voluntary initiatives

UK industry has made unilateral *voluntary commitments* in areas such as ozone-depleting substances, used tyres and reporting on GHG emissions and on waste and water. The Making a Corporate Commitment campaign encourages business to publicly set improvement targets in such areas.

Overall there are far *fewer voluntary agreements* in the UK than in other EU countries of comparable size and environmental performance. For example, nine agreements concerning climate change, water pollution and waste management had been negotiated in the UK by 1997, less than half the EU average. Most were not legally binding. Government and industry have negotiated agreements on energy efficiency in the chemical industry, pesticides, HFCs and cleaning products.

Firms often opt for voluntary initiatives as a way to *avoid or minimise regulatory costs*. A firm may expect to lower its pollution abatement costs by negotiating a lower environmental target, or to reduce its compliance costs through voluntary approaches that often allow greater flexibility in how to reach the target. Firms generally also opt for voluntary pollution abatement because of the benefits of product differentiation based on environmental performance and signalled to consumers via labelling. In the UK, however, large corporations point to cases where voluntary measures were taken but regulatory costs were imposed anyway, which has resulted in some distrust of voluntary approaches.

2.4   Environmental expenditure

The UK has only recently begun systematically collecting information on current or future *environmental expenditure*, whether public or private (Table 6.8). Thus there is a lack of comparable data over time. Recent analyses suggest, however, that from 1996/97 to 2000/01 average annual growth in public sector net expenditure on environmental protection was higher than GDP growth (7.0% compared to 4.8%) and thus the share in GDP slightly increased. Together with environmental expenditure by industry the share is of the order of 1.0% of GDP.

In 1999/2000, reported *pollution abatement and control (PAC) expenditure* totalled about GBP 7.4 billion, 48% of it public expenditure and 52% by industry (Table 6.8). Less than 15% of public gross expenditure was investment; for industry the share was 33%. In industry, the proportion of capital expenditure on integrated processes, as compared to end-of-pipe solutions, has increased significantly and is now about 50%. By far the biggest portion of public expenditure is for waste management. In industry, priority investment areas were air and climate (53%) and waste water treatment (20%), while for current expenditure waste water treatment accounted for the largest share. A breakdown of 1997 and 1999 *expenditure by firm size* shows that for current expenditure the split between large companies and small and medium-sized enterprises (SMEs, fewer than 250 employees) was roughly 65%

Table 6.8 **Environmental expenditure,** 1999-2000

		Total	Public			Industry		
			Total	Investment	Current expenditure	Total	Investment	Current expenditure[c]
Env. Expenditure[a]	(GBP million)	8 742	4 643	572	4 071	4 099	1 301	2 798
Share[b]	(%)	*100*	*53*	*7*	*47*	*47*	*15*	*32*
Per unit of GDP	(%)	*1.0*						
PAC expenditure	(GBP million)	7 436	3 546	466	3 080	3 890	1 275	2 615
Share[b]	(%)	*100*	*48*	*6*	*41*	*52*	*17*	*35*
Air and climate	(%)	*16*	*7*	*18*	*5*	*25*	*53*	*11*
Waste water	(%)	*23*	*6*	*8*	*5*	*39*	*20*	*48*
Waste	(%)	*49*	*78*	*13*	*88*	*22*	*8*	*29*
Soil and groundwater	(%)	*5*	*5*	*30*	*1*	*6*	*4*	*7*
Other env. expenditure	(GBP million)	1 305	1 096	105	991	209	26	183
Share	(%)	*100*	*84*	*8*	*76*	*16*	*2*	*14*

a) Covers PAC plus research and development, environmental education, nature and biodiversity conservation; excludes flood defence and water supply.
b) Parts may not add up to total, due to rounding.
c) Breakdown by media are OECD Secretariat estimates.
Source: DEFRA; OECD.

to 35% in both years. For capital expenditure, the SME share increased from 26% to 34% while the share of larger companies declined correspondingly, indicating that SMEs are gradually catching up.

In addition to PAC expenditure, *other environment-related costs* (e.g. R&D and education) total about GBP 1.3 billion for the public and private sectors. Some GBP 500 million of this is spent for conservation and management of nature and biodiversity; three-quarters of this expenditure takes the form of public sector current expenditure.

3.   Focus on Selected Topics

3.1   *Economic context*

The UK has experienced almost a decade of *continuous GDP growth*, exceeding both the OECD and EU averages (Figure 6.1). After a recession in 1991-92, output increased by an annual average of almost 2.5%. Per capita GDP has grown 20% in real terms. This robust expansion was primarily driven by rapid growth in the *service sector*, particularly transport, communication, finance and business services. Since 1995, service sector growth has exceeded 20% while *manufacturing* has grown by less than 5%. The service sector's share in total output increased by about 10 percentage points in the 1990s, to more than 70%, while industry's contribution dropped from one-third to one-quarter of GDP. This dematerialisation in the UK economy has helped ease some conventional pollution pressures. *Farming, forestry and fishing* together have dropped to under 5% of GDP, though their environmental significance is disproportionally important.

These sectoral shifts, with output stagnating in traditional manufacturing and agriculture, must be viewed against a background of *currency appreciation*. The real effective exchange rate of the pound is now roughly 25-30% higher than in the mid-1990s. This has helped bring inflation down to less than 2%, compared with a 1991 peak of about 9%. Employment has increased slowly but steadily, at about 1% per year. The unemployment rate, which during the 1991-92 recession climbed from 6% to over 10%, had dropped to about 5% by the end of 2000.

The increase in the value of the pound affects the UK's position in international markets. The *current accounts balance*, which had significantly improved during the first part of the 1990s and was almost balanced in 1997, has returned to a deficit of about 2% of GDP. As a result of strict control of public finances, the fiscal position (as a percentage of GDP) improved from an 8% deficit in 1993 to a 2% surplus in 2000. The overall *gross debt ratio* declined to around 40% of GDP, significantly below the EU Maastricht stability criterion of 60%.

Despite these positive overall trends, *low productivity* remains a feature of the UK economy. In part, this reflects a long period of public and private under-investment in human and physical capital. Through the early 1990s, *investment* as a percentage of GDP fell sharply, and although it recovered in the latter half of the decade, it remains low by OECD standards. General government gross investment is less than 1.5% of GDP, the lowest for any OECD country. A 1998 comparison showed investment per worker and education spending per student to be lower in the UK than in any other G7 country, on a purchasing power parity basis. UK businesses spend less per worker on R&D than most of their major competitors, and their relative position in this regard among OECD countries has deteriorated.

The quality of basic public infrastructure and key public services in the UK is low compared to that of other G7 countries. This is true not only for transport, health and education, where the UK's budget situation gives it flexibility; it also holds for important *environmental infrastructure and services* (e.g. management of waste and waste water), where greater use should be made of economic incentives, service pricing and charges to steer economic activity and consumer behaviour towards better environmental performance.

3.2 Appraisal of environmental impacts of policies: extending cost-benefit analysis

The UK Government is committed to systematic appraisal of its policies' environmental impacts. For many years, guidance from the Treasury on appraisal and evaluation of policies emphasised the importance of comparing the *costs and benefits* of proposed policy measures, including costs and benefits not easily valued, such as those relating to the environment. This initiative, supported by the Cabinet Office's Better Regulation Unit, has encouraged and institutionalised cost-benefit approaches.

The 1999 white paper on modernising government included a commitment to develop and apply an *integrated system of impact assessment and appraisal tools* in support of sustainable development. A "Policy Makers' Checklist" requires policy makers to screen policy proposals, taking account of government objectives and key issues related to sustainable development, health, environment, consumer impacts, scientific evidence, risk and human rights. The Cabinet Office, the Centre for Management and Policy Studies and individual departments are working to further develop the checklist.

The importance of presenting evidence on the costs and benefits of policy options was formalised in 1998 by the requirement to conduct a *regulatory impact assessment* (RIA) of proposed policies. RIA replaced a dual system of Compliance

Cost Assessment, concerned with costs of regulation to business, and Regulatory Appraisal, concerned with assessing regulations' benefits. The intent is for RIA to become an integral part of policy making so that, from the earliest stages, ministers can be shown the risks, benefits and costs associated with all options. The advantage of RIA is that it not only integrates costs and benefits but also takes a broader view of them, with clear recognition of environmental impacts.

The Advisory Committee on Business and the Environment recently produced a guidance note, "How Sustainable Is Your Business?", as part of its work to promote consideration of sustainable development issues in decision making in the *business sector*. The note was sent to the heads of 10 000 companies. In June 2000 the government relaunched its Making a Corporate Commitment campaign. While the first campaign focused on energy efficiency, "MACC2" encourages commitment to a much wider sustainability agenda. Over 50 organisations have signed up, making a public commitment to improvement targets and annual progress reports.

3.3   Institutions promoting sustainable development

Each UK government department has a *"green minister"* whose aim it is to promote sustainable development and environmental concerns within the department. The green ministers collectively work to promote integration of sustainable development within the public sector, to encourage environmental appraisals of policy and to improve the environmental performance of government operations. Twice a year, the green ministers report to the *Cabinet Committee on the Environment* about environmental policies and co-ordination of sustainable development policies. Among other steps, the green ministers have set targets for energy efficiency, greener transport and waste recovery. They have also helped departments adopt environmental management systems and promote environmentally friendly procurement.

In 1999, the government established the *Sustainable Development Commission* "to inspire sustainable development in government, the economy and society". It is a consultative body with 22 members from diverse backgrounds. The commission's role is to advocate sustainable development in all sectors, review progress and build consensus on the actions needed. Its initial focus is on five key themes: the economic paradigm, climate change, regeneration, sustainable food production and communication.

The House of Commons *Environmental Audit Committee* assesses the contribution of government policies, programmes and operations to environmental protection and sustainable development. The EAC audits performance against targets and can requisition evidence from any department. It can also review regional bodies and consider the impact of central government policies on local authorities' ability to deliver sustainable development locally. The EAC reports annually on environmental dimensions of taxation and expenditure and evaluates the various departments' performance on policy appraisal, operations and environmental reporting.

At the *sub-national level*, sustainable development in England is an important part of the responsibilities of the Countryside Agency, the Environment Agency (which has developed its own sustainable development guidance) and English Nature, which is the government's biodiversity adviser. The Scottish Parliament and the Welsh and Northern Ireland Assemblies also take responsibilities for supporting sustainable development. In addition, England's regional development agencies focus not only on economic development but have sustainable development as at least a secondary duty.

The 2000 Local Government Act gave *local authorities* powers to promote the economic, social and/or environmental well-being of their areas. Participation in recent initiatives such as the New Deal for Communities, Best Value and exercised sustainable development frameworks indicates that these powers are being taken up.

More than 25 *non-ministerial public bodies* are involved in advising on issues relating to sustainable development. They include the Advisory Committee on Business and the Environment and the Trades Union and Sustainable Development Advisory Committee. Many more bodies are involved in sustainable development at the sub-national, regional and local levels.

3.4   Institutional trends

The institutional framework for environmental management has undergone *significant changes* in recent years. A major *devolution of powers*, initiated in 1997, transferred some environmental policy authority from the central government to sub-national governments in Scotland, Wales and Northern Ireland. Legislative powers concerning environmental protection in Scotland were devolved from the UK Parliament to the newly established Scottish Parliament in 1998. While responsibility for international environmental agreements and green tax matters is still centralised, the sub-national administrations have assumed much responsibility for environmental policy formulation and virtually all responsibility for regulatory implementation and enforcement (Chapter 6, Section 3.5).

Concurrently, in England, there has been a strong trend towards *decentralisation* of environmental regulatory responsibility to regional and local levels. In 1994, eight regional entities were established in England. Among their mandates are promoting sustainable development and maximising regional competitiveness, prosperity and quality of life. Since 1998, each region has established a strategy and action plan on development, taking into account consultation with a range of stakeholders (e.g. business, trade union, educational and non-profit groups, including environmental NGOs). In addition, the Local Government Act expanded local authorities' powers to develop measures to improve environmental management.

At the central government level, the Department of the Environment handled environmental protection from 1970 to 1997. It was then merged with the Department of Transport to form the Department of Environment, Transport and the Regions (DETR). In a reshuffling of portfolios following the 2001 general election, the environment units of DETR were merged with the Ministry of Agriculture, Fisheries and Food to form the *Department for Environment, Food and Rural Affairs*. DEFRA's defined aim is to enhance the quality of life in the UK through the pursuit of sustainable development. To this end, it is to promote: i) a better environment; ii) thriving rural economies and communities; iii) diversity and abundance of wildlife; iv) a countryside for all to enjoy; and v) sustainable and diverse farming and food industries that work together to meet consumers' needs.

3.5   Sub-national authorities responsible for environmental regulation

England and Wales

The *Environment Agency* is responsible for environmental regulation and monitoring in England and Wales. Created by the 1995 Environment Act, the agency took over the functions of the National Rivers Authority and Her Majesty's Inspectorate of Pollution, as well as certain responsibilities of local authorities (e.g. regulation of waste management). The agency's principle aim is to protect and enhance the environment as a contribution to the UK's sustainable development. With a staff of 10 500, the Environment Agency regulates water and air quality and waste management using IPC (and, increasingly, IPPC) (Chapter 6, Section 2.1). Its other responsibilities include nature conservation, flood defence and management of water resources and fisheries. The agency's central office in Bristol develops policies and strategies, with operational objectives, while its eight regional offices are primarily responsible for implementation at the local level.

In 2000, 77% of the agency's total *operational budget* of GBP 655 million was funded by cost-recovery regulatory mechanisms (e.g. licences and inspection fees) and flood defence levies. The remainder came from government grants. Environment Agency expenditure in 2000 was dominated by flood defence (45%) and environmental protection (33%), followed by water resource management (15%), fisheries (4%), and recreation, conservation and navigation (3%).

Scotland

The *Scottish Environment Protection Agency* is the primary regulatory and enforcement body for pollution control in Scotland. It regulates air, water and land pollution control and the storage, transport and disposal of controlled waste and radioactive material. Established under the 1995 Environment Act, SEPA assumed the responsibilities of the River Purification Authorities and Her Majesty's Industrial Pollution Inspectorate, as well as some environmental management responsibilities of district and island councils (e.g. waste regulation and air pollution control). Its main aim is to provide "an efficient and integrated environmental protection system for Scotland which will both improve the environment and contribute to the Government's goal of sustainable development".

SEPA's *operating budget*, which includes income from charges and grants, rose from GBP 32 million in 1999 to GBP 40 million in 2001. Staff numbers increased from 670 to over 800 during the period. SEPA is phasing in the IPPC regime in Scotland, with some 2 000 installations expected to be covered by 2007 (including Part B installations). Charges for inspection and consultation are administered to recover regulatory costs, in conformance with the polluter pays principle.

Northern Ireland

The *Industrial Pollution and Radiochemical Inspectorate (IPRI)* is responsible for enforcing pollution control regulations at prescribed industrial sources in Northern Ireland. Under the Industrial Pollution Control (Northern Ireland) Order of 1997, IPRI inspectors issue permits and monitor operators' performance against the conditions therein. IPRI is also responsible for regulating the storage, use and disposal of radioactive material.

7

ENVIRONMENTAL – SOCIAL INTERFACE*

Recommendations

The following recommendations are part of the overall conclusions and recommendations of the Environmental Performance Review of the United Kingdom:

- take concerted action to reduce *disparities in risk exposure* and access to environmental services;

- monitor implementation and assure proper enforcement of *countryside access and rights of way*;

- further strengthen the *integration of environmental targets and actions* in initiatives to combat social exclusion and deprivation, and seek to ensure that social *compensation measures* do not undermine the effectiveness of environmental policies;

- assure effective integration of environmental objectives in *local partnership approaches* to sustainable development;

- provide for improved *legal standing of NGOs* in courts and pursue implementation of recent legislation concerning access to environmental information.

---

* The present chapter reviews progress in the last ten years, and particularly since the previous OECD Environmental Performance Review of 1994. It also reviews progress with respect to the objective "social and environmental interface" of the 2001 OECD Environmental Strategy.

© OECD 2002

Conclusions

The environmental-social interface has taken on new importance in the UK's sustainable development strategy. Improving environmental quality and resource efficiency is among the objectives of local initiatives to combat *social exclusion and deprivation*. Disparities in exposure to pollution and the distributive effects of environment-related measures are increasingly considered in policy design and assessment. Legislation concerning countryside access and rights of way has been reinforced. *Access to environmental information* has improved, and broad-based consultation is current practice. Extensive databases on the state of the environment have been established, and particular emphasis has been put on developing and using "headline" indicators of sustainable development. Consumer campaigns have helped raise *environmental awareness* and influence behaviour. Partnership approaches are promoted, and have helped improve environmental management and integration. *Environmental NGOs* are major actors in the environmental and sustainable development debate and activities, not only at the local, regional and national levels but also in international contexts such as the EU and the IUCN. Environmental and sustainable development *education* and learning have been reinforced by a wide range of measures, including an update of the national curriculum.

However, substantial *disparities in environmental quality* persist and generally are associated with socio-economic imbalances, resulting in significant inequality in health status and death rates. Distributive effects of environmental or environment-related policies are not systematically taken into account in planning. Countryside access and rights of way still require significant improvement to meet objectives. Regional development agencies have missed opportunities to promote truly integrated approaches to sustainable development with a strong environmental-social dimension. Local partnership approaches (e.g. Local Agenda 21 and community strategies) should be further strengthened, and performance assessment of local authorities in programmes such as Best Value should include systematic reviews of progress in environmental management and sustainable development. *Public support* for use of economic instruments is fading, partly because of inadequate communication strategies (e.g. concerning the roles of energy and transport taxation in achieving environmental objectives). Recent legislation concerning access to environmental information needs to be fully implemented. *Access to courts* is limited, de facto, for NGOs, which have no explicit right to stand on behalf of nature and the environment. Stakeholder participation in the *planning* of large-scale investment projects should not be restricted, but rather made more effective.

In designing and implementing its sustainable development strategy, the UK particularly emphasises the social dimension and its integration with the economic and environmental dimensions. Sustainable development itself is perceived as implying an improved social context (Chapter 7, Section 2.1), as reflected in the title of the strategy: "A Better Quality of Life". It puts much emphasis on *combating social exclusion and promoting sustainable communities*. Disparities in exposure to pollution and environmental degradation, as well as in the distributive effects of economic instruments used to help implement environmental policy, are major concerns. Environment is perceived not only as a problem but also as an asset, particularly in local development planning. Environmental quality and access to nature and the countryside are increasingly seen as conditions for enhancement of living and working conditions.

1.   Evaluation of Performance

1.1   Disparities in environmental quality

Disparities in exposure

Disparities in exposure to *pollution and environmental risks* are the subject of great concern in the UK. Studies have shown that poorer households are more exposed to industrial pollution. Thus, measures to reduce pollution from factories would clearly be socially progressive. In England and Wales, almost two-thirds of the most polluting industrial facilities are located in areas with below-average household income levels. Industrial facilities regulated under the integrated pollution control (IPC) system are concentrated in 1 300 of the country's 8 000 postcode areas. *Risky IPC sites* are found in 25% of neighbourhoods where average household income is below GBP 15 000, but in only 4% of areas with income above GBP 25 000. Exposure in low-income areas is 50% higher than it would be if IPC sites were randomly distributed, and in high-income areas it is 75% lower (Table 7.1). The correlation of environmental risk exposure and household income level is particularly strong in London and the north-east: over 75% of all IPC sites in these two areas are in districts with lower than average household income.

A study analysing spatial distribution of *air emissions of carcinogenic chemicals* in England found that, among 8 400 local community wards classified according to the Government's Index of Multiple Deprivation, the most deprived 20% of wards received over 80% of such emissions while the least deprived 50% of wards received less than 8%.

Analysis of some of the "headline" indicators of sustainable development in the English regions and Wales reveals: i) significant *territorial disparities*, in particular between the south of England and the north plus Wales; and ii) many *positive correlations* among economic, social and environmental factors. A comparison of economic, social and environmental conditions and trends in *south-eastern and north-eastern* England is most revealing. Expressed in percentage points against the England average, the gap in GDP per capita is 33%, after continuing to widen during the 1990s, with GDP per capita growth five percentage points higher in the south-east and seven points lower in the north-east. In the south-east only 7% of the working age population lives in workless households, while the north-eastern share is almost twice that. More than two-thirds of single elderly households live in fuel poverty in the north-east, against fewer than half in the south-east. The average rate of waste recycling is 13.6% in the south-east, 3.7% in the north-east. Only with respect to river water quality does the north-east outperform the south-east (Table 7.2).

Table 7.1   **Disparities in exposure to industrial pollution risk,** England and Wales

Areas[a]		Industrial facilities (number)	IPC facilities[b] (number)	Share (%)	Deviation from random distribution (%)	
					IPC sites	IPC processes
Low income areas	< GBP 10 000	406	104	26	54	64
	GBP 10-15 000	2 313	558	24	45	66
Medium income areas	GBP15-20 000	2 769	461	17	0	–5
High income areas	GBP 20-25 000	1 704	168	10	–41	–61
	> GBP 25 000	737	29	4	–76	–85
Total		7 929	1 320	17	0	0

a) Post code areas by average household income.
b) Industrial facilities regulated under the integrated pollution control system.
Source: Friends of the Earth; OECD.

Health effects of pollution exposure

The UK holds that reducing air pollution brings *substantial social benefits*. An economic analysis of the national air quality strategy objectives for 2005 concluded that the number of premature deaths would fall by some 18 500 per year, and that annual hospital admissions would fall by 22 000.

The government has commissioned several studies of the human *health effects of exposure to air pollution*. In urban areas of Great Britain (England, Wales and Scotland), exposure to PM_{10} was found to have caused the premature death of

Table 7.2   **Regional disparities in selected headline indicators,** England and Wales, late 1990s

	Economic performance and employment				Social exclusion and poverty		
	GDP per capita		Employment rate[c]	Workless people[d]	Crime rate[e]	Fuel poverty[f]	
	Level[a]	Change[b]					
England average (%)	100	15	75.0	11	1.34	60	
	Percentage point deviation from England average (+ desirable/– undesirable)						
London	27	2	–4.7	–3	–1.30	8	
South East	14	5	5.5	4	0.39	12	
South West	–10	0	3.6	2	0.44	–1	
East	11	0	3.1	3	0.52	6	
East Midlands	–7	–1	1.3	2	0.12	–1	
West Midlands	–11	–4	–1.8	0	–0.19	–2	
Yorkshire and the Humber	–14	–2	–1.1	–2	0.38	–13	
North East	–23	–7	–6.9	–2	0.33	–11	
North West	–14	–6	–2.1	–6	–0.01	–7	
Wales	–23	–7	–5.5	–5	–0.04	. .	

	Environmental management and quality		
	Brownfield rehabilitation[g]	Waste recycling[h]	River quality[i]
England average (%)	54	9.4	63
	Percentage point deviation from England average (+ desirable/– undesirable)		
London	28	–1.3	–37
South East	2	4.2	–5
South West	–19	5.0	15
East	–2	2.4	–35
East Midlands	–18	–0.4	–13
West Midlands	–4	–2.4	–7
Yorkshire and the Humber	–2	–3.3	–7
North East	–1	–5.7	22
North West	11	–3.0	–3
Wales	. .	–4.1	30

Note: Calculations based on regional data for selected headline indicators of sustainable development (H1 to H15):
a) H1   1998   GDP per capita (England = GBP 12 768).
b) H1   1990-98   GDP per capita growth (in real terms).
c) H3   2000   % of working age people in work (May-July).
d) H4   2000   % of working age people in workless households.
e) H8   1999-00   Violent crime per 100 inhabitants.
f) H4   1996   % of single elderly (aged > 60) households in fuel poverty.
g) H14   1996   % of new homes built on previously developed land.
h) H15   1998-99   % of household waste recycled or composted.
i) H12   1999   % of river length with "good" chemical river quality (average, England and Wales: 63%).
Source: DEFRA; OECD.

8 100 persons, and the figure for SO_2 was 3 500. High ambient concentrations of PM_{10} and SO_2 were associated with, respectively, about 10 000 and 3 500 additional hospital admissions per year for respiratory diseases in urban areas. The two together represent nearly 3% of total annual respiratory-related deaths and hospital admissions in urban Britain. The contribution of *ozone* was estimated at 12 500 premature deaths and 9 900 additional hospital admissions for respiratory disease during the summer months. Health impact estimates for other pollutants, including NO_x and CO, are considered less certain, but NO_2-related hospital admissions were estimated at 8 700 per year. With respect to *asthma and outdoor air pollution*, no significant association has been identified between high pollution events or locations and the initiation or aggravation of asthma. Thus, while asthma has increased sharply over the past three decades, this is probably not the result of changes in outdoor air emissions.

Health effects of climate change in the UK have also been studied. Cases of *skin cancer* are estimated to be increasing by 5 000 per year and cataracts by 2 000. *Flood disasters*, already on the rise, are projected to be much more significant. While in general the health effects of air pollution are seen as declining, cases of *high ozone levels* in summer are likely to grow more frequent, leading to several thousand extra deaths and hospital admissions. The UK now has the highest winter excess mortality in western Europe, with an estimated 60 000 to 80 000 cold-related deaths. Assuming a future increase of 1% per year in greenhouse gas emissions, cold-related deaths are expected to fall by 20 000 cases per year. In turn, *heat-related deaths* are likely to increase from 800 to 2 800 cases and the number of *food poisoning* cases is expected to double.

Between 1993 and 1997, the number of major and significant *water pollution incidents* fell by nearly 80%, from 7 000 to 1 500; presumably, associated human health risks have also declined, although to what extent has not been measured. Replacing lead water pipes will be a major issue in coming years, as the majority of housing stock is quite old. Complaints about *noise levels* have risen steeply since the early 1990s. About 200 000 noise-related complaints are received annually in England and Wales. Most are settled informally, with abatement notices served on around 15% of confirmed cases and prosecution on less than 1%.

Access to nature and rights of way

Access to the countryside and rights of way constitute an important feature of the UK debate on the environmental-social interface (Chapter 7, Section 2.3). Several laws grant rights to use footpaths and open space, but actual use and enforcement are subject to much controversy. With the 2000 *Countryside and Rights of Way Act*, the government is working to improve and reinforce public access. As a first step, detailed maps are being produced, indicating the areas of mountain, moor, heath, down and common land to which the new "freedom to roam" will apply. There has been full public consultation on the maps. The government is also providing moderate funding for NGOs to research "lost ways" that may ultimately be included on the definitive map of rights of way. Footpaths and bridleways dating from before 1949 but not recorded on the definitive map by 2025 will not be included. Authorities now have better legal bases on which to secure the removal of obstructions.

1.2   Distributive effects of environmental policy

Environment-related taxation

While the UK is committed to using economic instruments for achieving efficient resource use and integration of environmental externalities, there is scope for significant further steps to be taken. To some extent, this gap reflects a concern that strict internalisation of external environmental costs and benefits might conflict with social considerations on fairness and poverty. One example often cited is the decision in 2000 not to apply the *fuel duty escalator* automatically but to decide on duties annually. This action, however, was motivated only in part by social concerns, and no detailed assessment of the actual distributive effects was ever made. In fact, the higher fuel prices that led to the halt had more to do with international oil price rises than with the fuel duty. Opposition to further increases in the duty also stemmed from its being perceived as a revenue raising mechanism rather than as a tool for providing environmental guidance. In particular, critics noted that the revenue was not even partly earmarked for purposes such as promoting environmental management or public transport. This misunderstanding shows that the rationale for environment-related taxes needs to be properly communicated, based on sound analyses of the taxes' actual impact with respect to environmental effectiveness, economic efficiency and competitiveness, as well as to their social implications.

Tax relief and exemptions, often argued for on social grounds, can seriously undermine achievement of environmental objectives. Energy efficiency in the housing sector is an example (Chapter 8). In many other OECD countries, households tend to bear the main burden of adjustments required to combat climate change, but UK households are exempt from the *climate change levy*. Furthermore, instead of the standard *VAT rate* of 17.5%, the UK applies a reduced VAT of 5% to household heating fuel. The UK is the only EU country that applies no VAT to water supply, waste water and waste treatment services.

This suggests that any initiative to increase *economic incentives* for environmental management needs to be accompanied by convincing evidence and, if necessary, targeted measures assuring a double environmental-social dividend. The present policy response to the social concern about *fuel poverty* can be considered a step in the right direction. Rather than subsidising fuel use, the New Home Energy Efficiency Scheme (2000) provides targeted incentives to improve home energy efficiency, thus reducing heating costs, energy use and related emissions while improving comfort and health for the poor (Chapter 6).

Affordability, prices and charges

With the privatisation of water companies and reductions in water-related social assistance, *pricing of water and waste water* services became a key issue in the debate on social implications of environmental management. Between 1989 and 1992, discon-nections of households from the water supply as a result of unpaid bills increased from about 8 000 a year to over 20 000. After several measures to assure affordability of water charges, however, such service cuts were reduced to about 1 000 by 1998. The installation of some 15 000 prepaid water meters, leading to automatic disconnection if not paid, was judged illegal by the High Court in 1998. Now, under the 1999 Water Industry Act, water supply cuts to households are forbidden.

In England and Wales, the Office of Water Services (OFWAT) regulates the level of water prices. Between 1994 and 1998, the share of households spending more than 3% of their income on water charges fell from 22% to 18%. Since 1993, the ten private water companies in England and Wales have set up *water charity trusts* that offer assistance to people having difficulty paying their bills. The activities of these trusts often go even further, involving broader anti-poverty actions. In Scotland, the water industry has not been privatised, but water and sewerage charges have increased to fund necessary investments. The Scottish Executive has launched detailed analyses and consultations, with the aim of establishing a system of water and sewerage charges that is economically efficient, affordable and socially fair.

The Water Industry Act allows people who would benefit from a measured charge to opt for *metering*. OFWAT formally opposes universal domestic metering on cost-benefit grounds, but supports selective metering. It would be used where new resources are scarce (and hence expensive), where households consume significant amounts of discretionary water (especially for garden watering) and where the initial installation costs are relatively low (most notably for new homes). Two water companies, Anglian and Yorkshire, have had to cancel plans for compulsory metering in recent years because of determined public opposition.

1.3   Environment-related employment

Despite extensive economic analysis of environmental management and policy matters, the related *labour market implications* have not generally been studied in great detail in the UK. Both employer associations and trade unions assert that environmental improvement has not led to a net loss of jobs, but such assessments are based only on partial empirical evidence. So far research into the relationship between environment and employment in the UK has been promoted primarily by environmental NGOs and the European Commission.

A recent EU-wide study modelling the employment effects of pollution control and resource management concluded that in the UK some 465 000 jobs were directly or indirectly related to eco-industries, equivalent to 1.7% of total employment (Figure 7.1). Over 80% of the *environment-related jobs* were directly linked to pollution control (58%) and resource management (24%). While 70% of the direct employment stems from waste and waste water management, 30% is related to investment, particularly for water supply infrastructure. Regional development agencies in the UK have begun to pay greater attention to environment-related activities and employment in the private sector, estimating such employment to total 196 000 jobs. With respect to employment trends, the number of jobs in the water industry has declined steadily in the past decade, while in waste management and material recycling employment has increased and further growth is expected.

Several surveys have shown that *nature conservation* can have locally significant positive effects on employment, in particular if conservation strategies take economic and social concerns explicitly on board. A 1997 study calculated that nature conservation in Great Britain provides the equivalent of more than 10 000 full-time jobs. However, those who gain and those who bear the costs of nature conservation often do not coincide. In addressing such market failures, management agreements based on broad partnership approaches (e.g. involving local businesses, farmers, hunters, conservation NGOs, etc.) have generated promising results.

Other case studies, examining the potential employment effects of transition to more *sustainable production or transport*, concluded that, on balance, job losses tended to be more than offset by job gains, particularly where innovation leads to economic advantage. For example, one study analysed the employment implications of meeting the 2010 government target for road traffic reduction (–10% from the 1990 level), plus those of efficiency gains and shifts in transport modes. It calculated that the net direct employment impact would be up to 120 000 added jobs. In car-based industries more than 40 000 jobs would likely be lost, but with the introduction of new car technologies and higher leasing rates, the net loss could probably be limited to less than 10 000. The job gains would come primarily from rail investment and operation.

The New Deal programme to combat youth unemployment includes environmental activities: the *Environment Task Force* allows young people to get involved in a wide range of environmental projects and to acquire skills and experiences that can

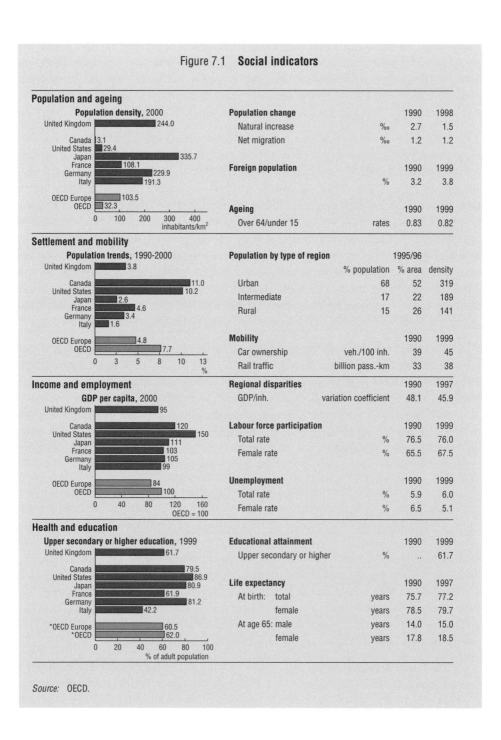

Figure 7.1   **Social indicators**

Source: OECD.

improve their employability. Although first evaluations show that only about half the participants found sustained employment immediately after taking part in the New Deal, the overall assessment is clearly positive, especially if compared to traditional unemployment assistance. Not only did recruits gain work experience, self-esteem and skills, but the environmental projects set up by local partnerships have improved environmental conditions both locally and beyond.

1.4   Environmental awareness and education

Awareness and attitudes

Over the past 15 years, regular surveys in England have monitored public attitudes to the environment. They have found *concern about the environment* increasing on all types of issues. In 2001, people were in general "very worried" about pollution, with disposal of hazardous waste topping the list (66%). Against the background of out-breaks of "mad cow" and foot and mouth disease, concern about livestock management methods increased significantly, to 59%. Pollution of rivers, bathing waters and beaches is also of major concern to more than half the people interviewed. Traffic emissions (congestion, noise, fumes), climate change and its effects, and air pollution were the three issues that people thought would cause the most concern in 20 years' time.

Awareness does not automatically translate into action. The percentage of people who declare themselves to be "actively *pursuing environment-friendly practices*" (e.g. recycling, water and energy saving) has shown no significant increase, and major variations exist, particularly among age groups. The percentage of people aged 18-24 undertaking environment-friendly activities is generally lower than that of other age classes. While concern about climate change is high, knowledge about potential causes is low. Fewer than half the people responding to a 1996/97 survey thought emissions from transport were a major factor in global warming. Only 12% thought household gas or electricity use was a major factor. These findings confirm the need for continued, well-targeted initiatives to strengthen environmental education and awareness raising.

Environmental and sustainable development education

Environmental education has figured on the *UK school curriculum* since the 1960s. Various national organisations were established to develop, promote and review environmental education practices and performance. With the 1988 Education Reform Act, the government assumed responsibility for setting the education agenda by establishing a national curriculum that formally recognised environmental educa-tion as a cross-curricular theme. Yet, in practice, it has often proved difficult to find a place for cross-curricular themes on schools' timetables. In the early 1990s, the government departments covering education and environment began to work together more closely. Nevertheless, a 1996 review of environmental education recommended better co-ordination between them and other stakeholders.

In 1998, the government created the *Sustainable Development Education Panel*, with members from business, local government, education and the voluntary sector. The panel's purpose is to identify gaps, opportunities, priorities and partnerships for action in providing sustainable development education in England, and to highlight good practices. The broadening of the remit from "environmental" to "sustainable development" education reflected a desire to increase attention to social and economic driving forces and impacts. The panel set up groups on schooling; higher and further education; the workplace; and the general public and households. The panel had significant input into the *1999 revision of the national curriculum*, which declares that pupils "should develop awareness and understanding of, and respect for, the environments in which they live, and secure their commitment to sustainable development at a personal, national and global level". The panel's *annual reports* provide detailed overviews on all dimensions of environmental and sustainable development education, dealing not only with formal education in schools, but also addressing informal and adult learning, professional training in the workplace, etc. Each report makes concrete recommendations for further improvement.

A network of newly established bodies, some employer-led (e.g. Sector Skills Councils), others linked to trade unions or academic institutions, has further promoted sustainable development learning in sectoral skills development and *workplace learning programmes*.

Consumer campaigns

In 1998, a review by the *National Consumer Council* criticised government activities aimed at raising environmental awareness as "somewhat diffuse and bitty", "failing to present a coherent, readily accessible message" and even "creating confusion in people's minds". In response, the government initiated a campaign called "*Are You Doing Your Bit?*" A similar initiative has been launched in Scotland under the slogan "*do a little – change a lot*". The aim is to motivate people to take action benefiting their local and global environment by making small but important behavioural changes in their everyday lives. Campaign messages are diffused through high-profile promotions in national media, including TV, radio and press advertising, posters and a mobile exhibition. Campaign literature, posters and websites (such as *www.doingyourbit.org.uk*) help disseminate the campaign's messages and support promotional activity. Surveys found that people are aware of the campaign (over 80%), its slogans (almost 70%) and its logos (over 50%), and that it had induced significant behaviour changes, especially where environmental improvement goes hand-in-hand with economic savings, such as improving energy efficiency.

1.5   Environmental information and reporting

Access to information

The UK has reinforced the legal basis for assuring improved access to environmental information and made *significant progress* in this respect, in line with OECD recommendations, EU directives and the Aarhus Convention. The 1991 Citizen's Charter aimed at making public bodies more responsive to requests from the public and allowing for greater openness. Following passage of the 1990 EU directive on freedom of access to environmental information, new statutory arrangements came into force, such as the 1992 Guidance on the Implementation of Environmental Information Regulations. The 1994 Open Government Code of Practice, although not statutory, provided guidance on what type of information could be obtained.

The 2000 *Freedom of Information Act*, being phased in from 2002, provides the public with legally enforceable rights to information, establishes an independent appeal mechanism and encourages proactive dissemination of information. It is a major step towards greater openness and accountability. Its implementation will require a significant change in administrative tradition, particularly as information requests are to be answered at no charge. In the past, high fees sometimes limited access to environmentally relevant information. For example, local authorities often charged GBP 100 or more for copies of planning applications and environmental statements (though inspection of such documents is free of charge).

Environmental data and indicators

The UK has a plethora of data and indicator sets on environmental conditions and trends, related socio-economic pressures and societal and policy responses. Several institutions are involved in environmental data collection, processing and dissemination at national, regional and local level. For England and Wales, a *National Forum for Environmental Monitoring* has been established, aiming at better co-ordination of environmental monitoring and reporting. The Environment Agency has recognised the need to improve environmental data management. On behalf of the Department for Environment, Food and Rural Affairs (DEFRA), the National Environmental Technology Centre manages the *National Air Quality Information Archive*, receiving hourly information on air pollution levels recorded at 112 sites across the UK. The Natural Environment Research Council, the Countryside Agency, devolved administrations and other bodies also maintain data sets.

With this *proliferation of environmental databases*, often not sufficiently harmonised, there is a risk of inconsistent and non-comparable results. To avoid gaps, overlaps and inconsistencies, better co-ordination is needed on activities related to monitoring, data collection, treatment and dissemination. Continued efforts are required to assure full coverage, comparability and consistency of environment-related indicators.

The UK has established a comprehensive set of *150 core sustainable development indicators*, now consistently used in all government reporting related to sustainable development performance (Chapter 7, Section 2.2). Among these are the *15 headline indicators* primarily aimed at raising awareness of key issues on the part of the public and policy makers. For England and Wales, this set is also broken down by region (Table 7.2). The Scottish Executive publishes a set of 24 sustainable development indicators with particular emphasis on resource use, energy, travel and social justice.

Dissemination and government reporting

Modern information technologies provide new opportunities for large-scale, cost-effective dissemination of environmental information. Through their websites, DEFRA and other ministries and agencies provide vast amounts of up-to-date information on environmental protection legislation, strategies, programmes and reports. The Environment Agency pollution inventory website, launched in 1999, provides extensive information on IPC sites, landfill sites, sewage works, river and bathing water quality, radioactive substances and flood risks, though time-series data for many environmental indicators are not available. The "What's in Your Backyard" feature on the Environment Agency website provides GIS-based maps, allowing the user to zoom from the national level to sub-national, regional and local. The number of electronic information requests to the Environment Agency is growing, from 680 000 visits to its website in 1997 to over 3 million in 2001.

The Environment Agency website has become the main channel for delivering *state of the environment reports*. The government emphasis in reporting has shifted from simple state of the environment reporting towards broader monitoring of sustainable development progress (Chapter 7, Section 2.2). The Environment Agency's annual "Spotlight on Business Environmental Performance" report creates a significant incentive for individual companies to ensure that they meet environmental standards. It ranks companies on lists of 30 "good performers" and "poor performers", based on number of court appearances, prosecuted offences and total amount of fines.

Private enterprise environmental reporting

To complement its own reporting, the government strongly encourages the business community to improve its environment-related reporting. In 2000, in a keynote speech to the Confederation of British Industry, the prime minister challenged the *top 350 companies* to be publishing annual environmental reports by the end of 2001. The impact of the challenge was marginal: by the deadline, 79 of the companies had actually produced such reports (of which 60 were already doing so) and only 24 of the others had indicated their intention to follow suit. Nevertheless, business reporting is likely to improve significantly in coming years since large *managers of large UK funds* have announced that they will make their investments dependent on environmental reporting.

The pressure on big firms to provide substantive environmental reports was further heightened by an amendment to the Pensions Act in 2000. *Pension trustees* now must state "the extent (if at all) to which social, environmental or ethical considerations are taken into account in the selection, retention and realisation of investments". Increasingly, funds are defining their investment policies and demanding proper reporting on performance with respect to environmental and social goals from companies in their portfolio. Concern for companies' reputations is likely to be a major impetus for providing sound environmental reporting rather than mere "greenwash" reports. The UK branch of the Association of Chartered Certified Accountants gives annual Environmental Reporting Awards to companies issuing high-quality reports.

1.6   Participation and access to courts

Environmental NGOs and other civil society groups

The UK has a *large number of strong environmental NGOs* engaged in practical projects and lobbying on policies related to environmental quality and biodiversity (Chapter 5). Some have a long history. For example, the Royal Society for the Protection of Birds was founded in 1889 to combat the extinction of bird species due to the plumage trade and use of feathers in fashion items. It is now Europe's largest wildlife conservation NGO and has an annual budget of about GBP 50 million. The UK branch of WWF also manages a significant annual budget (GBP 27 million). Membership in environmental NGOs has long been increasing. The UK branches of international environmental NGOs, such as WWF, Friends of the Earth and Greenpeace, are among the strongest in Europe in terms of *membership, resources and professional capacity* for analytical work and lobbying. The UK's environmental NGOs also tend to be very active internationally. Some have invested significant amounts of time, staff and money in setting up EU-wide NGO networks such as Birdlife International. Through *international knowledge transfer, capacity building and support* for practical projects, they support environmental initiatives and stakeholders in countries with weaker environmental NGOs.

Other civil society organisations are increasingly concerned about and actively dealing with environmental matters. In line with the principles of sustainable development, many social and economic development initiatives are integrating environmental issues and actions into their agendas. Neighbourhood regeneration programmes such as the Groundwork Trust combine efforts to combat social exclusion with those against environmental degradation. Housing associations such as the Peabody Trust deal with environmental issues related to sustainable construction and energy efficiency. Consumer groups, women's associations and others deal with environment-related food and health risks and issues such as waste management; an example is the Women's Environmental Network. Some groups address environmental issues with a special focus on ethnic minorities.

Stakeholder participation

Statutory provisions for public participation are long established in UK town and country planning. In other areas, such as pollution control, nature conservation and water resource management, fewer opportunities for public participation have been offered until recently. Setting standards and licensing under IPC was considered a primarily technical process, with no need for public input. In recent years, more active involvement of the public and other stakeholders has been facilitated through opinion surveys, consultation documents, public meetings and inquiries. For example, in setting up local biodiversity action plans, explicit measures were undertaken to encourage public and stakeholder participation in developing local strategies to help achieve national biodiversity targets.

There is concern, however, that participation might be leading to unproductive delays rather than improved decision making. Hence, the government intends to change *planning procedures* to provide a "fast track" for major infrastructure investments. Parliament could grant permission for a wide range of large-scale projects, such as quarries, open-cast mines, chemical plants, waste incinerators, nuclear plants, airports and major roads. The local population would no longer have the right to challenge at public hearings "the principle need for, or location of major developments". Instead, their influence would be limited to matters of local detail. NGO representatives question whether stakeholder participation is really delaying large-scale projects unreasonably. They note that only ten projects in the past 15 years had public consultation periods lasting more than three months. Where there are unproductive conflicts, these may result from *participation being phased in too late* in the decision-making process. Delays could thus be avoided by incorporating participation earlier, closer to the more strategic policy design and planning phases.

Access to courts

Under present UK legislation, *applicants* for planning permission, water discharge consents or IPPC licences can appeal unfavourable decisions. Other parties have such rights only if directly affected. Third parties, like environmental NGOs, normally have no chance to stand in court for the common interest, though they can launch a judicial review on the formal, procedural aspects of a decision. With respect to substance (merits appeal), parties have to prove that their immediate rights are at stake. This disparity in favour of the applicants has been interpreted as a "pro-development" bias. There is concern that existing arrangements for involving objectors in decision making may conflict with the spirit and objectives of the Aarhus Convention. The 2000 government green paper on planning concluded that a *third party right of appeal* could add to the costs and uncertainties of planning, a prospect not acceptable to the government. In contrast, the Royal Commission on Environmental Pollution, a high-level government advisory body, has argued that the costs represented by changes and delays would be a price worth paying to ensure that environmental considerations are given their proper weight. The commission predicted that improved quality in applications for development would result. It thus recommended that third parties should have a right of appeal against decisions on planning applications in certain circumstances, and that similar rights should be introduced for other forms of environmental regulation. It has also been proposed that establishing an *environmental court* or tribunal, as a "one-stop-shop" to handle all aspects of environmental disputes, would further strengthen public confidence. So far, no government initiative has been taken on this proposal.

1.7   Local Agenda 21 and community strategies

To achieve a better quality of life both now and in the future, the notion of sustainable development needs to be translated into real action and tangible results. The general concept of integration must be reflected in concrete decisions in which priorities are established, trade-offs optimised and synergies found. Local authorities, along with broad-based public-private partnerships, are playing an important role in moving towards more *sustainable community development*. UK local authorities were quick to respond to the request at the 1992 Rio summit for local sustainable development strategies. By 1996, the UK was recognised as a world leader in the preparation of *Local Agenda 21* plans. Of the 2 000 started worldwide by then, 300 were in the UK, and half of all UK local authorities were involved. Most of these early strategies focused primarily on environmental issues. This began to change when the government launched several other economic and social policies that also relied heavily on area-specific, participatory, bottom-up approaches to local development.

Since 1994, *local regeneration policies* have been integrating social, environmental and economic objectives. Government funding, hitherto channelled through 14 separate programmes, was integrated into a single regeneration budget to be used by local partnerships of key stakeholders. The problems of each area are unique, so priorities for local regeneration vary according to location. All local partnerships, however, must systematically tackle the following key challenges: poor job prospects; high crime levels; educational underachievement; poor health; housing problems; and pollution and environmental degradation. In 1997 the prime minister set up a Social Exclusion Unit to help improve government action in this area. It was instrumental in developing an integrated approach to the development of sustainable communities in deprived areas through the Neighbourhood Renewal programme. An Active Community Unit was also established to set targets and funding priorities for capacity building so that individuals and NGOs might become more actively involved in community development. The 1998 New Deal for Communities is working closely with 39 partnerships across England. The *Neighbourhood Renewal Fund* provides additional resources of GBP 900 million over three years for the 88 most deprived local authorities in England. Funding is not earmarked and can be used in any way that will tackle the deprivation in these areas.

All these initiatives have certain common features. With regard to *content*, they include better integration of social, economic and environmental concerns. With regard to *method*, there is a growing emphasis on local involvement and empowerment. It should be noted that environment is no longer identified only as a pollution problem, but increasingly is also understood as a development asset. This evolution is also reflected in the more recent Local Agenda 21 approaches. The prime minister set a target for all English and Welsh local authorities to have a Local Agenda 21 strategy in place by the end of 2000. Over 90% met the deadline. Building on that progress towards more integrated, participatory local development, the *2000 Local Government Act* requires local authorities to prepare community strategies. These must promote or improve the economic, social and environmental well-being of the local government area, thereby contributing to the achievement of sustainable development in the UK. Similar programmes for Scotland are under preparation.

Existing Local Agenda 21 strategies provide the starting point for community strategies. Each community strategy is being developed through "*local strategic partnerships*" that bring together the various parts of the public sector at local level as well as private business, the community and the voluntary sector. Much attention is paid to *monitoring progress in implementation* of all these initiatives. The Best Value system requires a local authority to review all its functions periodically, consulting local people and measuring its performance in a way that can be checked by an independent auditor. To assure proper coverage of the environmental dimension, the Best Value indicator set should be enlarged in line with the proposals in the handbook for local sustainable development indicators (Chapter 7, Section 2.2). To be effective, local initiatives need to operate in a supportive national and regional context. Sustainable development should thus become a more explicit priority in regional development planning and policy. In particular, the remit of the regional development agencies needs to be reviewed (Chapter 6, Section 1.2).

2. Focus on Selected Topics

2.1 Social context

Population trends

The UK *population* numbers close to 60 million (England: 49.9, Wales: 2.9, Scotland: 5.1, Northern Ireland: 1.7). With about 245 inhabitants per square kilometre, the country is *densely populated*. More than two-thirds of the inhabitants live in urban areas, including the London, Birmingham, Manchester, Liverpool, Newcastle and Glasgow metropolitan areas. In contrast, in parts of south-western and northern England, Wales, Northern Ireland and, in particular, Scotland, significant stretches of the countryside have well below 50 inhabitants per square kilometre.

During the 1990s, the UK population increased by 3.8%. The *natural balance*, although still positive, was shrinking, while *net migration* was rising. The percentage of *foreign population* rose from 3.2% to 3.8%. London and the south-east are the regions where international migration has the biggest impact on population growth; in 1999 their net balance was 136 000, compared to a UK total of 182 000. In internal migration, most of rural England experienced positive net migration. Here population growth was significantly higher than the national average, while rural Wales and Scotland continued to lose population. These changes in settlement correspond with new patterns of *commuting and mobility*. Car ownership increased from 39 to 45 vehicles per 100 inhabitants during the 1990s, and rail traffic rose from 33 to 38 billion passenger-kilometres (Figure 6.2).

Contrary to the situation in many other OECD countries, the UK *ageing index* (age > 64/< 15) remained almost stable at 0.82, not least because of the inflow of foreign population. Life expectancy at birth increased over the decade from 75.7 to 77.2 years. After age 65, men in the UK can now expect to live to 80, women to over 83. These figures, however, remain below the OECD average, and are the lowest among G7 countries. *Life expectancy varies significantly* by socio-economic status: those in professional and managerial occupations live almost ten years longer than those in partly skilled and unskilled occupations.

Poverty, unemployment and other social indicators

At USD 21 000, *per capita GDP* is 5% lower than the OECD average, and the lowest among the G7 countries. Regional variation is significant, with average per capita regional GDP differing by almost 50% from the national average, though this variation diminished somewhat over the 1990s. *Poverty* persists, with over 10% of households earning more than 50% below the median income level. The excess winter mortality rate, partly a result of inadequate housing and heating, is the highest in western Europe, at over 30 000 deaths per year. In 1996, 1.5 million homes (7.2% of the housing stock) were judged unfit to live in.

Labour force participation is 76% for those aged 15-64. Over the 1990s, male participation slightly declined, while female participation increased. Even as the total UK labour force increased by 1.5%, total employment rose by 3%. At close to 6% the *unemployment rate* is at about the OECD average. Unlike in most other countries, the unemployment rate is lower for women than for men. Youth unemployment is twice as high as the UK average.

Education levels of the adult population are close to the OECD average, with 62% of those aged 25-64 having upper secondary or higher education. However, compared to most other countries, over the past decade there has been little progress in improving this rate. The prevalence of *drug use* among the population aged 15 and above is the highest among EU countries, and drug-related death rates are close to US levels. *Crime rates* and incarceration rates are also among the EU's highest.

2.2   *Sustainable development indicators*

The UK has developed tools for quantitative measurement of progress towards sustainable development. Following the release of the 1994 sustainable development strategy, a set of 118 preliminary indicators was published, largely covering environmental issues. They were later reviewed and refined, with the social, economic and international dimensions of sustainable development better covered. Around 60% of the 118 initial indicators then remained. The 1999 sustainable development strategy set out a new *core set of 150 sustainable development indicators*, now consistently used by the various ministries in their annual reporting related to sustainable development performance. First results were published that same year in a comprehensive report called "Quality of Life Counts".

A sub-set of *15 headline indicators* was selected as a "quality of life barometer" (Table 7.3). In addition to measuring overall progress, it is intended as a communication tool, helping to raise awareness of key issues on the part of the public and policy makers. For most of these 15 indicators, some improvement was achieved in the 1990s. However, unsustainable development trends have also been observed, notably as regards investment (its GDP share fell three percentage points over the decade, to 17%), violent crime (up by almost 30%), wildlife biodiversity (the farmland bird population declined by 18%) and municipal waste generation (up by about 15%) (Table 6.1).

The headline indicators have been *broken down by region* to reveal territorial differences in sustainable development performance and trends (Table 7.2). To provide guidance for sustainable development reporting at the local community level, a handbook called "Local Quality of Life Counts" was developed jointly by the Department for Environment, Transport and the Regions (DEFRA's predecessor), the Local Government Association, the Improvement and Development Agency, the Audit Commission, local authorities and Local Agenda 21 groups. It proposes *29 local sustainable development indicators*. Eight of them concern environment, 16 deal with

Table 7.3 **Headline indicators of sustainable development**

		Tendency[a]	Change 1990-98[b] (%)	Indicator specification
Economic output		+	+14	Real growth in GDP per capita
Investment		−	−3%p	Share of investment in total GDP
Employment		0	−1%p	Share of working age population in work
Poverty		0	Little change	Poverty and social exclusion indices
Education		+	+22%p	Share of population aged 19 with level 2 qualifications
Health		0	Little change	Healthy life expectancy
Housing		0	−0.4%p	Share of homes unfit to live in
Crime	Vehicle	+	−18	Crime rates per 100 000 inhabitants
	Burglary	+	−13	
	Violent	−	+29	
Climate change		+		
	GHG		−9	GHG emissions
	CO_2		−7	CO_2 emissions
Air quality		+	−58	Days with moderate or higher urban air pollution
Road traffic		0	+12	Motor vehicle miles
River water quality		+	+2	River length with good chemical water quality
Wildlife		−		Bird population indices
	All species		−5	
	Woodland		−12	
	Farmland		−18	
Land use		0	+2%p	Share of new homes built on previously developed land
Waste	Household		+14	Total household waste generation
	Other		No data	

a) Key: + = Significant change, in direction of meeting objective. 0 = No significant change. − = Significant change, in direction away from meeting objective.
b) For some indicators, latest available data predates 1998. %p = Change in share expressed in percentage points.
Source: DEFRA; OECD.

social issues and five are economic indicators. They cover the following areas: prudent use of resources (four indicators); protection of the environment (four); better health and education for all (three); access to local services and travel (six); shaping our surroundings (four); empowerment and participation (three); and sustainable local economy (five).

2.3   *Countryside access and rights of way*

Countryside access and rights of way are key features of the social-environmental relationship in UK environmental policy, reflecting long tradition. Attempts to pass a *freedom to roam* bill were made every year from 1884 to 1914. In 1932, "ramblers" trespassed en masse in the Peak District, and were prosecuted for a criminal offence, an event that catalysed the ramblers' movement. The National Parks and Access to the Countryside Act was finally adopted in 1949, and the Peak District became the first national park in 1951. The 1968 Countryside Act widened the definition of open land to include woodland and riverside, yet no new access agreements have since been made. Given this history, proper implementation and enforcement of the 2000 Countryside and Rights of Way Act, as well as of similar provisions under the proposed land reform bill in Scotland, are important.

The *public rights of way network* in England comprises an estimated total of almost 190 000 kilometres, of which 3 000 kilometres, through particularly attractive landscapes, are designated as national trails. Ten such trails exist and three new ones totalling 600 kilometres are being developed. Local highway authorities have a statutory duty to keep a legal record of all public rights of way, in the form of a definitive map and statement. In 1998, however, fewer than 30% of authorities had a consolidated definitive map and most reported definitive map anomalies requiring rectification.

In 1987, the Countryside Commission and local authorities agreed to work together towards a national target of ensuring that by 2001 rights of way in England would be legally defined, properly maintained and well publicised. Surveys were undertaken to measure progress towards this target, judging, for example, whether paths were "easy to find", "easy to follow" and "easy to use". The 2000 *Rights of Way Condition Survey* found that none of the survey regions had attained the national target. The "easy to find" criterion, which stated that 95% of signposting require-ments must be met, was not attained in any region, and only 15% of the survey regions met both of the other two criteria. The situation as regards "easy to find" and "easy to follow" has improved since the 1994 OECD review: 66% of paths now meet signposting targets, compared with 34% in 1988 and 42% in 1994. On "easy to use", however, progress has been slight. Although walkers, cyclists and horse riders found almost 90% of the paths to be usable, they must expect to encounter serious obstacles, such as closed gates, walls or hedges, roughly every two kilometres. A major concern is the impact of cultivation on rights of way. Ploughing and crop growing has often made ways unusable.

Countryside access is also an important *economic development factor*. Visits to the countryside account for about 25% of domestic tourism and 22% of the total spent, amounting in 1999 to GBP 2.5 billion. Between 1993 and 2000, the number of tourist trips to the countryside grew by 50%. About half the tourists visit the countryside simply to enjoy it, and about 20% mention hiking, walking and rambling. The economic importance of countryside access for rural economies was clearly demonstrated during the 2001 outbreak of foot and mouth disease. The English and Welsh Tourist Boards estimated that rural businesses lost over GBP 5 billion in turnover to the outbreak.

SECTORAL INTEGRATION: CONSTRUCTION*

Recommendations

The following recommendations are part of the overall conclusions and recommendations of the Environmental Performance Review of the United Kingdom:

- further promote the *integration of environment-related measures* into strategies and programmes devoted to improving performance in the construction sector;

- amend the Building Act to address the operational *energy efficiency of existing buildings*, and launch a comprehensive policy, with clearly defined targets, to substantially upgrade energy efficiency in existing buildings;

- continue efforts to improve *resource efficiency and conservation* through increased recycling and reuse of construction materials and sites, and strengthen control of illegal disposal of construction and demolition waste;

- ensure that the public sector, through its *procurement policy*, sets a good example for sustainable construction and operation of buildings and infrastructure;

- add environmental indicators to the set of *construction performance indicators* and promote public awareness of *rating and labelling systems* such as SAP and BREEAM.

---

* The present chapter reviews the construction industry's progress towards environmental integration and sustainable development, focusing in particular on housing construction, repair and refurbishment. It also reviews progress with respect to the objective "decoupling environmental pressures from economic growth" of the 2001 OECD Environmental Strategy.

Conclusions

The UK recently adopted a *strategy for more sustainable construction* and has established institutions and procedures for improving the integration of environmental concerns into construction activities and policies. In close co-operation with the industry, several initiatives for technology diffusion have been set up. With respect to material use, a quantified target of increasing the use of construction waste and *recycled aggregates* was set: an increase of more than 80% by 2006, from the 1989 level. Landfilling of construction and demolition waste has fallen since the introduction of the *landfill tax*. The 2002 *aggregates levy*, which increased prices of sand, gravel and crushed rock by some 30%, is expected to provide additional incentive for recycling. The 2001 climate change levy should help improve energy efficiency in commercial buildings. Standards for *energy efficiency* in new buildings have gradually been raised through the application of revised building regulations, and there is now more technical flexibility in meeting them. To improve energy efficiency in the existing housing stock, an investment programme targeted at *"fuel poor" households* was launched. In the private sector, builders now have to display energy ratings for new homes. The environmental performance of buildings is rated through the Building Research Establishment Environmental Assessment Method (BREEAM). Already applied to about 25% of new office buildings, this *labelling system* has helped raise awareness of energy efficiency issues.

However, there is still considerable scope for progress. Despite repeated upgrades, energy efficiency standards for new dwellings remain below those of comparable EU countries, while the large potential for improved energy efficiency in the *existing building stock* is only now beginning to be addressed. Translation of positive experiences from pilot projects into standard practice should be accelerated. Awareness of energy saving potential is still low. Rating and labelling systems for buildings, such as BREEAM, should be promoted more actively. The public sector has not yet fully integrated sustainable construction objectives into its procurement policies as regards construction. Concerning waste streams, information is insufficient to review the impact of recent measures, though there is growing concern about *illegal disposal* of construction and demolition waste at unlicensed sites. The sustainable construction strategy does not contain *specific quantified targets*, but calls on the industry to measure baselines, set targets and publish results. The industry is developing sector- and product-specific performance indicators, yet the development and use of environmental indicators needs to be further encouraged. Environmental and sustainable development concerns and criteria are often not sufficiently integrated into decisions on the design, construction, operation and assessment of buildings. Overall, the restructuring and reorientation of the sector has been primarily driven by economic priorities and perspectives.

1.   Evaluation of Performance

1.1   Importance and impact of the construction sector

Trends in the construction sector

The UK construction sector accounts for about 5% of *GDP* and provides 7% of total *employment* (almost 2 million jobs). In the early 1990s, *construction output* dropped by about 10%. Since 1993, however, construction has recovered and output is back at about the same level as in 1990. Over the decade, construction of *infrastructure* and public non-housing buildings declined (–11%), while *housing* showed a moderate recovery (+5%), and construction of private *industrial and commercial* buildings experienced a major boom (+59%) (Figure 8.1).

Further increases are projected for all three type of construction. From an environmental perspective, it is particularly relevant that the number of households is increasing more rapidly than population (up more than 20% over 1990-2015, from 22 million to 27 million). Household size is declining, as is average dwelling size. It is estimated that *over the next 20 years, 3.8 million new homes* need to be built. During the 1990s, as total housing stock increased, the share of flats rose by more than 3 percentage points, to over 20%, while that of detached houses stayed at about 15%. From an energy efficiency point of view, this was a positive development, since average heat loss is more than twice as high in detached homes, and space heating is the largest category (57%) of residential energy consumption (Figure 8.2). While attention tends to focus on new construction, this has only a marginal effect on the total stock of buildings and infrastructure. With almost half its housing built more than 50 years ago, the UK has comparatively *old building stocks*. The UK ratio of *housing starts to stocks* is particularly low (Figure 8.1), making refurbishment, repair and maintenance (representing about 75% of activity in the sector) much more important than new construction.

Environmental and energy impact

The *environmental impact of construction* is particularly relevant with respect to land use, pressure on biodiversity, material use and waste management. Over the past decade, every year some 6 000 hectares were converted to urban use. For road and rail infrastructure, in particular, the *impact on land, landscape amenity and bio-diversity* reaches far beyond the area "sealed". Projections up to 2016 see a further acceleration of land use change. To limit urban sprawl, and to encourage urban regeneration, efforts are being made to increase the share of *construction on previously developed land*. In England the share of construction on such "brownfield"

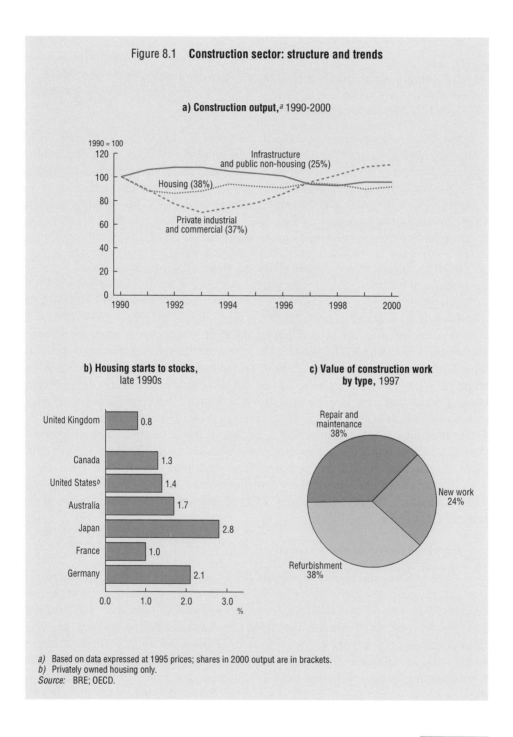

Figure 8.1 **Construction sector: structure and trends**

a) **Construction output,**[a] 1990-2000

b) **Housing starts to stocks,** late 1990s

c) **Value of construction work by type,** 1997

a) Based on data expressed at 1995 prices; shares in 2000 output are in brackets.
b) Privately owned housing only.
Source: BRE; OECD.

Figure 8.2   **Construction sector waste generation and energy consumption**

a) **Management of construction and demolition waste,** 1994

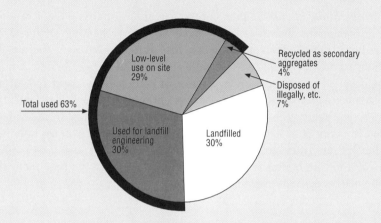

b) **Total final energy consumption,** 1996   c) **Residential energy consumption,** 1999

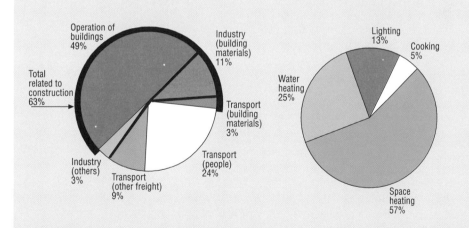

Source: DEFRA; BRE; Department of Transport and Industry.

sites increased from 51% in 1990 to 54% in 1996. The construction sector also has a major impact on *material and waste streams*. Annually the industry extracts some 260 million tonnes (Mt) of minerals. Total annual consumption of construction material is of the order of 350 Mt, or 6 tonnes per capita. In turn, the sector generates more than 70 Mt of construction and demolition waste annually, of which about two-thirds is reused or recycled (Figure 8.2).

The *operation of buildings* accounts for around half of the UK's total final *energy consumption*, mainly due to space and water heating (Figure 8.2). While advances have been made in reducing heat loss, further progress in thermal efficiency of the housing stock remains a key challenge. Even at present prices, *loft insulation* could be installed cost-effectively in 25-40% of houses. Only about 15% of homes are fully insulated, and about the same share is entirely without insulation (Figure 8.3). Since 1970, the share of housing with central heating, primarily from gas boilers, has increased from about 30% to 90%. Correspondingly, annual average internal temperatures have risen from below 13 °C to over 17 °C. Average *boiler efficiency* is around 76%; for old boilers it can be as low as 55%, while the best condensing boilers on the market achieve over 90%.

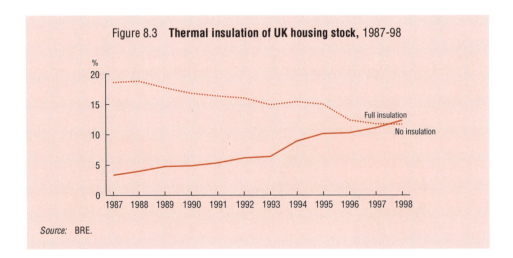

Figure 8.3   **Thermal insulation of UK housing stock, 1987-98**

Source: BRE.

1.2   *Objectives*

Reports and strategies

Since the early 1990s, the foundations and orientation of the UK construction sector have been reviewed on several occasions. Sponsored by both industry and government, several expert groups and task forces have produced influential reports that have led to a multitude of initiatives. Many of these are environmentally relevant, if not explicitly addressing environmental and sustainability concerns. Triggered partly by the recession of the early 1990s, the 1994 Latham report, "*Constructing the Team*", promoted a stronger focus on client value, partnership and standardisation. In 1998, the Egan report, "*Rethinking Construction*", outlined further steps to improve performance in the sector. While environmental concerns were not central to the report, the emphasis on improving efficiency (for example by reducing waste generation through improved processes) clearly had environmental implications.

In 2000, building on these reports and on extensive consultations with industry and other stakeholders, the government published a strategy for more sustainable construction, "Building a Better Quality of Life". This *sectoral strategy* aims to create a framework within which construction can contribute to the implementation of the UK's overall sustainable development strategy (1999). Several basic principles were established, including better protecting or enhancing the natural environment during construction and increasing the energy and natural resource efficiency of the sector. Covering a wide range of construction-related environmental issues, the strategy explores potential "win-win" situations where, by improving its environmental performance, the sector could also reap economic benefits.

The strategy lists *ten themes for practical action* by the construction industry: 1) reuse existing built assets; 2) design for minimum waste; 3) aim for "lean" construction; 4) minimise energy in construction and 5) maximise energy efficiency of operations; 6) do not pollute; 7) preserve and enhance biodiversity; 8) conserve water resources; 9) respect people and their local environment; and 10) set targets. These themes are reiterated in commitments for public procurement that are to be met by 2003.

Quantified targets

Overall, there has not been much progress so far in the setting of quantified targets. Despite the continual development of strategies for improving the sector's performance, considerable room remains for quantifying environmental objectives and rendering performance more measurable. The first steps have been taken, however. With respect to *land use*, the sustainable development "headline indicators" set a target of having the percentage of new homes built on "brownfield" sites reach 60% in England by 2008. For *construction and demolition waste and similar waste* from other sectors (e.g. colliery spoil, china clay, steel slag) the 1997 Mineral Planning Guidance set annual reuse targets increasing from around 30 Mt in 1989 to 40 Mt by 2001 and 55 Mt by 2006. With regard to *energy efficiency of new buildings*, the 1995 revision of the building regulations for England and Wales aimed at a 30% improvement.

The 2000 climate change programme projects how greenhouse gas (GHG) emissions will evolve from 2000 to 2010 and 2020, taking into account the effects of existing policy measures (Chapter 9, Section 2.1). It sees *GHG emissions from the residential sector* in 2010 being about equal to their 1990 level. In light of the expected growth in the housing sector, this projection implies significant improvement in energy efficiency and/or a shift in fuel mix.

The *2002 Energy Review* prepared by the Cabinet Office's Performance and Innovation Unit concluded that a dramatic improvement in energy efficiency was needed and set out a tentative *new target*: to ensure that domestic consumers' energy efficiency improves by 20% between 2000 and 2010 and by a further 20% between 2010 and 2020.

Monitoring progress

The 2000 sustainable construction strategy commits the government to measure progress and to report annually on achievements, using ten "*key performance indicators*". These indicators, endorsed by the government and all major players in the construction sector, focus almost exclusively on sectoral management, and environmental concerns are missing. In the context of overall reporting on the UK sustainable development strategy, *three of the 15 headline indicators* (air quality, wildlife and waste) and four of the 150 sub-indicators (construction and demolition waste going to landfill, aggregates per unit of output value, ratio of secondary or recycled to virgin material, CO_2 emissions by end user) are considered relevant for assessing progress in the construction sector. It is not clear how actual assessments can be made using the headline indicators, however, since they are influenced by many other forces. In the context of "Rethinking Construction", a working group developed a set of *six "environmental performance indicators for sustainable construction"* to be used by planners, designers, contractors, suppliers and users in support of benchmarking for various types of construction.

1.3   Institutional integration and regulations

Institutions and initiatives

All government initiatives to promote environmentally sensitive and sustainable construction have been developed in close collaboration with the industry and its stakeholders. Several bodies and initiatives have been established to promote performance and foster innovation and integration. Following publication of the Latham report, the *Construction Industry Board* was formed in 1995, bringing private and public suppliers and customers together with central government representatives to act on the report's recommendations. The *Construction Task Force*, which prepared the Egan report (1998), included representation from construction companies, major clients, academia, trade unions and financial institutions.

In response to this report, "Rethinking Construction", a network of experts called the *Movement for Innovation (M4I)* was formed. Staffed primarily via secondments from industry, it is currently managing 170 demonstration projects, some with explicit energy-related objectives. M4I was instrumental in developing the ten key performance indicators and six sustainability indicators. In addition, a "knowledge centre" provides an Internet portal for information related to innovation, best practice and services (www.knowledgeexchange.co.uk). Other institutions set up to assist in implementation of the construction strategy are the *Housing Forum*, the *Local Government Task Force* and the *Central Government Task Force*.

Another important institution actively involved in promoting innovation and improvement in the construction sector is the *Building Research Establishment (BRE)*. Founded in 1921 as a government agency, BRE was privatised in 1998. Through its laboratories and other facilities, with over 300 professional experts, it provides testing services and technical expertise related to construction. BRE has a strong focus on environment- and energy-related matters. It has developed and manages a labelling system for environmental rating of buildings, the BREEAM programme, described below.

The government and industry have collaborated to implement several policy instruments. For instance, the Construction Best Practice Programme, which aims to raise awareness of the benefits of best practices, is overseen by both the government and the construction industry, represented by the Construction Industry Board. The *Construction Research and Innovation Strategy Panel* provides a research and innovation focus for the Construction Industry Board, working to push issues up the industry agenda faster than they might otherwise rise.

Together, these and other institutions and initiatives such as the Construction Industry Research and Information Association and the Building Services Research and Information Association, are gradually changing the culture of the industry and helping increase awareness of the need to "rethink construction". The primary focus of most of these bodies is improving the sector's economic performance. While synergies with social and environmental objectives certainly exist, there is often scope for *more explicit reference to sustainable development concerns* and improved environmental integration.

Regulations and standards

Planning and building regulations are key policy instruments shaping the context for the construction sector. The *1984 Building Act* provides the legal framework for the building regulations, which have been frequently amended, most recently in 2000. From an environmental perspective the most relevant are: Part F, ventilation (indoor air quality); Part H, drainage and solid waste disposal (referring in particular to public health legislation); Part J, combustion appliances and fuel storage systems (dealing with fire, pollution and emission issues); and Part L, conservation of fuel and power. Builders and developers have to obtain a formal *building control approval*, an independent verification that the construction complies with the building regulations.

The building regulations set forth *energy efficiency standards* for new construction and large-scale building refurbishment projects. The standards were first included in the regulations in 1976, in response to the 1973 oil crisis. They were tightened in 1982, 1985, 1991, 1995 and 2000. Today they cover a wide range of design elements affecting a building's energy efficiency, such as insulation of walls, boilers, pipes and ducts, and control of space heating and cooling systems, hot water storage systems and lighting appliances. Under the 1995 *Home Energy Conservation Act,* local governments are the "energy conservation authorities" in charge of enforcing the upgraded standards and reporting on progress. While the Act referred to a "significant" improvement, without quantification, this has commonly been defined as a 30% increase in energy efficiency over ten years. A 1999 survey, however, reported that local authorities did not believe they were likely to meet this target; in the first four years an improvement of just over 6% was achieved.

As the energy efficiency standards have been tightened, *compliance processes have been made more flexible*, so as to avoid introducing inflexibility in building design or hampering technical innovation. Until 1991, the regulations for residential structures simply designated the minimum standard for the thermal performance of various building components, not making any allowances for trade-off in performance among components. Revisions since then incorporate new methods allowing for greater design flexibility. Despite the repeated upgrades, however, the UK's minimum energy efficiency standards for buildings are still considerably lower than those of other EU countries, leaving *room for further improvement*. Even the standards in place as of 2002 result in average energy use of about 140 kW/m^2, twice that recorded in European countries with more advanced energy efficiency requirements.

Since building regulations are relevant only for new constructions, *they do not affect the vast majority of the building stock* (two-thirds of housing and more than three-quarters of non-domestic buildings). This is where the biggest potential for cost-effective improvements lies. An amendment of the Building Act should thus be considered, allowing for building regulations that address not only the construction but also the operation of buildings.

Research and dissemination of best practices

The construction sector includes *many small firms*, which tend to be slow to absorb new technical expertise or construction practices. Seeking to promote better diffusion of best practices, and thus improve the industry's overall performance, the government and the construction industry have jointly implemented several programmes.

The *Construction Best Practice Programme* was launched in 1999 to raise awareness of the benefits of best practices and provide guidance and advice to construction and client organisations on how to bring about needed changes. Through the programme, the industry has received a wide variety of technical information on improving environmental performance. The government has also supported the promotion of research projects in the sector through the *Construction Innovation and Research Programme's* "Partners in Innovation Initiative", which has an annual budget of GBP 7 million.

Rating, labelling and procurement

Under the 2000 revision of the building regulations, home builders must *display energy ratings* for any new construction and make them known to potential buyers and to building regulators. The ratings are calculated according to the *Standardised Assessment Procedure* (SAP) method, which rates unit costs of a dwelling's space and water heating on a scale of 1 to 100; the higher the number, the more energy efficient the home. The aims of the rating system are to give prospective buyers information on the energy efficiency of new dwellings and to encourage builders to provide more efficient dwellings. To enhance the system's effectiveness, SAP ratings should be better communicated to potential buyers.

Another *environmental labelling programme, the Building Research Establishment Environmental Assessment Method (BREEAM)*, has been widely used and has helped increase awareness among both designers and their clients of the potential for improved environmental performance of buildings (Chapter 8, Section 2.1). Since its launch in 1991, some 25% of all new office buildings in the UK, in terms of total floor area, have been assessed under the BREEAM.

The BREEAM has also helped with the development of *green procurement* as regards construction. The central and local governments account for some 40% of the UK construction industry's output. In 2000, the government published a new procurement strategy for construction projects, "*Achieving Sustainability in Construction Procurement*". One of its main targets is that, by 2003, all new government-commissioned buildings should be rated "excellent" under the BREEAM or an equivalent rating system. Although the impact of the strategy is not yet discernible, the announcement of such a clear quantified target should support implementation of the government's green procurement policy.

Furthermore, in 2001, the government introduced the *Energy Efficiency Commitment* under the Utilities Act. It obliges electric and gas utilities to encourage their domestic and commercial customers to conserve energy, with a special focus on low-income consumers. To encourage utilities to improve their energy efficiency cost-effectively, targets are to be set in the form of fuel-weighted energy benefits, rather than specific energy efficiency measures to be implemented or a specified amount of investment to be made.

1.4   *Market-based integration and other measures*

Energy efficiency and fuel poverty

The government has declared the use of market-based approaches to be the centrepiece of any long-term carbon reduction policy in the UK. In practice, however, despite the scope for energy efficiency gains in the housing sector, there is considerable *reluctance to use economic instruments* such as taxes or charges to encourage energy savings by private households. In the early 1990s, the introduction of *VAT of 8% on domestic heating fuels* (the standard VAT rate is 17.5%) faced massive opposition and the rate was subsequently reduced to the EU minimum of 5%. Furthermore, domestic heating fuels are exempt from the *climate change levy* (Chapter 6, Section 1.4). Only in industrial and commercial buildings will the levy create incentives to realise cost-effective gains in energy efficiency.

"Fuel poverty" is a major policy concern in the UK. A household is considered to be in fuel poverty if, to maintain heating at a satisfactory level, it would have to spend more than 10% of its income. Since 1991 the number of households in fuel poverty has declined by roughly a third, but in 2000 some 4 million UK households (about 16%) were still considered fuel-poor. The 2001 *fuel poverty strategy* commits the central government and devolved administrations to end fuel poverty for vulnerable households by 2010. In an attempt to simultaneously address environmental, social and economic aspects of fuel poverty, the authorities are trying to generate *synergies in energy efficiency improvement*: saving energy, reducing pollution, upgrading housing comfort, improving health and strengthening purchasing power for households in greatest need.

An important policy instrument to combat fuel poverty in England and Wales is the *Home Energy Efficiency Scheme (HEES)*, providing grants for energy-saving measures. Similar programmes exist for Scotland and Northern Ireland. HEES was introduced in 1991, offering a limited number of energy efficiency measures for a large number of homes. Up to 1999, about 3 million homes were improved, but a review found that the programme had not reached many of the fuel-poor, and that the measures chosen had not always been those generating the biggest energy-saving benefits. Consequently, the *New HEES* was launched in 2000 to provide a more comprehensive package of measures that could be tailored to each property. It is aimed at the most vulnerable households: those of the old, disabled and chronically ill, as well as low-income families with children. In its first year of operation, the New HEES improved as many as 250 000 dwellings. Reviews indicate that the cost-effectiveness of upgrade projects has been greatly enhanced. On average, energy efficiency ratings improved by 19 SAP points to SAP 60, (on a 1 to 100 logarithmic scale) and a significant proportion exceeded SAP 80. In the short run, these efficiency gains will not fully translate into energy (cost) and emission savings, as poor house-holds generally opt for taking some of the gains in the form of greater comfort (warmer homes).

To further stimulate investment in measures to improve energy efficiency and reduce fuel poverty, since 2000 eligibility for the *5% VAT rate* has been extended to energy saving materials and installations in all houses, as well as to grant-funded maintenance, repair and installation of central heating.

Material use and waste management

The introduction of the *landfill tax* in 1996 had a large impact on the management of construction and demolition waste. Different rates were set for non-inert and inert waste, to reflect the different levels of environmental externalities associated with them (Chapter 4, Section 2.2). A rate of GBP 7 per tonne was applied to organic waste that on decomposition would lead to the emission of methane, an important GHG. The rate for inert waste (which covers most construction and demolition waste) is GBP 2 per tonne, since inert waste landfills produce less methane and leachate.

Although the tax rate for inert waste was quite low, its introduction meant a two- to three-fold rise in the cost of landfilling construction and demolition waste. A review concluded that the GBP 2 per tonne tax on inert waste has had a *significant guidance effect* leading to a substantial reduction in final disposal of construction and demolition waste. Consequently, the government decided not to increase the tax on inert waste, but it raised the rate for non-inert waste to GBP 10 per tonne in 1999 and plans incremental increases to GBP 15 per tonne by 2004.

Due to a lack of basic time-series data, in particular regarding the recovery rate for construction and demolition waste, proper evaluation of the precise effects of the landfill tax on such waste is difficult. For taxes to work effectively, their design must be reviewed in the light of precise information regarding targeted activities. In this sense, the *tax's effectiveness* could be further improved by establishing a reliable mechanism to regularly monitor how construction and demolition waste is actually managed, and to reflect findings in the periodic review of the tax. Concerns have been raised over potential negative aspects of the landfill tax. In particular, it is generally agreed that one reason the landfilling of such waste has fallen is that some of it is being *diverted from regulated landfills to sites* exempt from licensing (Chapter 8, Section 2.2). Illegal activities at such sites have been a source of growing concern. Stronger measures to restrict operations at such sites will be imperative for improving the management of construction and demolition waste.

Furthermore, the landfill tax so far has not led to increased use of secondary materials to substitute for primary construction materials. Most recovered material has gone to construction projects requiring materials of lesser quality. To encourage the use of recovered materials instead of new aggregates, an *aggregates levy* came into force in April 2002. Its aim is to reduce the environmental impact of quarrying and increase the recycling rate for construction materials. The flat-rate levy, applied to sand, gravel and crushed rock, is GBP 1.60 per tonne, which increases aggregates prices by nearly 30%. The introduction of this levy is a step towards more sustainable use of construction materials. Its economic costs and environmental benefits should be carefully monitored and assessed.

2.   Focus on Selected Topics

2.1   *Environmental labelling of buildings*

The *Building Research Establishment Environmental Assessment Method* is a voluntary environmental labelling programme for buildings, operated by the UK's Building Research Establishment. The BREEAM was first established in 1991 with the objective of providing independent practical guidance on minimising the damaging effects of new office buildings on the global and local environments. Since then, with revisions in 1993, 1998 and 2001, the scope of assessment criteria and coverage of buildings have been extended. Today the BREEAM covers office buildings (new and existing), supermarkets, schools and houses.

A building's *performance is assessed against criteria set by the BRE* (Table 8.1) for a range of building categories. The building is awarded "credits" based on its level of performance. The percentage of credits achieved under each category is then calculated and environmental weighting is applied to produce an overall score. The score is then translated into a BREEAM rating: pass, good, very good or excellent. Since 1991, some 25% of all new office buildings, in terms of total floor area, have been given BREEAM ratings.

Table 8.1   **Performance criteria under the BREEAM**[a]

Performance criterion	Description
Management	Overall policy, commissioning and procedural issues
Energy use	Operational energy and CO_2 issues
Health and well being	Indoor and external issues affecting health and well being
Pollution	Air and water pollution
Transport	Transport-related CO_2 and location-related factors
Land use	Greenfield and brownfield sites
Ecology	Ecological value of the site
Materials	Environmental implication of building materials
Water	Consumption and efficiency

a) Building Research Establishment Environmental Assessment Method.
Source: BREEAM.

2.2   *Waste management regulations and unlicensed sites*

Under the Waste Management Licensing Regulations, any party that proposes to deposit, recover or dispose of "controlled waste", including construction and demolition waste, must obtain a *waste management licence.* The Environment Agency issues licences only to applicants that satisfy criteria regarding environmental offence records, technical competence and financial means. Once a licence is issued, the agency periodically inspects the site to ensure that licence conditions are upheld and that the environment and human health are protected. In the interest of promoting recycling of inert waste, however, some exemptions to the regulations are made. Examples include sites where inert waste (including construction and demolition waste) is used in development of recreational facilities (e.g. golf courses) or to build, maintain or improve buildings.

The *planning permission system* is also used to control waste management. The development of waste disposal or recycling sites (whether exempted from licensing or not) requires planning permission. To protect the environment, the planning authorities, when granting permission, commonly put some conditions on the amount and quality of waste that can be brought to the sites.

Since the introduction of the landfill tax, a *large amount of construction and demolition waste has been diverted from licensed landfills to sites* exempted from licensing, because the tax is not levied on waste brought to these sites. There have been growing concerns over illegal activities at such sites. Reportedly, much more construction and demolition waste than permitted is brought to some golf course development sites, and in other cases, hazardous waste, including asbestos, has been dumped at such sites. The Environment Agency is required to undertake periodic inspections of any establishment carrying out an exempt activity. So far the fees paid by exempt operators have not covered the agency's inspection costs.

Part III

INTERNATIONAL COMMITMENTS

INTERNATIONAL COMMITMENTS AND CO-OPERATION*

Recommendations

The following recommendations are part of the overall conclusions and recommendations of the Environmental Performance Review of the United Kingdom:

- review and adjust, if appropriate, *economic incentives in the energy and transport sectors* to facilitate full implementation of the climate change programme;

- strengthen and further expand measures to limit *nitrate inputs* into regional seas, with particular attention to diffuse sources such as agriculture;

- strengthen enforcement and pollution control measures at *offshore installations and refineries* in line with internationally agreed control targets (e.g. under OSPAR, MARPOL, EU emission ceiling directive);

- continue to reduce *fishing fleet capacity* and related subsidies, and work to ensure that precautionary management strategies are applied to overexploited fish stocks;

- monitor the implementation of voluntary initiatives designed to assure integration of sustainable development concerns into *export credits and guarantees*;

- increase *official development assistance* towards the Rio commitment of 0.7% of GNI and establish clear procedures for mainstreaming environmental objectives into projects;

- ratify and implement recently signed *international environmental agreements* (Annex II).

---

* The present chapter reviews progress in the last ten years, and particularly since the previous OECD Environmental Performance Review of 1994. It also reviews progress with respect to the objective "global environmental interdependence" of the 2001 OECD Environmental Strategy. A number of other international issues are treated in other chapters: international trade in hazardous waste (Chapter 4), endangered species and conservation of habitats for migratory birds (Chapter 5), sustainable development (Chapter 6) and local Agenda 21 (Chapter 7).

Conclusions

Concerning *climate change*, the UK reduced its greenhouse gas (GHG) emissions by 13.5% from 1990 to 2000. The country thus has already made very good progress towards meeting its ambitious national target of cutting CO_2 emissions by 20% between 1990 and 2010, as well as its international target under the Kyoto Protocol (a 12.5% reduction in GHG emissions between 1990 and 2008-12). A comprehensive climate change programme was launched in 2000, with the aim of sustaining these emission reductions and meeting the national CO_2 target. Concerning *transboundary air pollution*, the UK has met all of its international reduction targets for NO_x, SO_x and NMVOC emissions. Concerning *marine issues*, the UK extended prohibitions regarding ocean dumping to industrial waste and sewage sludge in the 1990s, and has consistently ensured that at least 25% of the foreign ships calling at its ports are inspected for compliance with the Paris Memorandum of Understanding on Port State Control. It has also upgraded waste management facilities in its ports, anticipating international requirements. Performance on transposing and applying EU directives on environment has improved overall, although several issues of non-compliance have been taken to court (e.g. on nitrates and marine habitats). A major review in 2000 of *export credit programmes* led to the adoption of a Statement of Business Principles that determines how applications for support are assessed, taking into account sustainable development concerns.

However, to ensure that the *GHG reductions* are sustained, the country needs to vigorously pursue implementation of additional policies and measures outlined in the climate change programme. Attaining its targets concerning wider use of renewables and combined heat and power production would also help assure the country's longer-term performance (post-2010) with respect to climate protection, and to transboundary air pollution control (in line with the EU acidification strategy and national emission ceiling directive). Additional measures will also be necessary to moderate demand for road transport and electricity. Further technological control of air emissions at *refineries and offshore installations* will be necessary to meet future international emission reduction targets for SO_x, NO_x and NMVOCs. The UK's performance in reducing *nitrate discharges to regional seas* has fallen short of international commitments. Offshore installations have been slow in complying with OSPAR limits on oil content in discharges of produced water. As in other North Sea countries, about half the *fish stocks* exploited by the UK fishing fleet are classified as outside of biologically sustainable limits. Programmes aimed at reducing fishing capacity have had moderate impact. The UK's *official development assistance* (ODA) totals 0.32% of GNI, well under the Rio target of 0.7%. Attempts to "mainstream" environmental concerns into ODA projects have helped raise general awareness of the issues, but have so far not led to clear and practical guidelines, or use of best practices.

1. Evaluation of Performance

1.1   Objectives

The United Kingdom has made many *international commitments concerning environmental issues* as a party to a range of international agreements on the environment (Annex II). The country *ratified a number of agreements* (e.g. the Basel Convention on the Control of Transboundary Movements of Hazardous Wastes, the United Nations Framework Convention on Climate Change [UNFCCC] and the Convention on Biological Diversity), as recommended in the 1994 OECD Environmental Performance Review. It also ratified the Sofia, Geneva and Oslo Protocols to the Convention on Long-range Transboundary Air Pollution, and the London, Copenhagen, Montreal and Beijing Amendments to the Montreal Protocol. Working to strengthen and expand international instruments for *protection of the marine environment*, the UK has played a very active role in the development of the International Maritime Organization (IMO) and International Oil Pollution Compensation Fund agreements concerning liability for marine pollution, air pollution from ships and the control of harmful anti-fouling systems. It also became a party to the OSPAR Convention and the UN Convention on the Law of the Sea.

The *1994 Environmental Performance Review* recommended that the UK pursue:

– ratification of a number of international environmental agreements;

– continued support of innovative action within the European Community;

– cost-benefit approaches when applying the precautionary principle;

– assurance that the financial and human resources necessary to achieve the targets set in international agreements are made available;

– monitoring of progress in implementing action plans under Agenda 21;

– strengthening of legal instruments for protection of the marine environment, and preparation of new international agreements to reduce sea pollution and cope with liability;

– continued implementation of the Montreal Protocol, with more efficient recovery of CFCs;

– clear definition and prioritisation of the environmental component of aid.

1.2   Climate change

While the UK Government retains overall *responsibility for implementing climate change policy*, the Department for Environment, Food and Rural Affairs

(DEFRA) is the designated co-ordinating agency. Many of the means by which emissions can be reduced have been devolved to the Scottish Parliament, the National Assembly of Wales and the Department of the Environment in Northern Ireland. DEFRA plays a strong co-ordination role vis-à-vis these administrations. By the end of 2001, each of the devolved administrations had established a climate protection plan, consistent with the overall UK programme.

Intentions, actions and results

The UK has made *very good progress* towards meeting its greenhouse gas (GHG) reduction targets. Its ambitious national target is to reduce its CO_2 emissions to 20% below 1990 levels by 2010. Furthermore, as a result of the sixth Conference of the Parties to the UNFCCC in Kyoto in 1997 and the EU burden-sharing agreement, the UK has committed to reducing the weighted sum (in CO_2 equivalents) of its national emissions of the "Kyoto gases" (CO_2, CH_4, N_2O, HFCs, PFCs and SF_6) to 12.5% below 1990 levels by 2008-12. The UK ratified the Kyoto Protocol in 2002. In its third National Communication to the UNFCCC (2001), and its national inventory of GHG emissions (2000), the UK reported that it reduced its overall emissions of Kyoto GHGs by 13.5% between 1990 and 2000 (Table 9.1). Over the same period, CO_2 emissions decreased by 8%, methane emissions by 32% and N_2O emissions by 37%. Between 1995 (the UK's designated base year for fluorinated gases) and 2000, HFC emissions fell by 39% and PFC emissions by 33%, while SF_6 emissions increased by 33%.

The UK has made *significant progress in decoupling CO_2 emissions from economic growth*. Over 1990-2000, its CO_2 emissions fell by 8% while GDP rose by 24%. The CO_2 intensity of its economy, at 0.44 tonnes of CO_2/USD 1 000, ranks 14th among OECD countries (Figure 9.1). The progress in decoupling is largely due to *fuel switching*. While the share of solid fuels declined from 30% of the fuel supply in 1990 to 15% in 1999, natural gas grew from 22% to 37% and nuclear power from 8% to 11% (Figure 9.2). The so-called "dash for gas" after deregulation resulted in the share of gas-fired electricity generation growing from almost zero in 1990 to over 30% in 1999 while the more CO_2 intensive generation of electricity from coal declined from 65% to 35%. Preliminary government figures indicate that CO_2 emissions increased slightly in 2001 as higher gas prices increased the commercial attractiveness of coal use for power generation.

The *energy intensity* of the UK economy (0.19 tonne of oil equivalent per USD 1 000 GDP in 1999) is equal to the average for OECD Europe, and ranks 12th among OECD countries (Figure 9.2). Energy intensity registered an overall decrease of 10% between 1990 and 2000, with the largest gains made in the industrial

Table 9.1   **Estimated and projected GHG emissions,** 1990-2020

(MtC)

	Base year[a]	2000	2005[b]	2010[b]	2015[b]	2020[b]
By GHG						
CO_2	164.4	151.1	149.1	150.9	155.5	158.2
CH_4	21.0	14.3	12.7	11.6	10.9	10.1
N_2O	18.3	11.5	11.7	11.8	12.0	12.3
HFCs	4.1	2.5	3.1	2.9	3.0	3.0
PFCs	0.3	0.2	0.1	0.1	0.1	0.1
SF_6	0.3	0.4	0.3	0.3	0.3	0.3
Total	208.4	180.0	177.2	177.6	181.9	184.0
Change from base year (%)						
All GHGs		*–13.5*	*–15.0*	*–14.8*	*–12.7*	*–11.7*
CO_2		*–7.9*	*–9.3*	*–8.2*	*–5.4*	*–3.8*
By energy end user						
Business[c]	73.3	61.0	59.1	58.9	60.3	60.4
Industrial processes	15.4	6.6	6.1	5.5	5.3	5.5
Transport	39.7	41.6	44.9	47.8	50.4	53.0
Residential	43.2	40.4	39.3	39.5	40.6	40.9
Public	9.0	7.7	7.3	7.2	7.3	7.2
Agriculture	15.7	14.6	13.8	13.5	13.5	13.6
Land use change	5.3	4.1	3.4	2.8	2.3	1.9
Waste management	6.9	4.3	3.2	2.4	2.0	1.5
Total	208.4	180.3	177.2	177.6	181.9	184.0
By emitting source						
Energy supply	67.4	50.2	46.6	46.7	48.6	47.9
Business[c]	36.2	36.5	36.5	35.9	36.0	36.2
Industrial processes[d]	15.5	6.6	6.1	5.5	5.5	5.5
Transport	35.6	37.7	40.9	43.8	46.4	49.1
Residential	22.0	22.6	22.7	23.1	23.6	24.2
Public	4.4	4.4	4.4	4.4	4.4	4.4
Agriculture	15.2	13.9	13.3	13.0	13.1	13.2
Land use change	5.3	4.1	3.4	2.8	2.3	1.9
Waste management	6.9	4.3	3.2	2.5	2.0	1.6
Total	208.4	180.3	177.2	177.6	181.9	184.0
By sink						
Forests[e]	–2.9	–3.2	–3.6	–3.6	–3.2	–2.9
of which: Trees planted since 1990[f]	0	–0.3	–0.6	–0.7	–1.0	–1.4
Land use change[g]	–5.3	–4.4	–3.9	–3.7	–3.5	–3.2

a)   The base year is 1990 for CO_2, CH_4 and N_2O; 1995 for HFCs, PFCs and SF_6; 1990 estimates given for sinks.
b)   Baseline projections, which take into account the effects of measures taken since the approval of the Kyoto Protocol in 1997.
c)   Includes energy use by industry and commerce.
d)   Includes operational emissions from industry.
e)   Includes carbon accumulated: i) in forests by woody biomass, soils, litter; ii) by agricultural crops; and iii) in timber and forest products grown in the UK.
f)   Figures do not include increasing pool of carbon sequestered in timber products.
g)   Net change (sum of emissions and sinks) from transition between land use categories.
Source: UK's Third National Communication to the UNFCCC Secretariat.

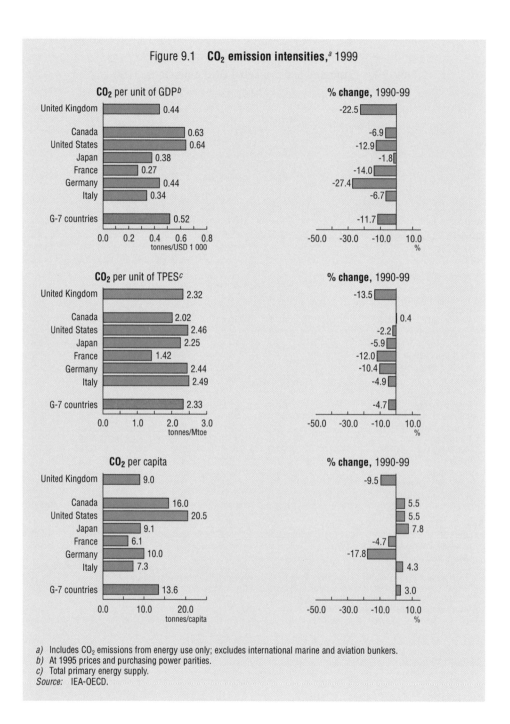

Figure 9.1 CO_2 emission intensities,[a] 1999

a) Includes CO_2 emissions from energy use only; excludes international marine and aviation bunkers.
b) At 1995 prices and purchasing power parities.
c) Total primary energy supply.
Source: IEA-OECD.

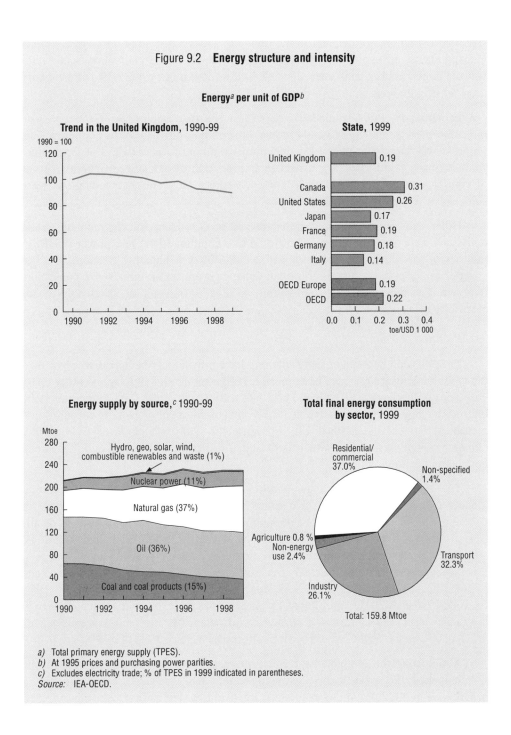

Figure 9.2 **Energy structure and intensity**

Energy[a] per unit of GDP[b]

Trend in the United Kingdom, 1990-99

State, 1999

Energy supply by source,[c] 1990-99

Total final energy consumption by sector, 1999

Total: 159.8 Mtoe

a) Total primary energy supply (TPES).
b) At 1995 prices and purchasing power parities.
c) Excludes electricity trade; % of TPES in 1999 indicated in parentheses.
Source: IEA-OECD.

sector. Growing energy demand in the transport and residential sectors largely offset gains in energy efficiency in other sectors. In 1999, the residential/commercial sector was the largest energy consumer (37.0%), followed by transport (32.3%) and industry (26.1%) (Figure 9.2).

In summary, the UK made *large strides towards meeting its GHG emission reduction targets*, and significantly reduced the carbon intensity of its economy. This progress was largely achieved by switching from coal to natural gas at large point sources (energy and industry), driven by exploitation of extensive offshore reserves of natural gas and liberalisation of energy markets. CO_2 emission reductions were achieved at relatively low marginal costs.

Other *"no regrets" measures* that played a significant role in reducing GHG emissions were the promotion of cost-effective combined heat and power (CHP) in industry, a road fuel duty escalator and a landfill tax (Chapter 6, Section 1.4). The costs of many policies related to climate change were borne directly by consumers (e.g. via the non-fossil fuel obligation, a levy in favour of renewable-source electricity).

Planned actions

The emission benefits of fuel switching have now largely been realised; in effect, the "low-hanging fruits" have been picked. Future reductions in CO_2 and other GHG emissions will be more difficult and costly to achieve. Whereas the UK is likely to be one of the few countries to reach its Kyoto commitment, it will need additional measures to meet its national CO_2 commitment. This is recognised in the 2000 *climate change programme*, which is designed to help the UK meet and then move beyond its Kyoto target.

The programme includes an *"additional policies and measures"* scenario to identify cost-effective measures that could help achieve the 2010 national target for CO_2 emissions and the 2008-12 international target for GHG emissions. It details several measures and estimates their emission impact (in MtC of avoided emissions) (Chapter 9, Section 2.1). As the cost of the measures is not examined in detail, however, it is difficult to estimate their actual cost-effectiveness. It is projected that the package of measures would reduce GHG emissions by 23%, and CO_2 emissions by 19%, between 1990 and 2010. Controlling CO_2 emissions appears to be the main challenge in the longer term. *Sequestration of carbon* by woodlands is expected to total 3.6 MtC in 2010, of which 0.6 MtC would be from afforestation since 1990 (Table 9.1).

Anticipating the establishment of an international emission trading system, the UK launched the world's first economy-wide *domestic GHG emission trading programme* in 2002. Voluntary reduction targets initiated in its first stage are expected to deliver annual emission savings of at least 2 MtC by 2007. Government funds totalling GBP 215 million are being made available for the first five years of the programme. In April 2002, 34 companies bid successfully in auction for a share of the incentive money in return for a total emission reduction of 4 Mt of CO_2 to be achieved by 2007. It is expected that the number of participants will increase, as around 6 000 companies under climate change levy agreements will be eligible to use the programme to meet their targets or to sell their overachievements.

1.3   *Transboundary air pollution*

Transboundary air pollution has long been an issue between the UK and its neighbours, as the UK is a *net exporter of acidifying air pollutants, by a large margin*: nearly seven times for SO_x and five times for NO_x. In 1999, some 70% of the UK's SO_x emissions and 80% of its NO_x emissions were exported. On the other hand, about 25% of the SO_x and 40% of the NO_x deposited in the UK originates abroad or from ships.

The UK has *met or surpassed its commitments* to reduce atmospheric emissions of SO_x, NO_x and NMVOCs under the Convention on Long-range Transboundary Air Pollution and its protocols (Chapter 9, Section 2.2). The UK has signed but *not yet ratified* the 1998 Aarhus Protocols on persistent organic pollutants and heavy metals, and the 1999 Gothenburg Protocol to Abate Acidification, Eutrophication and Ground-level Ozone. It has already largely met future targets under the Aarhus Protocols (Chapter 9, Section 2.2).

In the late 1990s, the *UK further strengthened its commitments* to limit acidifying air emissions in the framework of the EU Acidification Strategy (1997), which aims to halve overall acid deposition in the EU by 2010, from 1990 levels. The EU's national emission ceiling directive would cap SO_x, NO_x, VOC and NH_3 emissions in 2010 for each member state at levels stricter than those in the Gothenburg Protocol. Through early implementation of EU directives on the sulphur content of motor vehicle fuels, heavy fuel oil and gas oil, the UK has already reduced SO_x emissions from transport (Chapter 2, Section 1.4).

In 2000, the North Sea was designated as a *SO_x emission control area* when the IMO approved an amendment to MARPOL Annex VI. When the annex enters into force, new control technology will likely be required at UK refineries. A study commissioned by the Environment Agency in 2000 concluded that UK refineries do not match up to international best practice in pollution abatement, and have so far relied heavily on "sweet" low-sulphur North Sea crude oil to help meet tightened emission and fuel quality standards. The study concluded that the use of low-sulphur feedstock alone will not be sufficient to meet future EU fuel quality standards.

Furthermore, it was estimated that implementation of cost-effective measures to reduce the refining industry's emissions of SO_x and NO_x would add as much as GBP 26 million per year to its costs, and that full compliance with the 2001 EU directive on national emission ceilings would imply annual costs of up to GBP 190 million.

1.4   Marine pollution

In a speech in March 2002, the prime minister committed the UK to launching measures to improve marine conservation at home and abroad, and to publishing a series of *marine stewardship reports* to summarise goals and progress. The first report, "Safeguarding our Seas: A Strategy for the Conservation and Sustainable Development of our Marine Environment", was published in May 2002. It calls for an "ecosystem-based approach" to reconciling conservation objectives and economic needs. Estimating that marine-related activities (including fishing, tourism and off-shore oil and gas extraction) contribute 3-4% of the UK's GDP and directly employ around 423 000 people, the report establishes the overarching objective of maintaining the health of ecosystems alongside appropriate human use of the marine environment. After reviewing the UK's international engagements regarding marine conservation (e.g. under OSPAR, the Convention on Biological Diversity, the EU habitat and bird directives), the report describes general policy relating to economic activities in the marine environment (e.g. shipping and ports, offshore activities and renewable energy, fisheries) and sets out priorities for action.

Over the last ten years, the UK has worked within the frameworks of the OSPAR Commission for the Protection of the Northeast Atlantic and the North Sea Conferences to promote *coherent and sustainable management of marine resources*. The UK supported OSPAR's development of long-term strategies concerning the sustainable development of the marine environment, which set objectives and targets up to 2020 in five priority areas: hazardous substances, radioactive substances, eutrophication, protection of ecosystems and biodiversity, and offshore activities. The UK submits regular *reports on compliance* to the OSPAR Secretariat.

Before 1998, the control of marine pollution was the joint mandate of the Marine Safety Agency and the Coastguard Agency. In 1998, the two agencies were merged, with the aim of better integrating policy making and implementation. The resulting *Maritime and Coastguard Agency (MCA)* has general responsibility for developing, promoting and enforcing high standards of marine safety, responding to maritime emergencies and minimising the risk of pollution of the marine environment from ships and other sources.

Pollution from oil and gas production

The *largest producer of oil and gas in the North Sea*, the UK is also responsible for the majority of emissions from offshore installations in the OSPAR area. In the late 1990s, the country operated some 200 offshore installations discharging to the sea or air. UK production (113 billion m^3 of natural gas and 118 Mt of oil in 2001) constituted about half of total North Sea output, whereas hydrocarbons discharged from UK operations made up three-quarters of the OSPAR total. Concerning air emissions, UK facilities emitted 96% (14 kt) of the total SO_2 emissions from installations in the OSPAR area in 1998, and 64% (19.1 Mt) of the CO_2 emissions (in part due to continued flaring). Since 2000, the UK has been regulating large combustion plants on offshore platforms under the integrated pollution prevention and control system (Chapter 6, Section 2.1), which should help reduce air emissions.

Gas flaring by UK offshore operations decreased by 24% between 1995 and 2000, when a total of 4.76 million m^3 of gas was flared per day (about 3% of the UK's associated gas production). The government reduced the number of flaring consents issued over the period, and launched a flare-trading programme in 2001 to further restrict the practice. Most flaring now carried out is done for safety reasons.

Nearly 14% of UK offshore installations exceeded the *OSPAR limit on oil in effluents* (40 mg/litre) from 1994 to 1999, a rate of non-compliance nearly 45% higher than the OSPAR average during the period. In 2000, however, the performance of the UK operations vastly improved, with the rate of non-compliance falling to 2%. Of the 32 North Sea installations that exceeded the OSPAR limit in 1997, 19 were UK installations. Of those, five installations accounted for 95% of the effluent exceeding the limit. In 2001, all five were brought into compliance.

The major remaining source of oil discharge is *produced water*. As in other countries with mature developments, UK discharges of displacement and produced water have risen in recent years, from 408 203 m^3/day in 1993 to 652 188 m^3/day in 2000 (a 60% increase). The amount of oil associated with these discharges rose from 4 553 tonnes in 1993 to 5 395 tonnes in 2000 (18% growth). To reduce the amount of oil discharged in produced water by 15% between 2000 and 2006, and thus achieve the target set by OSPAR Recommendation 2001/1, the UK will have to further reinforce its control efforts.

In line with the OSPAR agreement to discontinue *discharges of oily drill cuttings*, the UK had stopped such discharges by 1997. UK operators switched to using synthetic drilling fluids until concerns following research into their biodegradability led to the decision to phase out such discharges by the end of 2000 (later reflected in OSPAR Decision 2000/3). The phase-out was initiated in the framework of a voluntary agreement between the government and UK offshore operators. In 2000, UK operators brought nearly 1 500 tonnes of synthetic fluids to shore for disposal, but still discharged 1 937 tonnes to sea.

The *frequency of oil spills at UK offshore installations* nearly doubled during the 1990s, although it appears to have stabilised at about 350 spills per year since 1997. The magnitude of the increase in the number of spills partly reflects improved reporting and surveillance introduced during the period. Most of the spills are small. In 1992, the average spill involved the release of 1.2 tonne of oil; in 2000, the average spill led to the release of only 0.2 tonne of oil, thanks to improved response times.

Reducing the *pollution intensity of oil refining* in the UK would significantly reduce loading to rivers and estuaries that drain to the North Sea. UK refineries account for almost one-quarter of the refining capacity of the 11 OSPAR countries. While the average pollution intensity of the UK's 14 refineries (none built since the 1970s) decreased by 83% between 1990 and 1997 to 3.3 tonnes of oil discharged per Mt of crude oil processed, UK refineries overall were still 50% more pollution-intensive than the OSPAR average (2.2 tonnes/Mt in 1997). UK refineries are also the most pollution-intensive in the OSPAR area for discharges of sulphides, ammonical nitrogen and phenolic compounds.

Pollution from ships

Since 1997, the *MCA's Enforcement Unit* has prosecuted 12 vessels found to be violating MARPOL and polluting UK waters. Fines have ranged from GBP 5 000 to 35 000. The maximum fine for pollution was GBP 250 000, which was reduced to GBP 25 000 on appeal. The MCA co-operates with its counterparts in neighbouring countries to enforce anti-pollution regulations and prosecute offenders under MARPOL. Enforcement efforts have been reinforced since 1999, when northwest European waters (including the North Sea and its approaches, the Irish Sea and its approaches, the Celtic Sea and the English Channel and its approaches) were accorded "special area" status under MARPOL Annex I. In such areas, any *discharge of oil or oily mixtures from oil tankers* and large ships (400 or more gross tonnes) is prohibited. Discharges of bilge water from machinery spaces of all ships, and discharges from ships of less than 400 gross tonnes, are also prohibited if the effluent's oil content exceeds 15 ppm.

In 1997, the UK introduced regulations requiring *ports and terminals* to provide adequate waste reception facilities, to some extent anticipating the 2000 EU directive on port reception facilities. In 2000, a survey of 35 UK ports concluded that the availability of and accessibility to disposal facilities was good, for all types of waste.

The UK has ratified MARPOL Annex IV concerning sewage from ships, and is participating in IMO activities aimed at developing on-board waste treatment techniques. In compliance with the Paris Memorandum of Understanding on Port State Control, the MCA inspects at least 25% of the foreign ships calling at UK ports, to check their conformance with MARPOL standards. After peaking at 34% in 1991, the percentage of ships inspected stabilised at 28% from 1996 to 2000.

DEFRA regulates the *disposal of waste in UK waters* through a system of licences under the Food and Environment Protection Act (1985). Disposal of most types of waste at sea is no longer allowed in the UK: dumping of radioactive waste was prohibited in 1982, of industrial waste in 1992 and of sewage sludge in 1998. The burning of waste at sea was banned in 1990. In accordance with the requirements of the OSPAR and London Conventions, the only materials now licensed for disposal at sea are dredged material and fish processing waste. Since the mid-1990s, the UK has issued about 150 permits per year for the dumping of dredged material. In 2000, the amount of dredged material dumped at sea by the UK totalled 33 Mt (dry weight). The dumping of fish processing waste is carried out on a much smaller scale (1 600 tonnes in 2000).

Oil spills, maritime accidents

In recent years, the UK has worked to strengthen international co-operation concerning *liability and compensation for pollution damage* from maritime accidents and oil spills. At the June 2001 Council of EU Transport Ministers, the UK and French ministers presented a strategy for strengthening EU-level co-operation concerning maritime liability, preparedness and response, in particular by fully implementing relevant international instruments (e.g. the 1996 Hazardous and Noxious Substances Convention [HNS], the 1996 Protocol on Limitation of Liability for Maritime Claims, the 2001 Bunkers Convention, the 1990 International Convention on Oil Preparedness, Response, and Cooperation [OPRC] and the 2000 OPRC-HNS Protocol), and by reforming the International Oil Pollution Compensation Fund. The UK supports setting higher liability limits and establishing more effective compensation arrangements for claimants and more secure funding mechanisms for pollution response activities.

The UK co-operates with other North Sea states in combating oil spills and monitoring marine waters, in compliance with the *Bonn Agreement* and with special bilateral arrangements. For example, an emergency towing vessel stationed at Dover is jointly funded by the UK and France, which co-operate in counterpollution efforts in the English Channel under the *Mancheplan*. The plan was successfully invoked after the chemical tanker *Ievoli Sun* sank on 31 October 2000 off Alderney in the Channel Islands. Similarly, the *Norbrit Agreement* between the UK and Norway establishes joint counterpollution procedures, particularly for spills from offshore installations in the North Sea south of latitude 62°.

After the grounding of the *Sea Empress* in 1996, and the consequent release of 72 000 tonnes of crude oil and 360 tonnes of fuel oil into Milford Haven and along the Pembrokeshire Coast, the UK reviewed and overhauled its *National Contingency Plan for Marine Pollution from Shipping and Offshore Installations*. In particular, the Secretary of State's Representative Model has been used to co-ordinate responses to major oil spills since October 1999. The MCA continues to develop the model by running training exercises in strategic locations and by reviewing all processes and actions during incident responses.

Scrapping of ships and platforms

According to UNCTAD, the UK had the *world's tenth largest shipping fleet*, totalling 19 million dead-weight tonnes, in 2000 (2.5% of world shipping capacity). Its merchant marine fleet includes 590 ships of over 100 gross tonnes, totalling 12 000 dead-weight tonnes. In the late 1990s several dozen large ships per year were withdrawn from the fleet, many sold to non-OECD countries. The government does not keep records on how many of these ships went to dismantling, but the number can be expected to rise significantly by 2010 as bulk and tanker ships commissioned in the 1970s approach the end of their service life. Most ships contain large quantities of hazardous substances, which pose serious disposal challenges in countries that have not developed the proper infrastructure, regulations and techniques. Recently the problem of *ships sold for scrapping* to countries with lower safety and environmental standards has attracted international attention. As a member of the IMO and a party to MARPOL and the Basel Convention, the UK supports the development of international safety and environmental requirements for ship scrapping.

In July 1998 at the first ministerial meeting of the OSPAR Commission, a new regime for the *decommissioning of offshore installations* was established. Since then the decommissioning of installations on the UK continental shelf has been conducted accordingly. The Department of Trade and Industry provides a list of approved decommissioning programmes at www.og.dti.gov.uk. Guidance notes for industry, available on the website, state that, in addition to adhering to the principles of the OSPAR decision, decommissioning proposals should take into account the precautionary principle, best available techniques, best environmental practices and waste hierarchy principles. In a number of approved programmes, installations have been reused. For example, it is standard practice to reuse floating production storage and offloading vessels. Pieces of platforms from the Brent Spar and Hutton fields were reused in quay extension projects. Over 99% of the steel from installations decommissioned since 1998 has been reused or recycled, the rest going to landfill. In 2000, tax allowance provisions applicable to decommissioning costs were modified to encourage reuse of materials from offshore structures.

Nutrients from land-based sources

The UK has not yet identified marine eutrophication problem areas and therefore is not technically subject to the 50% reduction targets for *nitrogen and phosphorous* adopted by other members of the North Sea Conference (originally for 1985-95). According to its report to the Fifth North Sea Conference (2002), however, the UK paralleled the performance of other North Sea countries, reducing its discharges of phosphorous to the North Sea by 43% between 1985 and 1999, but making little progress in reducing nitrogen inputs. Since 1990, when the integrated pollution control system started being applied to large point sources (Chapter 6, Section 2.1), discharges to UK coastal waters of nitrogen and phosphorus from sewage and industrial sources have decreased by 30% and 35%, respectively. The country's overall nitrogen inputs to the North Sea, however, have risen by 11% since 1985 (Table 9.2).

Diffuse pollution constitutes about 75% of the UK's nitrate input to water, with agriculture the main source. The UK has been slow to designate nitrate vulnerable zones under the EU nitrate directive and to put in place a national action programme to limit diffuse nitrate pollution from agricultural land. In December 2000, the European Court of Justice ruled that the UK had failed to comply with the nitrate directive. For full compliance, designation of significant additional areas as nitrate vulnerable zones will be necessary in England, Scotland and Wales. The UK should move quickly to define land and near-shore areas that are especially vulnerable to

Table 9.2   **Nutrient inputs to the North Sea,**[a] 1985-99

	1985 (kt)		1999 (kt)		Change, 1985-99 (%)	
	Nitrogen[b]	Phosphorus[c]	Nitrogen[b]	Phosphorus[c]	Nitrogen[b]	Phosphorus[c]
UK total	319	58	355	33	+11[d]	−43
Thames catchment[e]	40	11	29	6	−28	−45

a) Direct and riverine inputs only; excludes inputs via leaching and surface water runoff downstream of riverine monitoring points.
b) Measured as total-N.
c) Measured as orthophosphate-P ($PO_4 - P$).
d) A "worst case" scenario, as nitrogen inputs were probably underestimated in 1985. More reliable data for 1991-99 indicate stabilisation over the period.
e) 1999 data concerning inputs from the Thames catchment are smoothed to take account of annual flow variability.
Source: Department for Transport, Local Government and the Regions.

eutrophication, and to take adequate measures to limit diffuse discharges in these areas, as eutrophication affects some 80% of UK river catchments (Chapter 3, Section 1.3).

1.5   Management of living marine resources

During its 1998 EU presidency, the UK launched initiatives aimed at making the *Common Fisheries Policy* (CFP) more focused on sustainable management objectives. It introduced the Cardiff process, under which key sectors such as fisheries have since been required to produce strategies and reports detailing measures to integrate environmental considerations into sectoral policy. The UK has worked for an ecosystem-based approach to the management of shared stocks of living marine resources, and has ratified OSPAR Annex V. It has also worked actively within the EU to protect marine mammals, in particular supporting the 2002 *ban on the use of drift nets on the high seas* (because of the scale of accidental capture of dolphins).

Offshore fisheries

Capture fisheries and fish processing are economically significant to the UK. In 2000, the UK fishing fleet landed some 748 000 tonnes of marine fish worth about GBP 550 million, or 0.1% of GDP (about 5% of GDP comes from agriculture, fisheries and forestry). In addition, the UK imported fish and fish products valued at GBP 1.3 billion, nearly twice what it exported (GBP 700 million). The UK's substantial fish processing industry comprises some 540 businesses employing 22 000 persons.

The *European Union* has jurisdiction over the conservation and management of shared marine fish stocks in UK waters beyond the 12-mile national waters boundary. Under the CFP, the EU adopts rules and regulations that are then applied in member states. The UK can take measures in relation to local stocks found within 12 miles of the coastline, provided that these measures apply only to UK citizens and do not conflict with CFP objectives. Under the CFP, EU conservation policies are aimed at regulating quantities of fish landed through a system of total allowable catches allocated as quotas to member countries.

As is the case in other North Sea countries, the majority of fish stocks exploited by the UK fleet are classified as *"outside biologically sustainable limits"* according to spawning biomass estimates by the International Council for the Exploration of the Sea (Table 9.3). Thus, for over 50% of stocks, spawning levels are insufficient to guarantee stock replenishment. The Food and Agriculture Organization has attributed this unsustainable level of resource exploitation in large part to overcapacity of national fleets and has called on member states to reduce their fleet capacity and end production subsidies.

A series of *vessel decommissioning programmes* in the UK has helped reduce the number of fishing vessels by about 33% since 1990. One such programme in 1996 led to a 2% reduction in fleet capacity, involving 104 vessels with a total weight of 4 215 tonnes, at a cost of GBP 464 million. The UK fishing fleet numbered 7 809 vessels at the end of 1997 and 7 242 in 2000. While on the surface the decommissioning programme was successful, it had the unplanned effect of catalysing a

Table 9.3   **Biological status of key stocks in UK fisheries**

Species (stock)	Minimum spawning stock[a] (kt)	Estimated spawning stock biomass (kt)		Status of stock W/C/O[b]	Landings by the UK fleet in 2000	
		1999	2000		Quantity (tonnes)	Value (1 000 GBP)
Demersal species						
Anglerfish (N. Sea)	..	..	..	O	10 521	23 991
Anglerfish (W. Scotland)	..	..	..	O	1 541	3 408
Cod (N. Sea)	150	66	67	O	27 549	38 901
Cod (Irish Sea)	10	7	4	O	838	1 322
Cod (W. Scotland)	22	6	5	O	2 339	3 451
Haddock (N. Sea)	140	133	111	O	39 654	39 937
Haddock (W. Scotland)	30	32	32	C	6 134	6 200
Plaice (N. Sea)	300	222	271	O	20 711	21 022
Saithe (N. Sea)	200	120	134	W	6 719	2 698
Sole (N. Sea)	35	54	53	W	946	5 186
Sole (Irish Sea)	308	4	4	O	141	751
Sole (Eng. Channel)	8	12	11	W	1 045	6 602
Whiting (N. Sea)	315	151	224	O	18 943	11 463
Whiting (Irish Sea)	7	2	2	O	684	389
Whiting (W. Scotland)	22	13	9	O	28 818	2 764
Demersal catch					300 955	302 261
As % of total catch (demersal + pelagic)					*49*	*79*
Pelagic species						
Herring (N. Sea)	800[c]	906	908	O	40 825	5 613
Horse mackerel	..[d]	2 739	..	..	3 479	960

a) B_{pa} (precautionary approach spawning stock biomass).
b) ICES assessment, 2001; W = Within biologically sustainable limits; C = Close to limits; O = Outside biologically sustainable limits.
c) MBAL (minimum biologically acceptable level).
d) Previous ICES estimate of B_{pa} (500 kt), an underestimate, was withdrawn in 2001.
Source: ICES Advisory Committee on Fishery Management.

major shift towards large fishing vessels. From 1996 to 1997, the number and size of vessels less than 250 gross tonnes fell by 305 vessels and 9 100 tonnes, respectively, while the number and size of vessels greater than 250 gross tonnes increased by 41 vessels and 33 900 tonnes. In 1997, the average capacity per vessel, in both gross tonnage and kilowattage, was some 55% higher than the EU average.

Offshore habitats

Protection of *deep sea coral reefs and cetacean populations* in the "Atlantic Frontier" (north and west of Scotland) was the subject of a court battle between the UK Government and Greenpeace from 1997 to 1999. In 1996, the Atlantic Frontier was opened to exploration for oil and gas reserves by ten international oil companies. At the same time, the government continued to limit its application of the EU habitat directive to the area up to 12 nautical miles off its shores. In a landmark decision in 1999, the UK High Court ruled for Greenpeace, declaring that the UK's issuing of permits for off-shore oil exploration and development in areas further than 12 miles offshore implied a duty to apply the habitat directive in the entire 200-mile exclusive economic zone.

As a result of the High Court's ruling, the UK is to survey marine life in the area between 12 and 200 nautical miles from the coast, identify which sites contain habitats or species requiring protection, propose areas with vulnerable habitats or species as candidates for *special conservation areas* and put in place a strict system of protection for whales and dolphins. A 1998 survey by Greenpeace and the Whale and Dolphin Conservation Society suggests that the Atlantic Frontier is heavily populated by whales and dolphins, and that the animals may use the area for breeding, feeding, migrating and/or rearing, which all require protection under the habitat directive. Other research shows that the area contains unique and extensive deep sea coral reefs (*Lophelia pertusa*), which are important habitats to some 300 species.

1.6   Development assistance and the environment

Expressed as a share of gross national income (GNI), the UK's *official development assistance* was 0.32% in 2000, surpassing the OECD Development Assistance Committee (DAC) average of 0.22%. In 2000, the UK was the fourth largest donor among DAC countries (Figure 9.3). Yet, it is still far from reaching the *United Nations' ODA/GNI target* of 0.7%. At the present rate of growth of the ODA/GNI ratio (0.01% per year), it would take the UK four decades to reach 0.7%.

With the overall aim of bringing about lasting reductions in poverty, the UK development assistance programme seeks to promote *sustainable use and effective management of environmental resources* in developing countries. In a 2000 strategy

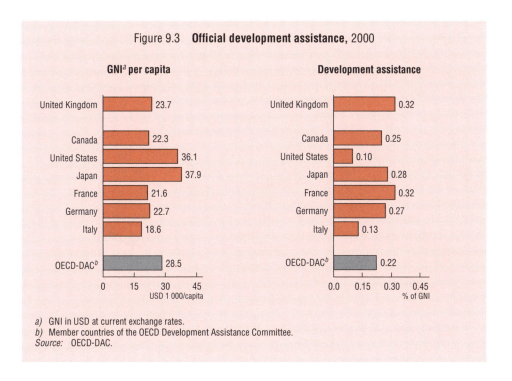

Figure 9.3 **Official development assistance,** 2000

GNI[a] per capita

Development assistance

a) GNI in USD at current exchange rates.
b) Member countries of the OECD Development Assistance Committee.
Source: OECD-DAC.

paper ("Achieving Sustainability: Poverty Elimination and the Environment"), the Department for International Development (DFID) outlined this approach, committing itself to structure aid programmes to promote economic growth that is both equitable and environmentally sustainable. Particular emphasis is put on promoting more effective management of natural resources as a means of improving the health and livelihoods of the poor and reducing their insecurity and vulnerability. In the 1990s, DFID devoted an increasing proportion of its budget to forestry projects, most of them including participatory and capacity-building provisions.

As early as 1989, DFID adopted a *Manual of Environmental Appraisal*, which has since been updated and expanded to help project staff take full account of environmental issues. Environmental appraisal is carried out for projects, programmes and policies in order to identify environmental constraints and opportunities. The process is progressive, with the level of detail being determined by the outcome of the initial stages. If initial screening indicates an activity could have a significant impact on the environment, then further investigation such as environmental analysis or a detailed environmental impact assessment (EIA) is required.

Thus, instead of being conducted as discrete, stand-alone studies, environmental investigations such as EIAs are now integrated into all project stages, first through screening and then through iterative assessment. For all projects subjected to EIA, an environmental management plan is prepared, indicating how environmental effects will be mitigated, managed and monitored during project implementation.

Despite the priority attached to environmental issues, *shortcomings* in DFID's programmes are apparent. A 2000 DFID review ("Environmental Evaluation Synthesis Study – Environment: Mainstreamed or Sidelined?") concluded that environment as a potential development opportunity (rather than as a risk to be minimised or mitigated) had not been systematically incorporated ("mainstreamed") into its bilateral programmes. Fully integrating environmental objectives in bilateral aid, designing measurable performance targets, and effectively promoting and monitoring environmental performance were identified as key challenges. Recent efforts to promote mainstreaming of environmental concerns into ODA included training programmes and guidance provided to project officers. DFID believes there is now a high level of awareness of the importance of environmental mainstreaming, although still considerable uncertainty as to how to do it in practice.

The UK channels much of its funding for international environmental issues through the *Global Environment Facility (GEF)*. For example, its contribution to the climate change and biodiversity conventions is distributed through the GEF. UK commitments totalled GBP 89.5 million under GEF 1 and GBP 85.25 million under GEF 2. Special funds, such as the Darwin Initiative (Chapter 5, Section 2.3), have also been set up by the UK to finance bilateral environmental initiatives.

1.7   Regional co-operation

The UK's performance in *transposing and implementing EU environmental directives* is about average, compared to other EU countries. Roughly speaking, out of every 15 environment-related cases being examined by the European Commission, one concerns the UK. Environment-related cases made up about 40% of the Commission's UK caseload in 2001, slightly higher than the EU average (34%). Most cases concerned failure to notify or nonconformity of national transposing measures. The UK ranked last among the 15 member states in 2001 concerning performance in notifying the Commission of national measures implementing environmental directives: only 81% of applicable directives had implementing measures by the deadline. Of complaints to the Commission concerning potential infringement of environmental directives, about one in three concerned nature conservation, one in four environmental impacts, one in six waste and one in ten water pollution.

Responsibility for the UK's co-operation with the *Republic of Ireland* on common environmental concerns has been devolved to the Northern Ireland Assembly. The UK shares its only *transboundary waterway* with Ireland. Although the UK has not yet ratified the 1992 UNECE Convention on the Protection and Use of Transboundary Watercourses and Lakes, the establishment of necessary cross-border mechanisms is well advanced. Ratification is expected to take place jointly with Ireland. Since 1990, the Irish Sea Forum (ISF), a non-profit organisation associated with the University of Liverpool, has organised several seminars per year on subjects concerning the *Irish Sea marine and coastal environment*. An ISF report of 2000 identifies several areas for future co-operation, including reduction of diffuse inputs of contaminants, reduction of litter from shipping and other sources, and development of regional ecosystem-based fishery management approaches.

The discharge of *radioactive waste into the environment from licensed nuclear sites* has been a source of concern with a few countries. The management and future development of spent nuclear fuel reprocessing at the UK's Sellafield facility is the subject of a legal dispute between Ireland and the UK. Arguing that the UK's decision to open a new mixed oxide fuel (MOX) facility in Sellafield violated Ireland's rights under the UN Convention on the Law of the Sea, Ireland petitioned the International Tribunal on the Law of the Sea to order the immediate suspension of the plant's authorisation in 2001. The Irish Government maintained that operation of the plant in the period leading up to arbitration under Annex VII of the convention (scheduled for 2002) would entail unacceptable risks of radioactive pollution of the Irish Sea, particularly from the transport of radioactive material to and from the plant. In December 2001, the tribunal ruled that the situation was not so urgent as to warrant a suspension of the plant's authorisation, but ordered Ireland and the UK to exchange further information with regard to possible impacts on the Irish Sea arising from commissioning of the MOX plant, and to jointly monitor the risks/effects of the plant's operation as regards the Irish Sea.

1.8   *Other global issues*[*]

Trade and the environment

The UK seeks to promote consistency between *trade liberalisation and environmental protection policies*, and to avoid conflicts between the multilateral trading system and environmental law. Within the EU, the UK actively seeks

---

[*]   Some additional global concerns are discussed in other chapters: international trade in hazardous waste (Chapter 4), endangered species and conservation of habitats for migratory birds (Chapter 5).

clarification concerning the legal interface between the rules of the World Trade Organization (WTO) and trade measures taken pursuant to multilateral environmental agreements (e.g. the status of eco-labelling measures vis-à-vis WTO rules, and the role of the precautionary principle within the multilateral trading system). Attaching priority to the *integration of environmental considerations into trade negotiations*, the UK sent its environment minister as part of its official delegation to the WTO's Seattle and Doha ministerial meetings.

The UK's Health and Safety Executive administers a national system of *prior informed consent (PIC)* to address concerns about the export of dangerous chemicals to developing countries. In compliance with the EU regulation on PIC, the government requires: i) notification of the intent to export chemicals that have been banned or severely restricted within the EU; ii) conformity with the *UNEP/FAO voluntary PIC procedure*; and iii) packaging and labelling of the chemicals in compliance with EU legislation, at a minimum, and in a suitable format for the importer. Since 1992, the UK has processed more than 300 export notifications. It has signed the *Rotterdam Convention*, which will eventually supersede the voluntary procedure.

A major review of the *Export Credits Guarantee Department* in 2000 revealed a need to more systematically assure the coherence of its activities with the UK's wider objectives (e.g. in the area of sustainable development). The review led to the adoption in December 2000 of business principles that determine how applications for export credit are assessed, addressing concerns of sustainable development (including environmental impacts), human rights, etc. Use of the business principles is compulsory on all applications for support; the challenge will be to ensure their implementation. In 2001, the department put in place a screening process to ensure that all applications take account of projects' environmental and social impacts. The environmental assessment process fully meets the requirements of the agreement on "Common Approaches on the Environment and Officially Supported Export Credit", which was accepted by the majority of OECD Export Credit Group members in November 2001.

Ozone-depleting substances

The UK diminished its use of ozone-depleting substances (ODS) in the 1990s to meet the progressively tighter deadlines set by the four EU regulations introduced since 1988. Issued in response to amendments to the *Montreal Protocol*, the regulations set stricter limits and deadlines than those defined in the protocol for developed countries. From 1 January 2002, Regulation 2037/2000 mandates recovery of all CFCs and HCFCs from discarded domestic refrigerators. In late 2001, the UK began strongly expanding its CFC recovery and destruction capacity to comply with the regulation. By May 2002, two mobile destruction plants were operating and two stationary plants were being built. As an interim measure, refrigerators were being exported to Germany for treatment, or stored at secure sites. How recovery and destruction will be financed in the longer term is an open question. Instruments for applying extended producer responsibility should be given consideration.

The UK contributed USD 13.8 million to the *Montreal Protocol Multilateral Fund* in the first commitment period (1991-93), USD 26.2 million in the second period (1994-96), USD 29.3 million in the third period (1997-99) and USD 23.0 million in the fourth period (2000-02). The UK emphasises the continued need to support and promote implementation of the Montreal Protocol, particularly in *developing countries*, and has called for strengthening of measures to limit smuggling of CFCs into the EU from developing countries where they are still produced.

Genetically modified organisms

The UK helped develop UNEP's *International Technical Guidelines for Safety in Biotechnology* (1995), which established common principles for risk assessment and management of genetically modified organisms (GMOs). While supporting a precautionary approach to the development and use of genetically modified crops, the UK has initiated a programme of *farm-scale trials* to study the environmental effects of their cultivation. There is no commercial cultivation of genetically modified crops in the UK.

Although *international co-operation on genetically modified food and crops* has become more turbulent since 1997, the UK has continued to press for international solutions. The UK supported international conferences on GMOs, in co-operation with the OECD and other international organisations, in Edinburgh (2000) and Bangkok (2001). Discussions focused on issues related to freedom of trade, the right of countries to refuse imports that may affect biodiversity and the consumer's right to choose. The UK signed the Cartagena Protocol to the Convention on Biological Diversity in 2000, and vowed to push for early ratification.

2.   Focus on Selected Topics

2.1   Climate change: the UK Programme

In its "*baseline with ongoing measures*" *scenario*, the UK's climate change programme ("Climate Change: The UK Programme", 2000) forecasts that national GHG emissions will be 15% below 1990 levels in 2010 (Table 9.4). The scenario takes into account the impact of measures implemented since the approval of the Kyoto Protocol in 1997 (e.g. the fuel duty escalator to 1999), as well as several measures set out in the programme (e.g. the climate change levy, the 10% renewables target). The scenario concludes that full implementation of present measures will comfortably allow the UK to meet its Kyoto target. However, as the national target to

Table 9.4 Summary of the Climate Change Programme

Measures	Sector	Avoided emissions (MtC)	Net change 1990-2010 (%)
Ongoing measures (since 1997)			
Fuel duty escalator (ended in 1999)	Energy	1-2.5	
Climate change levy	Energy	2	
Delivery of 10% renewables target	Energy	2.5	
All GHG emissions			*-15*
CO_2 emissions			*-9*
Additional measures[a]			
Climate change agreements with energy-intensive sectors	Business	2.5	
Energy efficiency measures under the Carbon Trust	Business	0.5[b]	
Voluntary reduction targets (1st stage of emission trading programme)	Business	At least 2[b]	
Reform of building regulations[c]	Business and domestic	1.3[b]	
EU-level voluntary agreements on CO_2 from motor vehicles	Transport	4	
Transport 2010: The 10 Year Plan	Transport	1.6	
Sustainable distribution strategy[d]	Transport	0.1	
Improved household energy efficiency (including Energy Efficiency Commitment)	Domestic	2.6-3.7[e]	
Upgrading of district heating systems	Domestic	0.9	
New household energy efficiency standards	Domestic	0.2	
Appliance standards and labelling	Domestic	0.2-0.4	
Afforestation	Domestic and public	0.6	
New central government, school and NHS[f] targets	Public	0.5	
Proposed changes to building regulations, new central estate target and NHSiS target	Public[g]	0.1	
All GHG emissions			*-23*
CO_2 emissions			*-19*

a) Additional measures necessitated by national target of reducing CO_2 emissions by 20% from 1990 to 2010.
b) Actual savings will depend on final design and take-up rate.
c) England and Wales only.
d) Scotland and Wales only.
e) Estimated scope for savings from cost-effective energy efficiency measures.
f) National Health Service.
g) Scotland only; NHSiS = National Health Services in Scotland.
Source: Climate Change: The UK Programme.

reduce CO_2 emissions by 20% between 1990 and 2010 is not attained in this scenario (which projects that CO_2 emissions will be 9% below 1990 levels in 2010), the programme also develops additional measures.

Measures to reduce energy consumption

The programme introduced several measures aimed at moderating energy demand. First, since 2001, a *climate change levy* is administered on all energy (except fuel oil and energy from renewable sources) consumed by the business and public sectors. The levy is designed to be broadly neutral between the manufacturing and service sectors of the economy, with no net gain for the Treasury. Thus, levy payments are partly offset by a 0.3 percentage point cut in employers' national insurance contributions. Also, from 2001 to 2004, the *Carbon Trust*, a non-profit company, will "recycle" GBP 100 million in levy receipts as grants to businesses that install low-carbon technologies. The Carbon Trust also administers an enhanced capital allowance programme for businesses, under which approved energy saving investments are eligible for 100% first-year capital allowance deductions (at an estimated cost of GBP 200 million, depending on uptake). *Energy-intensive industries* participating in voluntary agreements with the government (which specify quantitative targets for reducing operational energy intensity and GHG emissions) are granted an 80% discount in the levy rates. The programme estimates that the levy will lead to GHG emission reductions totalling about 2 MtC per year by 2010 (Table 9.4).

As part of the programme, the *energy efficiency requirements* of building regulations are being strengthened in England and Wales (Chapter 8, Section 1.3). The forecast is that implementation of the new norms, expected by 2004, will reduce GHG emissions by nearly 1.3 MtC per year by 2010. In April 2002, the government introduced the *Energy Efficiency Commitment*, under which energy utilities are required to encourage consumers to conserve energy. As low-income consumers tend to use a substantial proportion of the energy thus saved to improve comfort, the projected annual carbon savings from the Energy Efficiency Commitment (2002-05) are lower than originally supposed, at around 0.4 MtC.

Automobile manufacturers are working to improve *motor vehicle fuel efficiency* in line with voluntary agreements with the European Commission to reduce average CO_2 emissions from new cars by at least 25% below 1995 levels by 2008. A combination of fiscal measures has been launched with the aim of creating market signals in favour of *low CO_2-emitting passenger cars* (Chapter 2, Section 1.3). In 2001, the annual *vehicle excise duty* was differentiated in favour of lower-CO_2 vehicles, with vehicles being classified into four CO_2 emission "bands". *Company car taxation* has also been differentiated in favour of lower-CO_2 vehicles. It is estimated that the voluntary agreements and the changes to vehicle excise duty and company car taxation will lead to GHG emission reductions equalling about 4 MtC per year by 2010. Further reductions in transport-related GHG emissions (e.g. 1.6 MtC per year by 2010 for England) are forecast as ancillary benefits of Transport 2010: The 10 Year Plan, which features GBP 180 billion of planned investment (Chapter 6, Section 1.3).

Measures to "green" the energy supply

The Climate Change Programme sets quantitative targets concerning the development of *renewable energy sources*. For example, 5% of national electricity demand is to be met by renewables by the end of 2003, and 10% by 2010, on condition that this can be done without imposing unacceptable costs on consumers. Another target is to expand installed capacity of CHP to at least 10 000 MW by 2010, nearly double the 2000 level. It is projected that meeting the 10% renewables target would reduce GHG emissions by 2.5 MtC per year by 2010 (Table 9.4). There is scope to improve market signals in favour of the development of renewable fuels through fiscal adjustment (Chapter 6, Section 1.4).

2.2   *Performance under the long-range transboundary air pollution Convention*

Concerning *sulphur emissions*, the UK met its commitment under the Oslo Protocol to reduce SO_x emissions by 50% between 1980 and 2000, and is well on its way to meeting its Oslo commitments for 2005 and 2010 (Table 9.5). The 1999 Gothenburg Protocol, which the UK has signed but not yet ratified, would establish a ceiling on SO_x emissions (625 kt SO_2/year) for 2010 that is 36% stricter than the 2010 target set under the Oslo Protocol (980 kt/year). In 2000, the UK was well on its way towards the 2010 Gothenburg target for SO_x.

Concerning NO_x *emissions*, the UK exceeded its commitment under the 1988 Sofia Protocol to reduce its emissions to 1987 levels by 1994, achieving a 17% reduction during the period (Table 9.5). The UK did not sign the Sofia Declaration. Upon ratification of the Gothenburg Protocol, the UK would agree to cap its annual emissions of NO_x at 1 181 kt by 2010, a 56% reduction from 1990 levels. In 2000, it had already achieved 72% of the 2010 target reduction.

Concerning *NMVOC emissions*, the UK met its commitment under the 1991 Geneva Protocol, to cut emissions by 30% between 1988 and 1999, by a small margin (Table 9.5). Upon ratification of the Gothenburg Protocol, the UK would commit to capping its annual emissions of NMVOCs at 1 200 kt, representing roughly a 30% decrease from 1999 levels. Road transport and solvent use remained the major sources of NMVOCs throughout the 1990s, although major reductions were achieved (Table 2.3).

With ratification of the Gothenburg Protocol, the UK would agree to reduce its *emissions of ammonia (NH₃)* by 19% between 1990 and 2010. Given the slow rate of change between 1990 and 1999 (–5%), and the technical difficulties associated with reducing NH₃ emissions from agriculture, meeting this target may prove to be a challenge (Table 9.5).

The UK has also signed the 1998 Aarhus Protocol on heavy metals, and ratification is expected in 2002. Under the protocol, *emissions of cadmium, lead and mercury* would be capped at 1990 levels. These caps would not represent real constraints, as national emissions of these heavy metals in 1999 were already at least 65% lower than in 1990 (Table 9.5).

Table 9.5 **Performance under Convention on Long-range Transboundary Air Pollution**[a]

	Protocol[b]		Commitments		Performance	
			Target period	Target change (%)	Observed period	Change (%)
Sulphur dioxide (SO₂)	Helsinki	(1985)	1980-1993	–30	1980-93	–36
	Oslo	(1994)	1980-2000	–50	1980-99	–76
			1980-2005	–70	1980-99	–76
			1980-2010	–80	1980-99	–76
	Gothenburg[c]	(1999)	1990-2010	–83	1990-99	–68
Nitrogen oxides (NOₓ)	Sofia	(1988)	1987-1994	0	1987-94	–17
	Gothenburg[c]	(1999)	1990-2010	–58	1990-99	–42
Non-methane volatile organic compounds (NMVOCs)	Geneva	(1991)	1988-1999	–30	1988-99	–37
	Gothenburg[c]	(1999)	1990-2010	–51	1990-99	–34
Ammonia (NH₃)	Gothenburg[c]	(1999)	1990-2010	–19	1990-99	–5
Heavy metals	Aarhus[c]	(1998)				
Cadmium (Cd)			1990 cap[c]	0	1990-99	–69
Lead (Pb)			1990 cap[c]	0	1990-99	–80
Mercury (Hg)			1990 cap[c]	0	1990-99	–71
Persistent organic pollutants	Aarhus[c]	(1998)				
Polycyclic aromatic hydrocarbons			1990 cap[c]	0	1990-99	–454
Dioxins/furans			1990 cap[c]	0	1990-99	–230
Hexachlorobenzene			1990 cap[c]	0	1990-99	–61

a) 1979 Geneva Convention.
b) Date opened for signature indicated in parenthesis.
c) The UK has signed but not yet ratified the Gothenburg and Aarhus Protocols; base years are therefore provisional, to be confirmed during ratification.
Source: EMEP; UK National Atmospheric Emissions Inventory; OECD.

The UK has signed the 1998 Aarhus Protocol on *persistent organic pollutants*, and ratification is expected in 2002. Here again, the limits set would not represent real constraints. The 11 pesticides to be phased out under the protocol have either already been banned or were never authorised in the UK. In addition, hexachlorobenzene (HCB) and PCBs are scheduled for elimination in the UK in advance of the protocol deadlines, and as for the three groups of chemicals for which the protocol proposes a cap at 1990 levels (PAHs, HCB and dioxins), the UK has already achieved very large reductions, according to the national emission inventory (Table 9.5).

ANNEXES

ANNEX I.A: SELECTED ENVIRONMENTAL DATA (1)

	Ref	CAN	MEX	USA	JPN	KOR	AUS	NZL	AUT	BEL	CZE	DNK	FIN
LAND													
Total area (1000 km^2)		9971	1958	9364	378	99	7713	270	84	31	79	43	338
Major protected areas (% of total area)	2	9.6	8.2	21.2	6.8	6.9	7.7	23.5	29.2	2.8	16.2	32.0	8.4
Nitrogenous fertiliser use (t/km^2 of arable land)		3.9	4.8	6.3	11.2	23.4	2.1	38.0	8.7	17.7	6.3	10.6	7.2
Pesticide use (t/km^2 of arable land)		0.07	0.13	0.21	1.50	1.29	0.23	0.85	0.25	0.92	0.12	0.15	-
FOREST													
Forest area (% of land area)		45.3	33.4	32.6	66.8	65.2	19.4	29.5	47.6	22.2	34.1	10.5	75.5
Use of forest resources (harvest/growth)		0.4	0.2	0.6	0.3	0.1	..	0.6	0.6	0.9	0.7	0.6	0.8
Tropical wood imports (USD/cap.)	3	1.6	0.2	2.2	10.7	6.1	4.0	3.4	0.5	24.3	0.3	3.8	1.4
THREATENED SPECIES													
Mammals (% of species known)		19.2	33.2	10.5	23.5	17.0	14.9	15.2	35.4	31.6	33.3	24.0	11.9
Birds (% of species known)		10.8	16.9	7.2	12.9	15.0	6.4	25.3	37.0	27.5	55.9	10.6	6.7
Fish (% of species known)		6.4	5.7	2.4	25.3	1.3	0.4	0.8	65.5	54.3	29.2	18.2	11.9
WATER													
Water withdrawal (% of gross annual availability)		1.7	17.4	19.9	21.2	35.6	4.3	0.6	2.7	42.5	15.6	15.7	2.2
Public waste water treatment (% of population served)		78	22	71	62	53	..	80	75	27	59	87	77
Fish catches (% of world catches)		1.1	1.3	5.1	5.6	2.3	0.2	0.6	-	-	-	1.5	0.2
AIR													
Emissions of sulphur oxides (kg/cap.)		89.7	24.5	62.7	6.9	32.9	95.8	12.3	5.7	23.6	68.0	20.7	19.5
(kg/1000 USD GDP)	4	3.7	3.3	2.0	0.3	2.3	4.0	0.7	0.2	1.1	5.3	0.9	0.9
% change (1990-late 1990s)		-19	..	-20	-3	-7	-4	3	-50	-25	-63	-50	-61
Emissions of nitrogen oxides (kg/cap.)		67.8	17.3	84.4	15.8	27.6	135.2	45.9	21.0	32.8	41.1	46.9	50.5
(kg/1000 USD GDP)	4	2.9	2.3	2.6	0.6	1.9	5.7	2.6	0.9	1.5	3.2	2.0	2.4
% change (1990-late 1990s)		-5	..	5	8	36	17	22	-11	-3	-43	-12	-13
Emissions of carbon dioxide (t./cap.)	5	16.0	3.7	20.5	9.1	8.8	17.0	8.0	7.5	11.6	10.8	10.0	11.2
(t./1000 USD GDP)	4	0.63	0.47	0.64	0.38	0.58	0.71	0.45	0.32	0.49	0.86	0.40	0.50
% change (1990-1999)		16	21	15	10	76	24	33	6	12	-26	7	8
WASTE GENERATED													
Industrial waste (kg/1000 USD GDP)	4, 6	..	51	..	41	56	106	28	63	62	288	22	118
Municipal waste (kg/cap.)	7	500	310	720	410	400	690	350	510	480	310	560	410
Nuclear waste (t./Mtoe of TPES)	8	5.0	0.1	0.9	1.9	2.7	-	-	-	1.3	1.1	-	2.2
PAC EXPENDITURE (% of GDP)	9	1.1	0.8	1.6	1.6	1.7	0.8	..	1.7	0.9	2.0	0.9	1.1

.. not available.　- nil or negligible.　x data included under Belgium.

1) Data refer to the latest available year. They include provisional figures and Secretariat estimates.
　　Partial totals are underlined. Varying definitions can limit comparability across countries.
2) Data refer to IUCN categories I to VI; AUS, HUN, ITA, LUX, TUR: national data.
3) Total imports of cork and wood from non-OECD tropical countries.
4) GDP at 1995 prices and purchasing power parities.
Source: OECD Environmental Data Compendium.

OECD EPR / SECOND CYCLE

FRA	DEU	GRC	HUN	ISL	IRL	ITA	LUX	NLD	NOR	POL	PRT	ESP	SLO	SWE	CHE	TUR	UKD*	OECD*
549	357	132	93	103	70	301	3	42	324	313	92	506	49	450	41	779	245	34777
10.1	26.9	2.6	9.1	9.5	0.9	9.1	6.5	11.6	7.6	9.4	6.6	8.4	21.6	8.1	18.0	3.8	20.4	12.4
13.7	16.7	7.4	5.6	10.2	47.0	7.9	x	34.9	11.8	5.9	4.5	6.2	4.1	6.8	12.6	5.5	20.3	6.6
0.59	0.29	0.29	0.14	..	0.25	0.78	x	1.06	0.09	0.07	0.43	0.18	0.23	0.06	0.37	0.13	0.58	0.25
31.4	30.1	22.8	18.9	1.3	8.8	23.3	34.4	9.2	39.2	29.7	37.9	32.3	42.2	73.5	31.7	26.9	10.5	33.9
0.7	0.4	0.6	0.6	-	0.6	0.3	0.5	0.6	0.5	0.6	0.8	0.5	0.5	0.7	0.5	0.4	0.7	0.5
6.8	1.8	2.8	0.1	2.8	11.2	7.1	-	15.6	3.6	0.3	17.9	6.3	0.1	2.2	0.6	0.5	2.7	4.0
20.2	36.7	37.9	71.1	-	6.5	40.7	51.6	15.6	5.9	15.5	17.3	21.2	23.3	18.2	34.2	22.2	20.0	..
14.3	29.2	13.0	18.8	13.3	21.8	18.4	50.0	27.1	7.7	16.6	13.7	14.1	14.3	8.6	42.6	6.7	6.8	..
6.6	68.2	24.3	32.1	-	33.3	31.8	27.9	82.1	-	27.1	18.6	29.4	38.3	12.7	44.7	9.9	11.1	..
23.9	24.4	12.1	5.0	0.1	2.6	32.2	3.4	4.9	0.7	18.7	15.3	36.8	1.4	1.5	4.9	15.2	17.4	11.9
77	89	45	22	16	61	63	88	97	73	47	55	48	49	93	94	12	92	59
0.6	0.3	0.1	-	1.9	0.3	0.3	-	0.6	2.8	0.3	0.2	1.3	-	0.4	-	0.6	0.9	28.5
16.2	10.1	48.3	64.7	32.1	48.7	16.0	8.4	8.0	6.9	61.3	37.6	49.1	33.2	8.0	4.6	29.8	19.9	36.1
0.8	0.4	3.6	6.7	1.3	2.1	0.8	0.2	0.4	0.3	8.2	2.5	3.2	3.3	0.4	0.2	4.8	1.0	1.8
-24	-84	-	-35	6	-3	-46	-76	-38	-43	-26	4	..	-67	-48	-24	..	-68	-30
29.1	19.9	35.2	19.4	105.6	33.9	25.8	39.6	28.5	50.5	29.9	37.0	31.7	24.1	30.2	18.2	14.5	26.9	41.8
1.4	0.9	2.6	2.0	4.4	1.5	1.2	1.1	1.3	2.0	4.0	2.4	2.1	2.4	1.4	0.7	2.3	1.3	2.0
-10	-40	8	-17	9	6	-24	-27	-23	2	-10	17	..	-43	-23	-22	37	-42	-3
6.1	10.0	7.7	5.7	7.4	10.7	7.3	17.3	10.5	8.3	8.0	6.1	6.9	7.3	5.4	5.6	2.8	9.0	11.0
0.27	0.44	0.54	0.54	0.29	0.43	0.34	0.43	0.44	0.32	0.93	0.39	0.39	0.72	0.25	0.21	0.47	0.44	0.51
-	-15	18	-14	3	24	6	-28	6	30	-11	53	29	-29	-	-3	32	-6	10
84	38	47	72	1	65	19	136	26	27	72	3	24	81	86	8	87	53	70
590	460	370	490	650	560	490	590	560	600	320	440	390	320	360	600	330	560	510
4.5	1.3	-	1.9	-	-	-	-	0.2	-	..	-	1.2	2.4	4.7	2.4	-	3.4	1.5
1.4	1.5	0.8	0.7	..	0.6	0.9	..	1.8	1.2	1.1	0.9	0.8	..	1.2	1.6	..	1.0	..

UKD: pesticides and threatened species: Great Britain; water withdrawal: England and Wales.

5) CO_2 from energy use only; international marine and aviation bunkers are excluded.

6) Waste from manufacturing industries.

7) NZL: household waste only.

8) Waste from spent fuel arising in nuclear power plants, in tonnes of heavy metal, per million tonnes of oil equivalent
   of total primary energy supply.

9) Household expenditure excluded; HUN, POL: investments only.

ANNEX I.B: SELECTED ECONOMIC DATA (1)

		CAN	MEX	USA	JPN	KOR	AUS	NZL	AUT	BEL	CZE	DNK
GROSS DOMESTIC PRODUCT												
GDP, 2000 (billion USD at 1995 prices and PPPs)		818	814	9141	3126	774	470	71	196	254	133	137
% change (1990-2000)		30.6	41.0	38.9	14.4	80.8	42.7	29.1	24.2	23.4	-7.5	25.7
per capita, 2000 (1000 USD/cap.)		26.6	8.2	33.2	24.7	16.4	24.5	18.4	24.2	24.8	12.9	25.6
Exports, 2000 (% of GDP)		45.8	31.4	11.0	10.8	45.0	21.7	35.7	48.9	88.1	73.2	42.4
INDUSTRY	2											
Value added in industry (% of GDP)		33	28	26	36	45	26	26	33	27	43	26
Industrial production: % change (1990-2000)		29.1	48.4	49.0	2.2	131.8	27.5	30.8	45.6	16.6	-23.8	39.1
AGRICULTURE												
Value added in agriculture (% of GDP)	3	3	5	2	2	5	3	7	2	2	4	3
Agricultural production: % change (1990-1999)		26.4	29.1	22.4	-8.2	20.9	24.2	24.6	0.9	19.6	-23.0	4.6
Livestock population, 2000 (million head of sheep eq.)		101	270	785	55	29	285	104	20	29	15	24
ENERGY												
Total supply, 1999 (Mtoe)		242	149	2270	515	181	108	18	28	59	39	20
% change (1990-1999)		15.6	20.0	17.9	17.5	97.5	23.3	30.0	12.7	21.1	-18.6	12.4
Energy intensity, 1999 (toe/1000 USD GDP)		0.31	0.20	0.26	0.17	0.25	0.24	0.27	0.15	0.24	0.30	0.15
% change (1990-1999)		-7.3	-9.1	-10.9	4.4	18.9	-10.4	3.8	-6.3	2.1	-9.3	-7.9
Structure of energy supply, 1999 (%)	4											
Solid fuels		15.8	9.8	27.4	18.0	21.6	48.8	12.4	22.0	14.1	49.5	30.8
Oil		35.4	62.6	38.9	51.7	55.0	33.0	35.5	41.7	41.3	21.3	46.1
Gas		28.8	20.8	23.0	12.0	8.4	16.9	26.5	23.9	22.8	19.9	21.8
Nuclear		7.8	1.8	8.9	16.0	14.8	-	-	-	21.8	9.0	-
Hydro, etc.		12.2	5.2	1.8	2.2	0.2	1.4	25.6	12.4	0.1	0.4	1.3
ROAD TRANSPORT	5											
Road traffic volumes per capita, 1999 (1000 veh.-km/cap.)		9.4	0.6	15.8	6.0	1.8	9.3	8.0	7.8	8.7	3.0	8.4
Road vehicle stock, 1999 (10 000 vehicles)		1876	1459	21533	7003	1116	1195	231	485	512	373	223
% change (1990-1999)		13.3	47.7	14.1	24.0	228.9	22.2	25.2	31.3	20.2	43.7	17.9
per capita (veh./100 inh.)		62	15	79	55	24	63	61	60	50	36	42

.. not available.   - nil or negligible.   x data included under Belgium.

1) Data may include provisional figures and Secretariat estimates. Partial totals are underlined.

2) Value added: includes mining and quarrying, manufacturing, gas, electricity and water and construction;
   production: excludes construction.

Source: OECD Environmental Data Compendium.

OECD EPR / SECOND CYCLE

FIN	FRA	DEU	GRC	HUN	ISL	IRL	ITA	LUX	NLD	NOR	POL	PRT	ESP	SLO	SWE	CHE	TUR	UKD	OECD
124	1362	1905	158	113	7	103	1266	19	395	117	348	161	717	56	203	198	421	**1254**	24860
24.0	19.2	20.5	25.0	8.3	27.3	98.2	17.0	76.2	33.3	38.9	43.2	29.0	29.6	11.4	18.7	9.3	41.9	**24.3**	29.8
23.9	22.9	23.2	14.9	11.3	26.3	27.2	22.0	42.7	24.8	26.1	9.0	16.1	18.2	10.4	22.9	27.6	6.3	**21.0**	22.2
42.5	28.9	33.3	22.1	61.6	34.3	95.2	28.4	119.7	67.1	46.3	26.8	31.3	29.9	73.5	47.4	45.1	23.8	**27.2**	21.7
34	25	31	24	34	29	36	30	20	27	36	36	31	30	35	29	30	30	**30**	30
64.9	17.7	13.9	12.5	48.2	..	223.5	15.7	26.6	21.7	41.4	63.6	21.8	23.5	-7.7	42.6	25.8	51.3	**11.5**	<u>27.9</u>
4	3	1	8	5	10	4	3	1	3	2	4	4	4	5	2	2	15	**1**	3
-8.4	5.8	-5.6	14.5	-28.9	3.2	9.9	9.2	x	0.2	-9.5	-18.8	1.1	11.1	-23.9	-2.3	-2.7	7.6	**-0.7**	..
9	165	126	21	13	1	53	71	x	47	11	60	18	96	7	14	12	119	**126**	2687
33	255	337	27	25	3	14	169	3	74	27	93	24	118	18	51	27	70	**230**	5229
15.8	12.8	-5.2	23.5	-11.1	51.3	33.6	11.5	-2.2	11.4	23.9	-6.5	43.9	30.9	-17.0	9.5	6.5	33.6	**8.1**	15.9
0.29	0.19	0.18	0.18	0.23	0.44	0.15	0.14	0.20	0.19	0.23	0.28	0.15	0.17	0.33	0.26	0.14	0.18	**0.19**	0.22
-1.2	-2.3	-19.0	2.9	-13.7	23.1	-25.1	-1.9	-39.8	-13.2	-8.9	-32.0	15.1	5.1	-23.9	-4.5	0.8	0.9	**-10.4**	-7.0
35.7	10.2	24.8	36.4	18.3	1.8	19.0	8.3	4.9	12.0	9.5	69.1	21.1	19.8	29.1	21.7	5.8	38.3	**16.3**	23.7
32.1	34.6	40.1	57.1	27.8	26.5	58.9	54.1	73.0	38.8	33.8	21.1	67.6	54.0	17.5	27.8	48.0	41.9	**36.2**	41.3
10.3	13.2	21.4	4.5	39.3	-	21.5	33.6	21.8	47.7	17.8	9.5	8.2	11.3	32.2	1.4	8.9	15.1	**36.3**	21.1
18.5	39.4	13.1	-	14.6	-	-	-	-	1.4	-	-	-	13.0	19.0	37.1	24.5	-	**11.0**	11.0
3.4	2.5	0.7	2.0	0.1	71.7	0.6	4.1	0.3	0.1	38.9	0.2	3.1	1.9	2.2	12.1	12.9	4.7	**0.2**	2.8
8.9	8.3	7.4	7.3	3.5	6.5	8.3	9.0	8.9	7.0	7.2	4.5	5.7	4.3	2.2	8.4	7.2	0.8	**7.8**	8.0
239	3309	4503	389	274	17	148	3545	29	675	225	1104	461	2048	141	424	376	548	**3055**	57515
7.8	16.3	20.7	54.1	25.0	27.3	55.8	15.9	39.5	17.7	16.0	72.6	109.5	41.8	..	7.9	13.9	132.1	**16.2**	<u>22.0</u>
46	56	55	37	27	62	39	61	68	43	51	29	46	52	26	48	53	8	**51**	52

3) Agriculture, forestry, hunting, fishery, etc.
4) Breakdown excludes electricity trade.
5) Refers to motor vehicles with four or more wheels, except for Italy, which include
  three-wheeled goods vehicles.

ANNEX I.C: SELECTED SOCIAL DATA (1)

		CAN	MEX	USA	JPN	KOR	AUS	NZL	AUT	BEL	CZE	DNK
POPULATION												
Total population, 2000 (100 000 inh.)		308	991	2754	1268	472	192	38	81	102	103	53
% change (1990-2000)		11.0	22.0	10.2	2.6	10.1	12.3	13.9	4.8	2.8	-0.9	3.8
Population density, 2000 (inh./km^2)		3.1	50.6	29.4	335.7	475.2	2.5	14.2	96.4	335.5	130.3	123.8
Ageing index, 1999 (over 64/under 15)		64.1	15.5	59.2	113.0	31.4	59.2	51.0	90.4	93.5	79.3	81.1
HEALTH												
Women life expectancy at birth, 1998 (years)		81.5	77.6	79.5	84.0	78.1	81.8	80.4	80.9	81.1	78.1	78.8
Infant mortality, 1999 (deaths /1 000 live births)		5.3	14.5	7.2	3.4	7.7	5.7	6.8	4.4	5.3	4.1	4.2
Expenditure, 1999 (% of GDP)		9.2	5.3	12.9	7.5	5.4	8.6	8.1	8.2	8.8	7.4	8.4
INCOME AND POVERTY												
GDP per capita, 2000 (1000 USD/cap.)		26.6	8.2	33.2	24.7	16.4	24.5	18.4	24.2	24.8	12.9	25.6
Poverty (% pop. < 50% median income)		10.3	21.9	17.0	8.1	..	9.3	..	7.4	7.8	..	5.0
Inequality (Gini levels)	2	28.5	52.6	34.4	26.0	..	30.5	25.6	26.1	27.2	..	21.7
Minimum to median wages, 2000	3	42.5	21.1	36.4	32.9	23.8	57.9	46.3	x	49.2	30.4	x
EMPLOYMENT												
Unemployment rate, 2000 (% of total labour force)		6.8	2.3	4.0	4.7	4.1	6.6	6.0	4.6	7.0	8.8	4.8
Labour force participation rate, 2000 (% 15-64 year-olds)		77.4	56.3	67.2	78.1	65.2	75.3	65.4	77.5	63.7	79.7	80.5
Employment in agriculture, 1999 (%)	4	3.6	20.1	2.6	5.2	11.6	5.0	9.5	6.2	2.3	6.0	3.3
EDUCATION												
Education, 1999 (% 25-64 year-olds)	5	79.5	20.2	86.9	80.9	66.3	57.4	73.6	73.9	57.4	86.0	79.6
Expenditure, 1998 (% of GDP)	6	6.2	4.7	6.4	4.7	7.0	5.5	..	6.4	5.0	4.7	7.2
OFFICIAL DEVELOPMENT ASSISTANCE	7											
ODA, 2000 (% of GNP)		0.25	..	0.10	0.28	..	0.27	0.25	0.23	0.36	..	1.06
ODA, 2000 (USD/cap.)		57	..	36	107	..	51	30	52	80	..	312

.. not available.   - nil or negligible.   x not applicable.

1) Data may include provisional figures and Secretariat estimates. Partial totals are underlined.

2) Ranging from 0 (equal) to 100 (inequal) income distribution; figures relate to total disposable income (including all incomes, taxes and benefits) for the entire population.

3) Minimum wage as a percentage of median earnings including overtime pay and bonuses.

Source: OECD.

OECD EPR / SECOND CYCLE

FIN	FRA	DEU	GRC	HUN	ISL	IRL	ITA	LUX	NLD	NOR	POL	PRT	ESP	SLO	SWE	CHE	TUR	**UKD**	OECD
52	594	821	106	100	3	38	576	4	159	45	386	100	394	54	89	72	668	**598**	11220
3.8	4.6	3.4	4.6	-3.4	10.2	8.1	1.6	14.1	6.2	5.9	1.3	1.3	1.5	2.5	3.7	6.9	18.9	**3.8**	7.7
15.3	108.1	229.9	80.0	107.7	2.7	53.9	191.3	169.6	382.4	13.9	123.5	108.8	77.9	110.0	19.7	173.8	85.7	**244.0**	32.3
81.3	83.7	107.1	95.2	84.8	49.0	50.9	119.6	75.6	73.0	77.1	59.9	90.3	108.9	57.5	98.7	87.2	17.6	**81.6**	63.2
81.0	82.2	80.5	79.4	75.2	81.5	79.1	81.6	80.5	80.7	81.1	77.5	78.8	82.4	77.0	81.9	82.5	71.3	**79.7**	..
3.6	4.4	4.5	5.9	8.5	2.4	5.5	5.1	4.7	5.2	3.9	8.9	5.5	4.9	8.3	3.4	4.6	36.6	**5.8**	..
6.8	9.3	10.3	8.4	6.8	8.7	6.8	7.9	6.1	8.7	8.5	6.2	7.7	7.0	..	7.9	10.4	4.8	**6.9**	..
23.9	22.9	23.2	14.9	11.3	26.3	27.2	22.0	42.7	24.8	26.1	9.0	16.1	18.2	10.4	22.9	27.6	6.3	**21.0**	22.2
4.9	7.5	9.4	13.8	7.3	..	11.0	14.2	..	6.3	10.0	..	..	..	..	6.4	6.2	16.2	**10.9**	..
22.8	27.8	28.2	33.6	28.3	..	32.4	34.5	..	25.5	25.6	..	..	..	..	23.0	26.9	49.1	**32.4**	..
x	60.8	x	51.3	35.6	x	x	x	48.9	46.7	x	35.5	38.2	31.8	..	x	x	..	**x**	..
9.8	9.7	7.8	11.3	6.5	1.3	4.3	10.7	2.6	2.4	3.4	16.1	4.0	14.1	18.8	4.7	2.0	6.4	**5.5**	6.2
74.5	68.6	74.7	61.8	58.8	77.6	69.6	60.0	64.3	66.4	80.9	65.3	75.0	65.6	69.3	76.2	81.2	51.7	**76.1**	68.4
6.3	4.2	2.8	17.7	7.3	8.6	8.6	6.4	2.0	3.0	4.6	17.9	13.6	7.4	7.4	2.6	4.7	45.1	**1.6**	7.8
71.5	61.9	81.2	49.9	67.4	56.0	51.3	42.2	55.9	..	84.6	54.0	21.2	35.1	..	76.6	81.7	22.2	**61.7**	62.0
5.7	6.2	5.5	4.8	5.0	6.9	4.7	5.0	..	4.6	6.9	..	5.7	5.3	..	6.8	5.9	3.5	**4.9**	5.6
0.31	0.32	0.27	0.20	..	..	0.30	0.13	0.71	0.84	0.80	..	0.26	0.22	..	0.80	0.34	..	**0.32**	0.22
72	69	61	21	..	..	62	24	288	197	281	..	27	30	..	203	124	..	**75**	64

4) Civil employment in agriculture, forestry and fishing.
5) Upper secondary or higher education; OECD: average of rates.
6) Public and private expenditure on educational institutions; OECD: average of rates.
7) Official Development Assistance by Member countries of the OECD Development Assistance Committee.

ANNEX II.A: SELECTED MULTILATERAL AGREEMENTS (WORLDWIDE)

Y = in force S = signed R = ratified D = denounced

			CAN	MEX	USA	JPN
1946 Washington	Conv. - Regulation of whaling	Y	D	R	R	R
1956 Washington	Protocol	Y	R	R	R	R
1949 Geneva	Conv. - Road traffic	Y	R		R	R
1954 London	Conv. - Prevention of pollution of the sea by oil	Y	R	R	R	R
1971 London	Amendments to convention (protection of the Great Barrier Reef)	R				
1957 Brussels	Conv. - Limitation of the liability of owners of sea-going ships	Y	S			D
1979 Brussels	Protocol	Y				
1958 Geneva	Conv. - Fishing and conservation of the living resources of the high seas	Y	S	R	R	
1960 Geneva	Conv. - Protection of workers against ionising radiations (ILO 115)	Y				R
1962 Brussels	Conv. - Liability of operators of nuclear ships					
1963 Vienna	Conv. - Civil liability for nuclear damage	Y		R		
1988 Vienna	Joint protocol relating to the application of the Vienna Convention and the Paris Convention	Y				
1997 Vienna	Protocol to amend the Vienna convention					
1963 Moscow	Treaty - Banning nuclear weapon tests in the atmosphere, in outer space and under water	Y	R	R	R	R
1964 Copenhagen	Conv. - International council for the exploration of the sea	Y	R		R	
1970 Copenhagen	Protocol	Y	R		R	
1969 Brussels	Conv. - Intervention on the high seas in cases of oil pollution casualties (INTERVENTION)	Y		R	R	R
1973 London	Protocol (pollution by substances other than oil)	Y		R	R	
1969 Brussels	Conv. - Civil liability for oil pollution damage (CLC)	Y	R	D	S	D
1976 London	Protocol	Y	R	R		R
1992 London	Protocol	Y	R	R		R
1970 Bern	Conv. - Transport of goods by rail (CIM)	Y				
1971 Brussels	Conv. - International fund for compensation for oil pollution damage (FUND)	Y	D	D	S	D
1976 London	Protocol	Y	R	R		R
1992 London	Protocol	Y	R	R		R
1971 Brussels	Conv. - Civil liability in maritime carriage of nuclear material	Y				
1971 London, Moscow, Washington	Conv. - Prohib. emplacement of nuclear and mass destruct. weapons on sea-bed, ocean floor and subsoil	Y	R	R	R	R
1971 Ramsar	Conv. - Wetlands of international importance especially as waterfowl habitat	Y	R	R	R	R
1982 Paris	Protocol	Y	R	R	R	R
1987 Regina	Regina amendment	Y	R	R		R
1971 Geneva	Conv. - Protection against hazards of poisoning arising from benzene (ILO 136)	Y				
1972 London, Mexico, Moscow, Washington	Conv. - Prevention of marine pollution by dumping of wastes and other matter (LC)	Y	R	R	R	R
1996 London	Protocol to the Conv. - Prevention of marine poll. by dumping of wastes and other matter		R		S	
1972 Geneva	Conv. - Protection of new varieties of plants (revised)	Y	R	R	R	R
1978 Geneva	Amendments	Y	R	R	R	R
1991 Geneva	Amendments	Y			R	R
1972 Geneva	Conv. - Safe container (CSC)	Y	R	R	R	R
1972 London, Moscow, Washington	Conv. - International liability for damage caused by space objects	Y	R	R	R	R
1972 Paris	Conv. - Protection of the world cultural and natural heritage	Y	R	R	R	R
1973 Washington	Conv. - International trade in endangered species of wild fauna and flora (CITES)	Y	R	R	R	R
1974 Geneva	Conv. - Prev. and control of occup. hazards caused by carcinog. subst. and agents (ILO 139)	Y				R
1976 London	Conv. - Limitation of liability for maritime claims (LLMC)	Y		R		
1996 London	Amendment to convention		S			
1977 Geneva	Conv. - Protection of workers against occupational hazards in the working environment due to air pollution, noise and vibration (ILO 148)	Y				
1978 London	Protocol - Prevention of pollution from ships (MARPOL PROT)	Y	R	R	R	R
1978 London	Annex III	Y			R	R
1978 London	Annex IV					R

OECD EPR / SECOND CYCLE

Y = in force S = signed R = ratified D = denounced

KOR	AUS	NZL	AUT	BEL	CZE	DNK	FIN	FRA	DEU	GRC	HUN	ISL	IRL	ITA	LUX	NLD	NOR	POL	PRT	ESP	SLO	SWE	CHE	TUR	UKD	EU
R	R	R	R			R	R	R	R			D	R	R		R	R			R			R	R		R
R	R	R				R			R	R			R	R	R		R	R			R			R	R	R
R	R	R	R	R	R	R	R	R		R	R	R	R	R	R	R	R	R	R	R	R	R	S	R	R	R
R	R	R	R	R		R	R	R	R	R		R	R	R		R	R	R	R	R		R	R			R
	R	R				R	R	R	R	R				R			R					R	R			R
	D			D		D	D	D	D		R		S	R	D	D	R	R	R		D	R				D
	R			R			S		S					R		R	R	R			R					D
	R	S		R		R	R	R			S	S		R		R	R			R					R
			R	R	R	R	R	R	R	R			R		R	R	R	R	R	R	R	R	R	R	R	R
			S				S				S		R		R										
			R				R			R						R		S	R							S
			S	R	R	R	S	S	S	R			R		R	R	R	S	S	R		R	S	S	S
			S				S			S			S		S			S							
R	R	R	R	R	R	R	R		R	R	R	R	R	R	R	R	R	R	S	R	R	R	R	R	R
			R			R	R	R	R			R	R			R	R	R	R	R		R				R
			R			R	R	R	R			R	R			R	R	R	R	R		R				R
S	R	R		R		R	R	R	S		R	R	R			R	R	R	R	R		R	R			R
	R	S		R		R	R	R	R			R	R			R	R	R	R	R		R	R			R
D	D	D		D		D	D	D	D	D		D	D	D	R	D	D	D	D	R	D		D	D	D
R	R			R		R	R	R	R	R		R	D	R	R	R	R	R	R	R		R	R			D
R	R	R		R		R	R	R	R	R		R	R	R		R	R	R	R	R		R	R			R
		R	R	R	R	R	R	R	R	R		R	R	R	R	R	R	R	R	R	R	R	R	R	R	R
D	D	D		D		D	D	D	D	D		D	D	D		D	D	D	R	D		D	D			D
	R			R		R	R	R	R	R		R	D	R		R	R	R	R	R		R				D
R	R	R		R		R	R	R	R	R		R	R	R		R	R	R	R	R		R				R
			R			R	R	R	R			R		R	R		S	R		R					S
R	R	R	R	R	R	R	R		R	R	R	R	R	R	R	R	R	R	R	R	R	R	R	R	R
R	R	R	R	R	R	R	R	R	R	R	R	R	R	R	R	R	R	R	R	R	R	R	R	R	R	R
R	R	R	R	R	R	R	R	R	R	R	R	R	R	R	R	R	R	R	R	R	R	R	R	R	R	R
R	R	R	R	R		R	R	R	R	R	R	R	R		R	R	R	R			R	R	R	R	R
			R			R	R	R	R	R		R				R			R	R		R			
R	R	R		R		R	R	R	R	R	R	R	R	R	R	R	R	R	R	R	R	R	R	R	R
	R	R	S		R	S		R			S	R			S	R			R			S	R		R
R	R	R	R	R	R	R	R	R	R	R		R	R	R		R	R	R	R	R		R	R		R
R	R	R	R			R	R	R	R	R		R	R		R	R	R	R			R	R	R		R
R	R					R	R		R						R					R		R			R
R	R	R	R	R	R	R	R	R	R	R	R		R	R	R	R	R	R	R	R	R	R	S	S	S	R
R	R	R	R	R	R	R	R	R	R	R	R	R	S	R	R	R	R	S	R		R	R	R		R
R	R	R	R	R	R	R	R	R	R	R	R	R	R	R	R	R	R	R	R	R	R	R	R	R	R	R
R	R	R	R	R	R	R	R	R	R	R	R	R	S	R	R	R	R	R	R	R	R	R	R	R	R	R
			R	R	R	R	R	R		R	R	R	R		R		R		R	R	R	R			
	R	R		R		R	R	R	R	R			R		R	R	R		R		R	R	R	R	R
				S	R	S	R							S	N					S				R
			R	R	R	R	R	R				R		R			R	R	R	R	R	R		R
R	R	R	R	R	R	R	R	R	R	R	R	R	R	R	R	R	R	R	R	R	R	R	R	R	R	R
R	R	R	R	R	R	R	R	R	R	R	R	R	R	R	R	R	R	R	R	R	R	R	R	R	R	R
		R	R	R	R	R	R	R	R			R	R			R	R	R	R	R	R	R				R

ANNEX II.A: SELECTED MULTILATERAL AGREEMENTS (WORLDWIDE) (cont.)

Y = in force S = signed R = ratified D = denounced

		CAN	MEX	USA	JPN
1978 London	Annex V	Y	R	R	R
1997 London	Annex VI				
1979 Bonn	Conv. - Conservation of migratory species of wild animals	Y			
1991 London	Agreem. - Conservation of bats in Europe	Y			
1992 New York	Agreem. - Conservation of small cetaceans of the Baltic and the North Seas (ASCOBANS)	Y			
1996 Monaco	Agreem. - Conservation of cetaceans of the Black Sea, Mediterranean Sea and Contiguous Atlantic Area	Y			
1996 The Hague	Agreem. - Conservation of African-Eurasian migratory waterbirds	Y			
1982 Montego Bay	Conv. - Law of the sea	Y S	R		R
1994 New York	Agreem. - relating to the implementation of part XI of the convention	Y S		S	R
1995 New York	Agreem. - Implementation of the provisions of the convention relating to the conservation and management of straddling fish stocks and highly migratory fish stocks	R		R	S
1983 Geneva	Agreem. - Tropical timber	Y R		R	R
1994 New York	Revised agreem. - Tropical timber	Y R		R	R
1985 Vienna	Conv. - Protection of the ozone layer	Y R	R	R	R
1987 Montreal	Protocol (substances that deplete the ozone layer)	Y R	R	R	R
1990 London	Amendment to protocol	Y R	R	R	R
1992 Copenhagen	Amendment to protocol	Y R	R	R	R
1997 Montreal	Amendment to protocol	Y R			
1999 Beijing	Amendment to protocol	R			
1986 Vienna	Conv. - Early notification of a nuclear accident	Y R	R	R	R
1986 Vienna	Conv. - Assistance in the case of a nuclear accident or radiological emergency	Y S	R	R	R
1989 Basel	Conv. - Control of transboundary movements of hazardous wastes and their disposal	Y R	R	S	R
1995 Geneva	Amendment				
1999 Basel	Prot. - Liability and compensation for damage				
1989 London	Conv. - Salvage	Y R	R	R	
1990 Geneva	Conv. - Safety in the use of chemicals at work (ILO 170)	Y	R		
1990 London	Conv. - Oil pollution preparedness, response and co-operation (OPRC)	Y R	R	R	R
1992 Rio de Janeiro	Conv. - Biological diversity	Y R	R	S	R
2000 Montreal	Prot. - Biosafety	S	S		
1992 New York	Conv. - Framework convention on climate change	Y R	R	R	R
1997 Kyoto	Protocol	S	R	S	R
1993 Paris	Conv. - Prohibition of the development, production, stockpiling and use of chemical weapons and their destruction	Y R	R	S	R
1993 Geneva	Conv. - Prevention of major industrial accidents (ILO 174)	Y			
1993	Agreem. - Promote compliance with international conservation and management measures by fishing vessels on the high seas	R	R	R	R
1994 Vienna	Conv. - Nuclear safety	Y R	R	R	R
1994 Paris	Conv. - Combat desertification in those countries experiencing serious drought and/or desertification, particularly in Africa	Y R	R	R	R
1995 Rome	Code of conduct on responsible fishing				
1996 London	Conv. - Liability and compensation for damage in connection with the carriage of hazardous and noxious substances by sea	S			
1997 Vienna	Conv. - Supplementary compensation for nuclear damage			S	
1997 Vienna	Conv. - Joint convention on the safety of spent fuel management and on the safety of radioactive waste management	Y R		S	
1997 New York	Conv. - Law of the non-navigational uses of international watercourses				
1998 Rotterdam	Conv. - Prior informed consent procedure for hazardous chemicals and pesticides (PIC)			S	S
2001 London	Conv. - Civil liability for bunker oil pollution damage				
2001 Stockholm	Conv. - Persistent organic pollutants	R	S	S	

Source: IUCN; OECD.

OECD EPR / SECOND CYCLE

Y = in force   S = signed   R = ratified   D = denounced

KOR	AUS	NZL	AUT	BEL	CZE	DNK	FIN	FRA	DEU	GRC	HUN	ISL	IRL	ITA	LUX	NLD	NOR	POL	PRT	ESP	SLO	SWE	CHE	TUR	**UKD**	EU
R	R	R	R	R	R	R	R	R	R	R	R	R	R	R	R	R	R	R	R	R	R	R	R	R	**R**	
																	S			S						
	R			R	R	R	R	R	R	R			R	R	R	R	R	R	R	R		R	R		**R**	R
			S	R	R	R	R	R		R			R		R	R	R	R		R		R			**R**	
			R			R	R		R				R			R				R		R			**R**	S
						S	S		S				S				S	R				S		S		S
			S			R	R	S	R	S			S		S	R			R	R	R	R			**R**	S
R	R	R	R	R	R	S	R	R	R	R	R	S	R	R	R	R	R	R	R	R	R	R	S		**R**	R
R	R	R	R	R	R	S	R	R	R		R	R	R	R	R	R	R	R	R	R	R	R	S		**R**	R
S	R	R	S	S		S	S	S	S	S	S		R	S	S	S	S	R	S	S	S	S			**S**	S
R	R	R	R	R		R	R	R	R	R			R	R	R	R			R	R		R	R		**R**	R
R	R	R	R	R		R	R	R	R	R			R	R	R	R			R	R		R	R		**R**	R
R	R	R	R	R	R	R	R	R	R	R	R	R	R	R	R	R	R	R	R	R	R	R	R	R	**R**	R
R	R	R	R	R	R	R	R	R	R	R	R	R	R	R	R	R	R	R	R	R	R	R	R	R	**R**	R
R	R	R	R	R	R	R	R	R	R	R	R	R	R	R	R	R	R	R	R	R	R	R	R	R	**R**	R
R	R	R	R	R	R	R	R	R	R	R	R	R	R	R	R	R	R	R	R	R	R	R	R	R	**R**	R
R	R	R	R	S	R	R	R		R			R	R		R	R	R	R		R	R	R			**R**	R
	R			R		R							R		R										**R**	
R	R	R	R	R	R	R	R	R	R	R	R	R	R	R	R	R	R	R	R	R	R	R	R	R	**R**	
R	R	R	R	R	R	S	R	R	R	R	R	S	R	R	R	R	S	R	S	R	R	R	R	R	**R**	R
R	R	R	R	R	R	R	R	R	R	R	R	R	R	R	R	R	R	R	R	R	R	R	R	R	**R**	R
	R			R	R	R							R	R	R		R	R	R				S	S	**S**	
						R		S		R				S			S	R	R		S		R		**R**	
																R						R				
R	R			R	R	R	R	R	R		R	R	R	R	R	R	S		R		R	R			**R**	
R	R	R	R	R	R	R	R	R	R	R	R	R	R	R	R	R	R	R	R	R	R	R	R	R	**R**	R
S		S	S	S	S	S	S	S	S	S	S	S	S	S	S	S	R	S	S	S	S	S	S	S	**S**	S
R	R	R	R	R	R	R	R	R	R	R	R	R	R	R	R	R	R	R	R	R	R	R	R	R	**R**	R
S	S	S	R	R	R	R	R	R	R		R	R	R	R	R	R	S	R	R	R	S		R	S	**R**	R
S	R	R	R	R	R	R	R	R	R	R	S	R	R	S	R	R	R	R	R	S	R	R	S	S	**S**	
				S											R						R					
															R						R					R
R	R			R	R	R	R	R	R	R	R	S	R	R	R	R	R	R	R	R	R	R	R	R	**R**	
R	R	R	R	R	R	R	R	R	R	R	R	R	R	R	R	R	R	R	R	R	R	R	R	R	**R**	R
				S	S		S								S	S					S			**S**		
S			S									S														
S	S			R	S	R	R	R	R	R	R		R	S	R	R	R	R		R	R	R	R		**R**	
				R		S		R					S	R	R		S			R						
S	S	S	S	S	R	S	S	S	R	S	R			S	S	R	R	S	S	S		S	R	S	**S**	S
S	S	S	S	S	S	S	S	S	S	S	S	S	S	S	R	S	S	S	S	S	S	S	S	S	**S**	S

ANNEX II.B: SELECTED MULTILATERAL AGREEMENTS (REGIONAL)

Y = in force   S = signed   R = ratified   D = denounced

		CAN	MEX	USA	JPN
1933 London	Conv. - Preservation of fauna and flora in their natural state	Y			
1946 London	Conv. - Regulation of the meshes of fishing nets and the size limits of fish	Y			
1958 Dublin	Amendments	Y			
1960 London	Amendments	Y			
1961 Copenhagen	Amendments	Y			
1962 Hamburg	Amendments	Y			
1963 London	Amendments	Y			
1950 Paris	Conv. - Protection of birds	Y			
1956 Rome	Agreem. - Plant protection for the Asia and Pacific region	Y			
1957 Geneva	Agreem. - International carriage of dangerous goods by road (ADR)	Y			
1975 New York	Protocol	Y			
1958 Geneva	Agreem. - Adoption of uniform conditions of approval and reciprocal recognition of approval for motor vehicle equipments and parts	Y			
1959 Washington	Treaty - Antarctic	Y	R	R	R
1991 Madrid	Protocol to the Antarctic treaty (environmental protection)	Y	S	R	R
1960 Paris	Conv. - Third party liability in the field of nuclear energy	Y			
1963 Brussels	Supplementary convention	Y			
1964 Paris	Additional protocol to the convention	Y			
1964 Paris	Additional protocol to the supplementary convention	Y			
1982 Brussels	Protocol amending the convention	Y			
1982 Brussels	Protocol amending the supplementary convention	Y			
1988 Vienna	Joint protocol relating to the application of the Vienna Convention and the Paris Convention	Y			
1964 Brussels	Agreem. - Measures for the conservation of Antarctic Fauna and Flora	Y		R	R
1964 London	Conv. - Fisheries	Y			
1966 Rio de Janeiro	Conv. - International convention for the conservation of Atlantic tunas (ICCAT)	Y	R	R	R
1967 London	Conv. - Conduct of fishing operations in the North Atlantic	Y	S	S	
1968 Strasbourg	Agreem. - Restriction of the use of certain detergents in washing and cleaning products	Y			
1983 Strasbourg	Protocol	Y			
1968 Paris	Conv. - Protection of animals during international transport	Y			
1979 Strasbourg	Protocol	Y			
1969 London	Conv. - Protection of the archaeological heritage	Y			
1972 Oslo	Conv. - Prevention of marine pollution by dumping from ships and aircraft	Y			
1983	Protocol	Y			
1972 London	Conv. - Conservation of Antarctic seals	Y	R	R	R
1973 Oslo	Agreem. - Conservation of polar bears	Y	R	R	
1974 Paris	Conv. - Prevention of marine pollution from land-based sources	Y			
1986 Paris	Protocol	Y			
1992 Paris	Conv. - Protection of North-East Atlantic marine env. (replace Oslo-1972 and Paris-1974)	Y			
1978 Ottawa	Conv. - Future multilateral co-operation in the Northwest Atlantic fisheries (NAFO)	Y	R	R	R
1979 Bern	Conv. - Conservation of European wildlife and natural habitats	Y			

OECD EPR / SECOND CYCLE

Y = in force S = signed R = ratified D = denounced

KOR	AUS	NZL	AUT	BEL	CZE	DNK	FIN	FRA	DEU	GRC	HUN	ISL	IRL	ITA	LUX	NLD	NOR	POL	PRT	ESP	SLO	SWE	CHE	TUR	UKD	EU
			R					S				R					S	R							R	
			R		R			R	R		R	R				R	R	R	R			R			R	
			R		R			R	R		R	R			R	R	R	R	R			R			R	
			R		R			R	R		R	R			R	R	R	R	R			R			R	
			R		R			R	R		R	R			R	R	R	R	R			R			R	
			R		R			R	R		R	R			R	R	R	R	R			R			R	
			R		R			R	R		R	R			R	R	R	R	R			R			R	
		S	R					S		S		R		R	R	R			S	R		R	R	R		
R	R	R						R								R			R						R	
			R	R	R	R	R	R	R	R	R			R	R	R	R	R	R	R	R	R	R		R	
			R	R			R	R	R	R		R			R	R	R	R	R	R		R	R		R	
			R	R	R	R	R	R	R		R			R	R	R	R	R	R	R	R	R	R		R	
R	R	R	R	R	R	R	R	R	R	R	R			R		R	R	R		R	R	R	R	R	R	
R	R	R	S	R	S	S	R	R	R	R	S			R		R	R	R		R	S	R	S		R	
			S	R		R	R	R	R	R				R	S	R	R		R	R		R	S	R	R	
			S	R		R	R	R	R					R	S	R	R			R		R	S		R	
			S	R		R	R	R	R	R				R	S	R	R		R	R		R	S	R	R	
			S	R		R	R	R	R					R	S	R	R			R		R	S		R	
			S	R		R	R	R	R	R				R	S	R	R		R	R		R	S	R	R	
			S	R		R	R	R	R					R	S	R	R			R		R	S		R	
			S	R	R	R	R	S	S	S	R			R		R	R	R	S	S	R	R	S	S	S	
	R	R	R					R						R			R	R							R	
			R		R			R	R				R	R	S	R		R	R	R		R			R	
R								R						R			R	R							R	
			R		R			R	R		R	S	R		R	R	S	R	R			R			R	
			R		R			R	R		R	R	R			R			R				R		R	
								R		S				R	R				R				S		R	
			R	R	R	R	R	R	R		R	R	R	R	R	R			R	R		R	R	R	R	
			R	R	R	R	R	R	R		R	R	R	R	R	R			R	R		R	R	R	R	
			R	R		R		D	R	R		R			R	R			D	R		D	D		D	
			R		R	R	R	R			R	R			R	R			R	R		R			R	
			R		R	R	R	R			R	R			R	R			R	R		R			R	
	R	S	R					R	R				R			R	R								R	
			R													R										
			R		R			R	R		R	R	S	R		R	R		R	R		R			R	R
			R		R			R	R		R	R			R	R			R	R		R			R	R
			R		R	R	R	R			R	R		R	R	R			R	R		R	R		R	R
R						R		R				R				R	R	D	D							R
	R	R	R	R	R	R	R	R	R	R	R	R	R	R	R	R	R	R	R	R	R	R	R	R	R	R

ANNEX II.B: SELECTED MULTILATERAL AGREEMENTS (REGIONAL) (cont.)

Y = in force S = signed R = ratified D = denounced

		CAN	MEX	USA	JPN
1979 Geneva	Conv. - Long-range transboundary air pollution	Y	R		R	
1984 Geneva	Protocol (financing of EMEP)	Y	R		R	
1985 Helsinki	Protocol (reduction of sulphur emissions or their transboundary fluxes by at least 30%)	Y	R			
1988 Sofia	Protocol (control of emissions of nitrogen oxides or their transboundary fluxes)	Y	R		R	
1991 Geneva	Protocol (control of emissions of volatile organic compounds or their transboundary fluxes)	Y	S		S	
1994 Oslo	Protocol (further reduction of sulphur emissions)	Y	R			
1998 Aarhus	Protocol (heavy metals)		R		R	
1998 Aarhus	Protocol (persistent organic pollutants)		R		S	
1999 Gothenburg	Protocol (abate acidification, eutrophication and ground-level ozone)		S		S	
1980 Madrid	Conv. - Transfrontier co-operation between territorial communities or authorities	Y				
1995 Strasbourg	Additional protocol	Y				
1998 Strasbourg	Second protocol	Y				
1980 Canberra	Conv. - Conservation of Antarctic marine living resources	Y	R		R	R
1980 Bern	Conv. - International carriage of dangerous goods by train (COTIF)					
1980 London	Conv. - Multilateral co-operation in North-East Atlantic fisheries	Y				
1982 Paris	Memorandum of understanding on port state control	Y	R			
1982 Reykjavik	Conv. - Conservation of salmon in the North Atlantic Ocean	Y	R		R	
1983 Bonn	Agreem. - Co-operation in dealing with poll. of the North Sea by oil and other harmful subst.	Y				
1989 Bonn	Amendment	Y				
1983 Cartagena	Conv. - Protection and development of the marine environment of the wider Caribbean region	Y		R	R	
1983 Cartagena	Protocol (oil spills)	Y		R	R	
1990 Kingston	Protocol (specially protected areas and wildlife)	Y		S	S	
1985 Rarotonga	Conv. - South Pacific nuclear free zone treaty	Y				
1986 Noumea	Conv. - Protection of the natural resources and environment of the South Pacific region	Y		R		
1986 Noumea	Protocol (prevention of pollution by dumping)	Y		R		
1986 Noumea	Protocol (co-operation in combating pollution emergencies)	Y		R		
1989 Geneva	Conv. - Civil liab. for damage caused during carriage of dang. goods by road, rail, and inland navig. (CRTD)					
1990 Lisbon	Agreem. - Co-op. for the protection of the coasts and waters of the North-East Atlantic					
1991 Espoo	Conv. - Environmental impact assessment in a transboundary context	Y	R		S	
1992 Helsinki	Conv. - Transboundary effects of industrial accidents		S		S	
1992 Helsinki	Conv. - Protection and use of transboundary water courses and international lakes	Y				
1999 London	Prot. - Water and health					
1992 La Valette	European Conv. - Protection of the archaeological heritage (revised)	Y				
1993 Lugano	Conv. - Civil liability for damage resulting from activities dangerous to the environment					
1993 Copenhagen	Agreem. - Co-op. in the prevention of marine poll. from oil and other dangerous chemicals	Y				
1994 Lisbon	Treaty - Energy Charter	Y			S	
1994 Lisbon	Protocol (energy efficiency and related environmental aspects)	Y			S	
1998 Aarhus	Conv. - Access to envtal information and public participation in envtal decision-making	Y				
1998 Strasbourg	Conv. - Protection of the environment through criminal law					
2000 Florence	Conv. - European lanscape convention					

Source: IUCN; OECD.

OECD EPR / SECOND CYCLE

Y = in force   S = signed   R = ratified   D = denounced

KOR	AUS	NZL	AUT	BEL	CZE	DNK	FIN	FRA	DEU	GRC	HUN	ISL	IRL	ITA	LUX	NLD	NOR	POL	PRT	ESP	SLO	SWE	CHE	TUR	UKD	EU
		R	R	R	R	R	R	R	R	R	R	R	R	R	R	R	R	R	R	R	R	R	R	R	**R**	R
		R	R	R	R	R	R	R	R		R	R	R	R	R	R	R	R	R	R	R	R	R	R	**R**	R
		R	R	R	R	R	R		R				R	R	R	R						R	R	R		
		R	R	R	R	R	R	R	R		R	R	R	R	R	S		R	R	R	R		R	R		**R**	R
		R	R	R	R	R	R	R	S	R		R	R	R	R		S		R	R	R	R		R	R	**R**	S
		R	R	R	R	R	R	R	R	S		R	R	R	R	S		R	R	R	R		R	R	**R**	R
		S	S	S	R	R	S	S	S	S	S	S	S	S	R	R	R	S	S	S	S		R	R	**S**	R
		S	S	S	R	S	S	S	S	S	S	S	S	S	R	R	R	S	S	S	S		R	R	**S**	S
		S	S	S	S	S	S	S	S	S		S	S	S	S	S	S	S	S	S	S		S	S	**S**	
		R	R	R	R	R	R		R	S	R	R	R	R	R	R	R	R	R	R		R	R	R		
		S	S			R	R			S		S	R	R			S		R	R	R				
						S	R			S		R	R			S		R	R	S					
R	R	R		R			R	R	R	R			R		R	R	R		R		R			**R**	R
								R																		
				R				R					R	R	R	R		R								R
		R		R	R	R	R	R		R	R		R	R	R	R	R		R			**R**			
		R	R				R					R						R					R			R
		R		R		R	R					R	R					R			**R**	R				
		R		R		R	R					R	R					R			**R**	R				
				R								R						R			**R**	S				
				R								R						R			**R**					
				S								R						S			**S**					
	R	R		S																S						
	R	R		R																S						
	R	R		R																R						
	R	R		R																S						
				S																						
						R											R	S								R
	R	R	R	R	R	R	S	R	R	S	S	R	R	R	R	R	R	R	R	R		R	R	**R**	R
	R	S	R	R	R	S	R	R	R		R	R	S	R	S	S	R		R	R		R	R	**S**	R
	R	R	R	R	R	R	R	R	R		R	R	R	R	R	R	R	R	R	R		R	R	**S**	R
	S	R	S	S	S	S	S	R	S		S	R	S	S	S	S	S	R	S	S		S		**S**	
	S	R	S	R	R	S	S	R		R	S	S	S	R	R	R	S	R	R	R	R	R	**R**			
				S			S		S	S	S	S				S										
				R	R				R					R				R			R					
S		R	R	R	R	R	R	R	R	S	R	R	R	R	S	R	R	R	R	R	R	R	**R**	R		
S		R	R	R	R	R	R	R	R	S	R	R	R	R	S	R	R	R	R	R	R	R	**R**	R		
		S	S	S	R	S	S	S	S	S	S	R	S	S	S	S	S		S	S	**S**	S				
		S	S		S	S	S	S		S	S			S	S			S								
				S	S	S		S				S	S		R	S	S	S		S	S	S				

Annex III
SELECTED ENVIRONMENTAL EVENTS (1994-2001)

1994

- Her Majesty's Inspectorate of Pollution (HMIP) issues eight guidance notes setting out how inorganic chemical processes will be regulated when they come under integrated pollution control (IPC) on 1 May.

- The government publishes a sustainable development strategy, fulfilling a commitment made at the Rio Summit in 1992.

- The government publishes "Climate Change: The UK Programme", a strategy for complying with the 1992 UN Framework Convention on Climate Change.

- The government publishes "Biodiversity: The UK Action Plan", a strategy to conserve, promote and monitor biodiversity, in line with the UN Convention on Biological Diversity.

- The government publishes "Sustainable Forestry: The UK Programme", a plan for forest management, following the adoption of the Statement of Forest Principles made at Rio.

- The government announces a review of countryside agencies in England and the possibility of merging the Countryside Commission and English Nature.

- The environment secretary announces that government policy will henceforth favour new shops in town centres rather than large out-of-town developments.

- The government announces that it will accept the ban on dumping low- and intermediate-level radioactive waste at sea as adopted at the consultative meeting of the London Convention in November 1993.

- A Health and Safety Commission report criticises the safety level of the nuclear reactors at Sellafield.

- A chemical leak from a factory in Wem, Shropshire, pollutes the water supplies of nearly 250 000 people in Worcestershire and Gloucestershire.

- The Donaldson report on shipping safety standards and marine pollution by ships is published.

- The third annual white paper reporting progress on the 1990 paper "This Common Inheritance" is published.

- The UK ratifies the Convention on Biological Diversity.

- The environment secretary signs a protocol in Oslo in which the UK agrees to reduce its SO_2 emissions by 80%, from 1980 levels, by 2010.

- The EU habitat directive becomes law in the UK.

- At least 100 000 fish die when slurry spills into the River Camel, near Camelford, Cornwall.

- A Friends of the Earth survey reveals that more than 700 designated wildlife sites in England and Wales are under threat from pollution or other pressures.

- The Royal Commission on Environmental Pollution publishes "Transport and the Environment", reviewing the environmental effects of transport systems and highlighting the implications of rapid growth in road and air travel.

- The Natural Environment Research Council reports that vehicle emissions have affected air quality even in rural areas.

- The government announces plans to set up an Environment Agency to take over the work of HMIP and the National Rivers Authority, along with the waste regulation functions of local authorities.

- Thousands of fish are killed by a cyanide spill into the River Wye, Buckinghamshire.

1995

- The environment secretary launches "Going for Green", an initiative to increase public awareness of sustainable development issues.

- The official nature conservation agencies in England, Scotland, Wales and Northern Ireland publish a list of 280 proposed Special Areas of Conservation. Complete designation of such areas under the habitat directive is expected to take several years.

- The government's fourth annual report in the "This Common Inheritance" series is the first on progress regarding commitments in the 1994 sustainable development strategy.

- The government approves plans for two community forests: Bristol/Avon Forest and Watling Chase in south Hertfordshire.

- The government publishes *A Guide to Risk Assessment and Risk Management for Environmental Protection*. The guide is intended to reflect the latest thinking on risk assessment and explores for the first time a practical realisation of the precautionary principle.

- The Environment Act receives the royal assent. The Act provides for the establishment of the Environment Agency and the Scottish Environment Protection Agency, among other purposes.

- The environment secretary announces stricter planning rules for out-of-town shopping centres.

- The Tamar Valley is designated an area of outstanding natural beauty.

- The government publishes a white paper on the English countryside, "Rural England: A Nation Committed to a Living Countryside", analysing the issues facing rural areas and making several recommendations.

- The UK biodiversity action plan is published. It sets targets for the conservation of 116 declining or endangered species of wild animals, birds, insects and plants, and for 14 "priority wildlife habitats".

- "Making Waste Work", the government's strategy for sustainable waste management in England and Wales, is published.

- The government publishes a white paper on the Scottish countryside, "Rural Scotland, Prosperity and Partnership".

1996

- The tanker *Sea Empress* runs aground at the entrance to Milford Haven, leaking 72 000 tonnes of crude oil.

- The Royal Commission on Environmental Pollution publishes "Sustainable Use of Soil", recommending that the government draw up and implement a soil protection policy.

- With publication of "Indicators of Sustainable Development for the United Kingdom", the UK becomes one of the first countries to construct sustainable development indicators that explicitly try to link environment and development concerns.

- The government publishes the fifth report in the series "This Common Inheritance".

- The European Court of Justice rules that Britain acted illegally in 1993 in excluding part of the Lappel Bank reserve on the River Medway, Kent, from being listed as a special protection area under the EU bird directive, thereby favouring economic interests over environmental ones.

- The government publishes a white paper on the Welsh countryside, "A Working Countryside for Wales".

- The Environment Agency starts operating on 1 April.

- The 1996 Wild Mammals (Protection) Act takes effect. It provides for the protection of wild mammals from certain acts of cruelty and extends protection to any wild mammal not otherwise protected by UK legislation (excluding domestic or captive animals).
- The 1995 Home Energy Conservation Act takes effect.
- The Biodiversity Action Plan receives formal government approval.
- The 1996 Energy Conservation Act and Noise Act take effect.
- The UK Management Plan for Exports and Imports of Waste takes effect.
- The Climate Change Impact Review Group publishes "Review of the Potential Effects of Climate Change in the UK", a sector by sector analysis of the impact of climate change on sea level, the natural environment, energy and transport for the 2020s and 2050s in the UK.
- The environment secretary announces a national air quality strategy, including new targets for reducing the level of eight hazardous pollutants in the atmosphere by 2005.
- Europe's largest wind farm opens at Carno in the county of Powys, Wales.
- Morecambe Bay in Lancashire, Foulness in Essex, the Alde-Ore Estuary and Benacre to Easton Bavents in Suffolk are classified as special protection areas under the bird directive. The first three are also listed as Ramsar wetlands.
- Leading environmental groups publish a report entitled "High and Dry", stating that 300 wildlife sites are under threat from policies pursued by water companies, industry and agriculture.

1997

- Two tankers collide 40 miles off the Kent coast, leaking 1 500 tonnes of gasoline into the English Channel.
- The government publishes the sixth "This Common Inheritance" report.
- The government publishes a national air quality strategy, setting standards for the main air pollutants and specific air quality objectives to be met by 2005.
- A report commissioned by the Department of the Environment shows a sharp decline in at least 12 varieties of farmland birds in the past 25 years. The report calls for reduced use of chemicals and other changes in agricultural practice.
- After meeting representatives of the water industry and its regulators, the deputy prime minister announces mandatory targets for repair of leaking pipes and a review of licences for withdrawals causing significant environmental damage.

- At the special "Rio+5" session of the UN in New York, the UK agrees to reverse the decline in the amount of aid given to developing countries and to reduce greenhouse gas (GHG) emissions to 20% below 1990 levels by 2010.

- Council Regulation (EC) No. 338/97 on the Protection of Species of Wild Fauna and Flora by Regulating Trade Therein comes into force in the UK, covering some 30 000 plant and animal species.

- The government publishes a statement of intent signalling its commitment to introduce environmental taxes as long as they are effective and do not damage the UK's competitiveness.

- The government publishes a consultation paper outlining options for achieving an integrated transport policy that would reduce the use of private cars.

- The government backs proposals that discharges of hazardous and radioactive substances into the sea be reduced to as close to zero as possible by 2020.

- The Royal Commission on Environmental Pollution publishes "Transport and the Environment: Developments Since 1994". It reports few signs of change in trends identified in the previous report, and sets out requirements for an integrated transport system.

- The government establishes the Sustainable Development Education Panel to identify gaps, opportunities, priorities and partnerships for action in providing sustainable development education.

- The UK ratifies the amendment to the Basel Convention banning exports of hazardous waste by developed countries.

- The government announces that the UK will cut its CO_2 emissions by 20% by 2010 from the 1990 level.

- Twenty-two wildlife conservation bodies sign a charter proposing better protection for sites of special scientific interest and other protected sites.

- The government publishes "Eliminating World Poverty: A Challenge for the 21st Century", reaffirming its commitment to meet the internationally agreed target of halving world poverty by 2015.

- The House of Commons establishes an Environmental Audit Committee to consider how policies and programmes of government departments and non-departmental public bodies contribute to environmental protection and sustainable development.

1998

- The UK begins its six month presidency of the Council of the European Union.

- The government launches a review of planning regulations.

- A consultation document on a new sustainable development strategy is published.

- The government announces that the Countryside Commission and the Rural Development Commission will be merged.

- The government launches "Are You Doing Your Bit?", a campaign designed to encourage small but important changes in everyday actions to benefit both people and the local and global environment.

- Wealden Heath in southern England and the Duddon Estuary in Cumbria are listed as special protection areas under the bird directive. The Dudden Estuary is also listed as a Ramsar wetland.

- The government signs the Kyoto Protocol.

- The government announces that the UK will reduce its GHG emissions by at least 12.5% of the 1990 level by 2010 as its contribution to the EU commitment to cut emissions by 8%.

- The UK and 14 other countries sign an agreement in Sintra, Portugal, under which the remaining Magnox nuclear power stations in Britain would close by 2010 and discharges from Sellafield would be reduced to "close to zero" by 2020.

- The government publishes a white paper on the future of transport, "A New Deal for Transport: Better for Everyone".

- Government safety inspectors report many chronic safety problems at the Dounreay nuclear complex.

- The 1998 Pesticides Act takes effect. It amends the Food and Environment Protection Act in respect of powers concerning pesticides and enforcement of provisions relating to pesticide control.

- A draft climate change consultation paper is published.

- "Conclusions of the Review of Energy Sources for Power Generation and Government Response to Fourth and Fifth Reports of the Trade and Industry Committee" is published.

- The Royal Commission on Environmental Pollution publishes "Setting Environmental Standards".

- The government publishes "Planning for Sustainable Development: Towards Better Practice", advising local authorities on how to build sustainable development into development plans and planning decisions.

- The 1998 Waste Minimisation Act takes effect. It amends the 1990 Environmental Protection Act to give certain local authorities powers to take steps to minimise waste generation in their area.

- The government launches consultation on proposals for "headline indicators" of sustainable development.
- The second London Oceans Workshop concludes that the main problems facing the marine environment come from fishing practices and pollution and other degradation from land-based activities.
- The government publishes "British Shipping: Charting a New Course", a strategy for sustainable shipping.

1999

- The UK stops dumping sewage sludge at sea.
- The Milford Haven Port Authority is fined GBP 4 million after admitting responsibility for the *Sea Empress* disaster of 1996.
- A major acid spill caused by a faulty drain at a company in Hartlepool contaminates Greenabella Marsh, a protected area in the Tees Estuary.
- The prime minister says there is no scientific case for a moratorium on the sale of genetically modified foods in the UK.
- The government publishes "Down to Earth", outlining major sustainable development issues for Scotland.
- The government publishes "Tomorrow's Tourism", a strategy for sustainable tourism in England.
- The environment minister announces that the government will honour an election pledge to give the public the right of access on unenclosed land in England and Wales.
- The government publishes "Taking Water Responsibly", which sets out forthcoming changes to the licensing system for water withdrawals in England and Wales.
- The government publishes "New and Renewable Energy: Prospects for the 21st Century", a consultation document on future renewable energy policy.
- The government publishes "Sustainable Distribution", a strategy on freight transport.
- The merger of English Heritage and the Royal Commission on the Historical Monuments of England is completed.
- The Countryside Agency is established following the merger of the Countryside Commission and parts of the Rural Development Commission.

- The government launches its revised sustainable development strategy, "A Better Quality of Life".

- Environmentalists call for a five-year freeze on the planting of genetically modified crops in the UK.

- The 1999 Water Industry Act takes effect.

- A draft waste strategy, "A Way with Waste", is published. It includes targets for reducing industrial and commercial waste to landfill, and for increasing municipal waste recovery and household waste recycling.

- The government publishes its first set of climate change indicators, which show that climate change is already taking place.

- The 1999 Pollution Prevention and Control Act takes effect.

- The government publishes summaries of responses to its climate change consultation paper of October 1998.

- The government publishes "Framework for Action on SSSIs", acknowledging that sites of special scientific interest continue to suffer damage and deterioration, and presenting proposals to improve their protection and management.

- At the fifth Conference of the Parties to the UNFCCC, the deputy prime minister calls for ratification and entry into force of the Kyoto Protocol by 2002.

- The Highways Agency publishes "Towards a Balance with Nature", a strategic plan aiming to minimise the impact of roads on the built and natural environment.

- The government publishes "Quality of Life Counts: Indicators for a Strategy for Sustainable Development for the United Kingdom". This "baseline assessment" elaborates on the indicators introduced in "A Better Quality of Life" in May 1999.

- The government's chemical strategy, "Sustainable Production and Use of Chemicals", is published.

- The UK signs the Gothenburg Protocol on acidification, eutrophication and ground level ozone.

2000

- The government publishes an air quality strategy for England, Scotland, Wales and Northern Ireland, setting out action to reduce air pollution.

- The phase-out of leaded gasoline is completed.

- The Northumbrian coast and the Breydon Water Extension in Norfolk are classified as Ramsar wetlands and as special protection areas for birds.

- The government publishes its draft climate change programme for consultation. This describes how the UK would meet its Kyoto target to cut greenhouse gas emissions to 12.5% below 1990 levels during 2008-12. It also shows how the government proposes to meet its domestic goal to cut CO_2 emissions by 20% by 2010.

- The Thames Estuary and Marshes are classified as a special protection area for birds and a Ramsar wetland.

- The new regime for contaminated land under Part IIA of the 1990 Environmental Protection Act comes into force. This provides, for the first time, a statutory definition obliging local authorities to identify contaminated land and require its remediation.

- The government publishes "Building a Better Quality of Life: A Strategy for More Sustainable Construction".

- The government publishes a waste strategy for England and Wales that includes statutory targets for recycling.

- The Royal Commission on Environmental Pollution publishes "Energy: The Changing Climate".

- The government issues "Transport 2010: The 10 Year Plan", a GBP 180 billion investment package to modernise the nation's transport system.

- The government releases "Guidelines for Environmental Risk Assessment and Management", a revision of guidelines first published in 1995, with a new chapter on the social aspects of risk.

- The IPPC regime begins to replace the IPC and local air pollution control systems to implement the EU's IPPC directive.

- Thorne and Hatfield Moors in Yorkshire and the Humber are classified as a special protection area for birds, as are Lee Valley and South West London Waterbodies.

- The Sustainable Development Commission is launched. It subsumes the British Government Panel on Sustainable Development and the UK Round Table on Sustainable Development, which date from 1994.

- The government publishes "Climate Change: The UK Programme", setting out a wide range of policies and measures to reduce UK greenhouse gas emissions.

- The government publishes "Our Countryside: The Future", a strategy for revitalising the English countryside, and "Our Towns and Cities: The Future", a strategy for improving the quality of English urban life.

- "Countryside Survey 2000", a national audit of habitats and landscape features, is published.

- The National Assembly for Wales adopts "A Sustainable Wales: Learning to Live Differently", which sets out how Wales is to meet its legal obligations on sustainable development.

- The 2000 Countryside and Rights of Way Act takes effect. It gives people access for the first time to over 4 million acres of open countryside.

- The 2000 Transport Act takes effect.

2001

- The government publishes its first review of progress towards sustainable development, "Achieving a Better Quality of Life: Government Annual Report 2000".

- An outbreak of foot and mouth disease is confirmed.

- The government launches the UK Emissions Trading Scheme.

- The newly formed Department for Environment, Food and Rural Affairs takes over responsibility for agriculture and the food industry from the former Ministry of Agriculture, Fisheries and Food, and for environment, rural development, countryside, wildlife and sustainable development from the former Department for the Environment, Transport and the Regions, as well as for animal welfare and hunting from the Home Office.

- The Energy Efficiency Commitment 2002-05 is published. It requires energy suppliers to promote improvements in energy efficiency by household consumers.

- Marazion Marsh and parts of the Isles of Scilly in the south-west and Sandlings in Suffolk are designated as special protection areas.

- The government launches the Policy Commission to take a fresh look at the emphasis and direction of farming policies in England.

- The fisheries decommissioning programme begins. Its aim is to reduce the English fishing fleet by 5% and thus help protect fish stocks.

- The DEFRA deputy minister convenes the UK's first waste summit, and the government orders the Performance and Innovation Unit to undertake a new review of waste strategy.

- DEFRA lifts restrictions on the last remaining foot and mouth infected area.

- The government launches consultation on plans to review, modernise and simplify laws on animal welfare. The objective is a much needed rationalisation of various legislation, some of which dates back 100 years.

- New "arable options" are made available in the Countryside Stewardship Programme, providing more opportunities for farmers to benefit from biodiversity, especially as regards farmland birds.
- The government and devolved administrations publish a consultation paper on the management of radioactive waste.
- The government introduces a new round of the Agriculture Development Scheme, designed to improve the marketing performance and competitiveness of agricultural sectors affected by foot and mouth disease.
- The tree planting target is increased in the DEFRA-sponsored National Forest in 2001/02 to a record total of nearly 600 hectares.
- The government publishes a consultation paper outlining options for reducing nitrate pollution from agriculture.
- The government publishes the neighbourhood renewal implementation strategy.
- The Environmental Impact Assessment (Uncultivated Land and Semi-natural Areas) (England) Regulations 2001 are introduced, taking effect from February 2002.
- Fur farming Act is banned under a government order that will come into force on 1 January 2003.

Annex IV

PHYSICAL CONTEXT

The *United Kingdom of Great Britain and Northern Ireland* consists of England, Scotland, Wales and Northern Ireland. It is an island country, with total land area of 244 000 km^2. No part of the country is more than 200 kilometres from the sea. Its only land boundary is with the Republic of Ireland. With a population of 60 million in 2000, the population density was 245 inhabitants per square kilometre, quite high for OECD Europe. Over 80% of the population resides in England and Wales, with half concentrated in south-eastern England and the Midlands. Parts of Scotland and Wales, on the other hand, are rather sparsely populated.

The United Kingdom has a *temperate maritime climate*, largely influenced by the Gulf Stream. Mean annual temperatures range from 7 °C in the Shetland Islands to 12 °C in the Scillies. Annual rainfall ranges from 40 cm in the Thames estuary to 240 cm in the Welsh uplands and Scotland. The territory encompasses woodlands; heath; grasslands; salt marshes, sand dunes and estuaries; marine areas; freshwater habitats; peatlands; farmland; and built-up areas.

About *70% of the UK's total surface area is agricultural land*. Of this, dairy farming and livestock grazing account for over 70% while the rest is under cultivation. About 10% of the country is covered by forests and woodlands. Another 10% is urbanised. Since 1990, agricultural land area has decreased by 3% and forest cover has increased by 16%. Urban areas have also grown. Some 58 000 hectares of brownfield land was unused and potentially available for redevelopment in England in 1998. This amounts to 0.4% of the land area, about the size of Manchester. The Environment Agency estimates that an area of land larger than Greater London is contaminated, much of it in the north near former coal mining and heavy industry sites.

Rivers in the UK are generally short. Several in the east drain into wide estuaries. Deeply glaciated rock basins in the Scottish Highlands have created many large lochs. The frequency and severity of river flooding increased significantly in the late 1990s. In England, about 10% of the population and 12% of farmland is located in flood prone areas.

Few species are endemic to the United Kingdom (one vertebrate species, 43 higher plant species, 20 lower plant, nine invertebrates) and there are relatively few species in

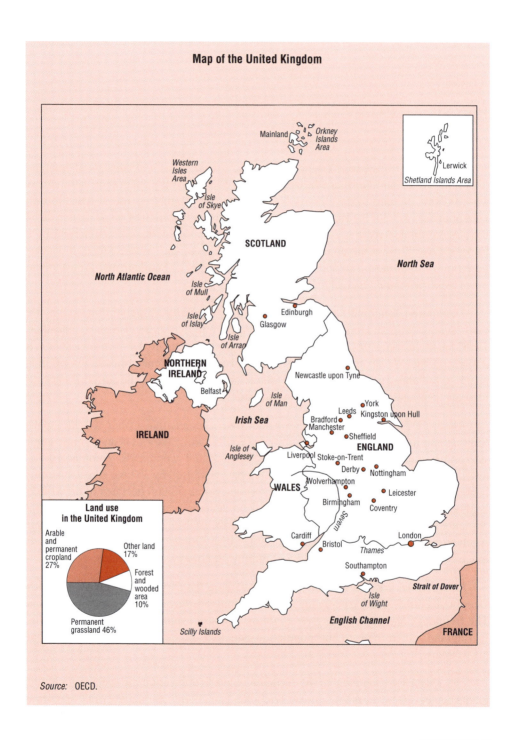

Map of the United Kingdom

Land use in the United Kingdom

- Arable and permanent cropland 27%
- Other land 17%
- Forest and wooded area 10%
- Permanent grassland 46%

Source: OECD.

© OECD 2002

the country overall. Nevertheless, the country harbours a number of species of major international importance, either being home to a high proportion of the total population or offering important habitat (e.g. wetlands and coastal habitats) to international migratory populations. This applies in particular to migratory birds and to sea mammals such as the grey and common seals, the bottlenose dolphin and the harbour porpoise. Commercial fisheries such as those for cod, haddock, sole and whiting play an important economic and social role in the country.

The United Kingdom has extensive *energy resources*. The majority of its energy supply comes from domestic oil and gas fields on the continental shelf. In 1999, oil and gas accounted for nearly 75% of the energy supply (evenly split between the two), followed by coal (15%) and nuclear energy (11%). Hydropower, geothermal energy, solar and wind power, combustible renewables and waste together accounted for 1% of the total energy supply in 1999.

Annex V

SELECTED WEBSITES CONCERNING ENVIRONMENTAL MANAGEMENT

Website	Host institution
www.defra.gov.uk/	Department for Environment, Food and Rural Affairs
www.sustainable-development.gov.uk	UK Government
www.dft.gov.uk/	Department for Transport
www.dti.gov.uk/	Department of Trade and Industry
www.parliament.uk/commons/selcom/eahome.htm	House of Commons Environmental Audit Committee
www.rcep.org.uk/	Royal Commission on Environmental Pollution
www.environment-agency.gov.uk/	Environment Agency
www.sepa.org.uk/index.html	Scottish Environmental Protection Agency
www.ehsni.gov.uk/environprotect/	Northern Ireland Industrial Pollution and Radiochemical Inspectorate
www.rspb.org.uk/flash.html	Royal Society for the Protection of Birds
www.nationaltrust.org.uk/main/	National Trust
www.foe.co.uk/	Friends of the Earth – England, Wales and Northern Ireland
www.greenpeace.org.uk	Greenpeace – UK

OECD PUBLICATIONS, 2, rue André-Pascal, 75775 PARIS CEDEX 16
PRINTED IN FRANCE
(97 2002 18 1 P) ISBN 92-64-19849-0 – No. 52669 2002